Best
Financial
Wishes !

Sincerely,
Robert L. Oshlundw, CFP.

404-803-0474 C
404-933-9401 D

WISE MONEY

HOW THE SMART MONEY INVESTS

WISE MONEY

Using the Endowment
Investment Approach to Minimize
Volatility and Increase Control

DANIEL WILDERMUTH

New York   Chicago   San Francisco   Lisbon   London   Madrid   Mexico City
Milan   New Delhi   San Juan   Seoul   Singapore   Sydney   Toronto

The **McGraw·Hill** Companies

1 2 3 4 5 6 7 8 9 0   DOC/DOC   1 8 7 6 5 4 3 2 1

ISBN   978-0-07-179804-4
MHID   0-07-179804-8

e-ISBN   978-0-07-179805-1
e-MHID   0-07-179805-6

McGraw-Hill books are available at special quantity discounts to use as premiums
and sales promotions or for use in corporate training programs. To contact a representative, please e-mail us at bulksales@mcgraw-hill.com.

This book is printed on acid-free paper.

Contents

From the Author

WHY WRITE, OR READ, ANOTHER BOOK ON INVESTING? THERE ARE countless books on the market, so hasn't enough been said on the subject already? Besides, what has been said hasn't appeared to be very helpful. Some investors believe the past few years highlighted the futility of investment planning and possibly even investing in general. The horrendous losses suffered by many in the 2008 global stock market crash seemingly confirmed the shortcomings of so many investment approaches.

The facts are ugly. The U.S. stock market declined nearly 40 percent in 2008 and dropped 55 percent from its high on October 9, 2007, to its low on March 6, 2009.[1] Possibly even worse for many investors, these declines were the second major market crash of the decade. The broad stock market indexes produced negative returns over a 10-year period. Weak bond returns over the same period didn't help. The result? Too many investors earned zero or negative returns over an entire decade while enduring terrible volatility.

But this is only part of the investment story. While many individual investors struggled, college endowments generally enjoyed success over the same period. These organizations recognized years ago the many limitations of traditional investment approaches that depend almost entirely on stocks and bonds. The endowments developed and implemented a very different investment approach generally referred to as the "endowment model." This investment strategy seeks to increase return *and* decrease volatility.

By nearly any measure, this approach has been a tremendous success. It has performed very well relative to virtually all other models over any reasonable time frame and has consistently proven its value over very long periods of time. To be fair, no model, strategy, or method of investing outperforms in every environment or circumstance, and the endowment model is no exception. But this investment strategy has shown remarkable consistency in outperforming in a wide variety of market conditions including bull and bear markets, markets that favor various sizes of companies, markets that benefit value or growth stocks, conditions that advance international versus domestic stocks, inflationary periods, and many other types of economic and market conditions. In addition, the model's outperformance has also been achieved with a lower chance of experiencing losses relative to many common strategies.

While even some institutions lagged in their adoption of the approach, today some form of the endowment model nearly always anchors the investment strategy employed by college endowments, institutions, and wealthy investors worldwide. Unfortunately, most individual investors continue using dated, simplistic strategies that have yielded very poor results and a very wild ride, especially during the past decade.

This brings me to my reason for writing this book. My experience and research has convinced me that smaller investors can replicate many of the same principles and practices successfully employed by institutions and wealthy investors. No individual investor will duplicate the exact performance of the endowments. Even different endowments don't earn the same results as one another. Yet I believe the basic principles and strategies can be transferred to much smaller portfolios, and their adoption can provide individual investors attractive rewards. Hopefully, your belief that this may be true will provide you enough motivation to find out more.

A small warning: While none of this material is particularly challenging or revolutionary, applying the strategy may require an adjustment to your thinking. This strategy departs from the traditional, tired approach of using only U.S. stocks and bonds. It doesn't just tweak the existing logic, it completely discards major parts of it. This doesn't mean it's difficult to understand or implement. But it is a different approach. With that caveat, I invite you to explore a new, and I believe much better, investment approach that may help you significantly better yourself financially while also increasing your confidence and comfort with your finances.

$$\underline{\hspace{3cm}}\!\!\!\!\!\bigcirc\!\!\!\!\!\underline{\hspace{3cm}}$$

The Need for a New Strategy

THE YEARS 2008 AND 2009 TREATED THE AVERAGE INVESTOR VERY poorly. Stock market losses in 2008[1] were horrific at 37.0 percent for the Standard & Poor's 500 Index (S&P 500)[2] while the average equity sector mutual fund lost 39.70 percent.[3] The average American worker lost over one-quarter of his or her 401(k) retirement plan savings in 2008.[4] The beginning of 2009 continued the trend with the market declining more than 26 percent[5] before sharply reversing as general panic subsided. The market actually ended up 26.5 percent[6] in 2009.

The tremendous losses and volatility of these months and years left most investors not only frustrated but also often completely bewildered and overwhelmed. In addition, many supposedly safe investments suffered rough rides. In 2008, even investment-grade corporate bonds lost 5.3 percent.[7] Almost the only place to hide seemed to be certificates of deposit or government bonds because they were the only assets seen as riskless during a time of tremendous uncertainty.

During this period of continuous tumult, I heard investors, journalists, and pundits echo similar sentiments that emphasized the horror of the situation and the futility of avoiding it. Others chose to dwell on the obvious challenges that only seemed to heighten the current panic. The overemphasis on near-term problems often

1

resulted in recommendations to sell when challenges looked the worst and asset valuations were the lowest. The results were disastrous as far too many people, especially individual investors, unloaded their severely discounted investments at exactly the wrong time.

Of course, the drop in the markets brought out inevitable claims that we should have seen this coming and somehow timed the sale of investments. While this sounds wonderful, clairvoyance eludes nearly all of us. How do we know ahead of time that corporations will lose money, banks will stop lending, or people will panic?

This simple answer seems to be that we can't, and we don't. I don't believe this situation will change. Moreover, the same reality apparently applies to even the world's most sophisticated and resourced investors. During this downfall, much of the downward pressure on the markets resulted from professionals unloading their holdings. The world's largest banks and hedge funds often sold at huge losses at the worst possible time to deleverage their balance sheets. They needed cash at all costs just when cash was most expensive.

If the experts and investment insiders couldn't get it right and in this downturn often contributed to the disaster, how can individual investors avoid disasters? Unfortunately, I believe it's nearly impossible unless you completely avoid any type of investment vehicle. In most cases, however, a risk-free portfolio mandates holding only CDs or government bonds. Over a longer time frame, the loss of purchasing power resulting from lack of return can pose a greater risk to nearly any investor than potential investment losses. As a result, most people must assume some type of risk in order to generate real investment returns.

Yet when pondering investments in stocks, the question isn't *will* the stock market crash or *will* we have another crisis. It's a matter of *when*. The economy will almost certainly experience major challenges in the future and new technology developments will disrupt established industries or even national economies. In fact, the accelerating pace of change in seemingly every area of life suggests more frequent crises and challenges. The stability of 20, 30, or even 50 years is probably just a memory rather than a likely future. The introduction of the microchip into our daily lives likely ensures that nearly everything will permanently move at a faster and faster pace, including economic ups and downs.

So, if I'm saying that you can't avoid or foresee problems well enough to completely avoid them, and avoiding risk isn't really a viable strategy, what options are there? After all, more traditional investment approaches that emphasize stocks and bonds have provided both poor returns and tremendous volatility over the past decade. Given this environment and the likely unpredictability of global markets in the future, what can investors do?

Very simply, I believe more consistent and predictable success requires a different investment approach. The strategy utilized must be capable of weathering inevitable storms regardless of size and duration. The approach must provide the performance and stability most investors need while also satisfying income and liquidity requirements. Of course, this sounds wonderful, but is it possible?

I believe the answer is yes. The strategy I'm referring to has been developed and successfully employed by many of the world's wealthiest and most successful university endowments as well as institutions and private wealth managers across the globe. Endowments and institutions, with very large amounts of money at stake and very substantial intellectual capital, believed there was a better way to excel in a rapidly changing world. They developed an approach often referred to as the "endowment strategy," which deviates significantly from the traditional stock and bond models of yesteryear. The strategy isn't new; it's just not familiar to most individual investors.

Sophisticated endowments recognized that changes in the global economy and investment landscape provide new opportunities to increase returns while also lowering portfolio volatility. Moreover, these same institutions determined that success requires breaking from dated models and strategies developed for a dramatically different world and historical context.

Their performance illustrates their success. The average U.S. investor with a 60 percent stock and 40 percent bond portfolio earned exactly 0.00 percent for the 10-year period starting January 1, 2000, assuming modest fees of 2.0 percent for stocks and 0.5 percent for bonds.[8] Unfortunately, most studies reveal that the average individual didn't do nearly this well, as the performance of most investors dramatically trail that of broad market indexes. By contrast, Yale, Harvard, and Stanford's endowments enjoyed a solid run over the same time period with returns across the three averaging just under 10 percent per year, including all fees.[9]

You may be thinking that this strategy must be too complex or difficult for the average investor to adopt. Or, your lack of billions must prevent you from accessing the investments that have enabled the endowments to achieve their success. Not only do I believe the average investor can successfully employ this strategy, various other experts do too.

A broad study by the *Journal of Wealth Management* highlights investor possibilities. Very simply, the journal claims that investment returns earned by endowments resulted primarily from strategies replicable by individual investors. More specifically, after a very thorough review of Yale's performance during the 20-year period ending in fiscal year 2007,[10] the *Journal of Wealth Management* concluded that even Yale's endowment management showed little skill or luck in selecting managers outside of the category of private equity. Their review of the 10-year data supported the same conclusion.

The source of the Yale endowment's success is critical. It results from the asset classes the institution invests in rather than the superior management of the funds within the asset class. With the exception of private equity for Yale, success derives from original investment choices, not contacts, managers, or skills out of the reach of any individual investor.

This conclusion bears repeating. Success results from strategy, not exceptional skills, access, or experience. The implications to individual investors are tremendous because individuals can copy strategy, and the rapid expansion of investments has provided individuals access to similar types of investments used by endowments.

This conclusion is exciting and encouraging. It strongly suggests that anyone willing to adopt the strategy can hope to experience similar results. Of course, we have to be careful here. Obviously, this study doesn't claim that everyone will enjoy similar success, and they add the caveat that Yale's private equity success has been an exception because its returns have been phenomenal. Furthermore, there are considerable differences in investment success experienced by endowments themselves, and individuals will almost certainly see similarly varying results. For instance, other institutions following the endowment model have achieved excellent success without duplicating Yale's private equity performance.

Understanding that the success of endowments generally doesn't come through special access to out-of-reach experts or unfathomable complex techniques is wonderfully liberating. The strategy is the key, and it's available to anyone willing to adopt it.

The report also mentions that a major part of these endowments' success is "consistent exposure to diversified, risk-tilted, equity oriented assets."[11] They follow up this conclusion with the simple statement that this strategy is easy for investors to emulate.

I'll jump in here with some editorial comments. *Easy* by their definition means something different than most of us understand in common conversation. *Easy* indicates that investors willing to put the effort into understanding and planning can create a similar strategy. In other words, the strategy is not beyond the reach of individual investors. Developing a vastly improved approach, however, isn't the same as pushing the big red Easy button. Some effort is required.

Regardless, the conclusion that the model can be emulated via widely available strategies remains very notable. While I've referenced this study specifically, there's tremendous additional research that decisively supports the same conclusion, and so do the results of my own professional experience. Anyone can do it!

The key to the strategy's success is including far more asset classes than typically make up an individual investor's portfolio while reducing holdings that are likely to provide poorer performance, such as traditional bonds. In fact, domestic stocks and bonds often comprise less than a quarter of an endowment's portfolio versus all, or nearly all, of the typical investor's. Instead, endowments diversify their portfolios through adding multiple investments with strong performance potential that are expected to perform more independently of one another. Their investments can include foreign developed market stocks, emerging market stocks, institutional quality real estate, commodities, private equity, hedge funds, managed futures, and debt-driven instruments. I realize that the list can appear daunting, especially if you haven't heard of many of these investments, but don't let the labels intimidate you. A decade ago, high-quality versions of many of these investments were difficult or impossible for individuals to access; today, excellent choices are readily available to individual investors.

The performance-oriented assets share two important character-istics. First, given the performance label, it's not surprising that all of the assets are projected to provide high average performance over time. Second, and just as important, they are expected to provide strong returns in different ways at different times according to various influences such as economic ups and downs, stages in the business cycle, current and future inflation, interest rates, global events, market volatility, and employment levels. Because the diverse assets contribute varying returns to the portfolio over time, with some assets performing well when others struggle, the overall port-folio performance tends to be much smoother than that delivered by a portfolio that depends on only domestic stocks to boost returns. In addition, the possibility of total portfolio losses should be much lower.

As did individual investors, endowments held U.S. stocks during the first decade of the millennium, and their domestic stock holdings usually suffered like those held by individuals. Yet, unlike far too many individual investors, endowments enjoyed success over the pre-vious decade because other assets in their portfolios performed well while stocks languished.

Endowments also avoid large exposure to bonds because they believe that bonds lack high long-term return potential. While most investors probably agree with this assessment, many individuals continue to hold large bond positions to lessen their overall portfolio volatility. This practice makes sense if a portfolio holds only one other volatile and unpredictable asset: domestic stocks. In contrast, endowments seek to lower volatility through broadly diversifying their performance assets rather than simply reducing these holdings.

Like many individual investors, endowments also depend on their portfolios to satisfy present-day financial needs. If required, a good portfolio design should consistently and predictably supply nec-essary income. The most obvious means to generate funds is through inclusion of investments that produce income directly. But for many individual investors, and for nearly all endowments, yields from income-producing investments aren't high enough to cover total funding needs, and additional income must be generated through sale of some holdings. When asset sales augment total portfolio income, it's imperative that assets are available that can be easily converted to cash with no, or very little, risk of loss.

While endowments have used multiple assets to deliver portfolio income for years, some individual investors are just waking up to the simple fact that bond yields are probably not high enough to provide sufficient portfolio income no matter how much of the portfolio they make up. As a result, income needs greater than a percent or two of total portfolio assets require that a portfolio be constructed to enable predictable and profitable sales of assets. The multiple assets within an endowment's portfolio offer a high probability that income needs can be advantageously met via the sale of an appreciated investment. In the rare but possible case that every performance-oriented asset in an endowment's portfolio declines, minimal holdings of safer and highly noncorrelated assets, such as bonds, provide a safety value that can cover immediate funding requirements. A good portfolio design satisfies current income needs *and* offers much higher long-term performance potential than is possible with a simple domestic stock and bond approach. Endowments appear to have developed an excellent investment model that delivers strong performance over reasonable time frames regardless of market and economic conditions while also satisfying significant income demands.

The rest of this book looks at various ways that this strategy can be applied and adapted to individual investors' specific situations. All of us are unique, and we all have different financial and emotional desires and needs. The financial landscape constantly changes, which presents evolving opportunities and challenges. Successful application of the endowment model requires your molding this strategy to your particular needs. Fortunately, I believe designing and implementing the strategy is well within your reach and likely presents an excellent opportunity to improve your investment success no matter how you define it.

2

The Standard Investment Approach

FOR MANY DECADES, A VERY TRADITIONAL INVESTMENT APPROACH has permeated everything from investment advice columns to financial models to standard investment recommendations. The story goes like this: If you are very young, you hold a high percentage of stocks in your portfolio because you can wait out expected volatility. As you move through your career and approach retirement, you add bonds to your portfolio to lessen the volatility and produce more income. The older you get, the more bonds you hold. So simple, so neat.

The only major disagreements with this model center around the percentage of your portfolio placed in bonds. At retirement, many standard recommendations emphasize splitting a portfolio between stocks and bonds. An aggressive portfolio might hold 60 percent stocks while a more conservative one has only 40 percent stocks. Very conservative investors might shun the stock market entirely, but then these individuals weren't really considered investors. Overly aggressive investors refuse to scale back stock holdings. Their stocks exceed percentages deemed appropriate for investors their age, which earns them condemnation from the investment world establishment. Of course, following this model requires little thought, and applications of this strategy are easy to explain, understand, and implement.

Building portfolios from stocks and bonds became accepted practice during the 1950s with the development of modern portfolio theory (MPT). The wealthy used these investments in much earlier times, but MPT made these investments understandable to a much wider public.

Some explanation might be helpful here. While I will avoid nearly all acronyms, I'm using MPT because it's the standard term employed in nearly all investment literature. It's a good term to know if you read much in this field.

Also, in different parts of the book, I'll be referring to various data and statistics related to public stock and bond markets. In many areas, I'll just refer to "the market," "emerging markets," or "bonds." To simplify later sections, I'll specify my meaning and data sources up front rather than repeatedly referring back to them. When I mean something other than what is defined here, or when data are gotten from different sources, I'll be specific.

U.S. stocks and *the market* refer to the S&P 500, the capitalization weighted index published in its current form since 1957. This index tracks the prices of the 500 largest, most actively traded firms in the United States and is widely viewed as the most representative index of the U.S. stock market. *Capitalization weighted* means that the components, or companies, that comprise the index are weighted according to the total market value of their outstanding shares.

You may be surprised that I don't use the very common Dow Jones Industrial Average (DJIA). While the DJIA is certainly a solid and well-known index, most studies and academic works refer to the S&P 500, partly because it includes 500 stocks rather than the 30 in the Dow Jones Industrial Average. Using the broader S&P 500 is much easier because information is so much more widely available. All data I use was supplied directly by Standard and Poor's, the owner and maintainer of this index.

For foreign developed stock market performance, the MSCI EAFE Index is used. This index includes a selection of over 6,000 stocks from 24 developed markets but excludes equities from the United States and Canada.[1] The MSCI EAFE acronym stands for Morgan Stanley Capital International, Europe, Australasia, and Far East. Like the S&P 500, the index is market capitalization weighted. All data was supplied by MSCI (www.msci.com), the firm that owns and maintains the index.

Since 1988, MSCI has also created the standard benchmark for emerging markets, predictably named the MSCI Emerging Markets Index. Because emerging markets have grown and evolved considerably over the last few decades, this index has been much more fluid than most others. As of this writing, the index includes over 2,700 securities in 21 countries that are currently classified as emerging market countries.[2] MSCI (www.msci.com) owns, maintains, and supplied the data for this index as well.

Price and yield performance for general bond returns are defined by the Barclays Capital U.S. Aggregate Bond Index, formerly known as the Lehman Aggregate Bond Index. After Lehman Brothers collapsed in April 2008, Barclays Capital bought the rights to this index from the defunct Lehman Brothers and now maintains it. This index provides a measure of the U.S. investment grade bond market performance and includes investment-grade U.S. government bonds, investment-grade corporate bonds, mortgage pass-through securities, and asset-backed securities publicly offered for sale in the United States. All bond data were supplied directly by Barclays Capital, the new owner and maintainer of this index. Now let's return to covering the standard investment approach.

MPT provided a simple investment framework. Risk and return could be easily understood across the investment community and within investment circles. It incorporated various unfamiliar concepts, including the efficient market hypothesis, a theory that assumes that all investors are rational and all markets are efficient. The all-encompassing nature of the model as well as its elegance made it easy to understand and communicate. You've probably already been exposed to this model through information on your 401(k) or various other investment explanations, although you may not have known its name.

The model's key contribution is its clear explanation of the risk-versus-reward trade-off between stocks and bonds. The premise is simple. Stocks and bonds usually don't move in the same direction at the same time and, when they move, they don't move in the same manner. Stocks are assumed to move up and down more sharply while bond values and returns vary less. In addition, because the returns of stocks and bonds have low or even inverse correlations, matching them in a portfolio helps to reduce the overall portfolio's volatility. By holding stocks and bonds with weak or even inversely correlated performance, the application of MPT sought to reduce the total volatility of a portfolio. In addition, the concept could be shown in a simple graph illustrating the trade-off in risk versus reward, depending on the percentage of stocks versus bonds in a portfolio (see Figure 2.1).

It's difficult to overemphasize the concept's impact. If you have money invested in nearly any tradable asset, you've been affected by this model. The concepts are ubiquitous, and investment professionals and most investors take them for granted. Nearly all investors assume that stocks are riskier than bonds but offer more performance potential. Conversely, we assume bonds are probably safer but offer less upside possibility. These beliefs result largely from MPT.

Today, most investors employ the concept on a regular basis starting in their 401(k) and 403(b) retirement accounts. Even the most unsophisticated investors assume that a higher percentage of stocks in their portfolio increases the expected return and risk while the addition of bonds reduces volatility and probable returns.

Figure 2.1 Traditional Definition of Risk versus Reward

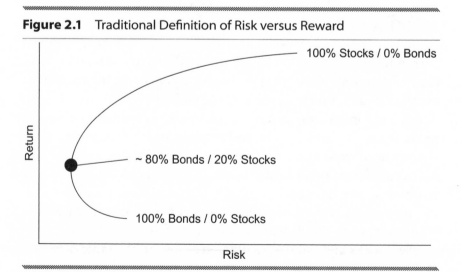

While the model has been widely adopted, that doesn't protect it from substantial criticism. For instance, external events tend to affect individual stocks and markets differently, and markets don't tend to be as efficient as assumed. Nevertheless, MPT's central assumption of the desirability of holding both stocks and bonds in varying amounts to maximize return for a given level of risk has held up remarkably well for many decades.

MPT's penetration of the global investment community has also vastly contributed to investor comfort with stocks and bonds. Sixty years ago, individuals rarely owned individual stocks, and even mutual funds were virtually nonexistent. Only the wealthiest investors and institutions invested in public markets.

Today, the majority of Americans invest in the stock market, often starting with their participation in retirement accounts. There are obviously many reasons for the change, including the vast reduction in fees and ease of ownership, but certainly the average individual's understanding of stocks and bonds plays a significant role.

The primary corporate retirement accounts, 401(k)s and 403(b)s, have also been the perfect place to apply the MPT concepts. Retirement accounts allow investors to hold only mutual funds invested in stocks or bonds, and these accounts provide many individuals their first, and sometimes only, investment experience. It's not surprising that so many investors are very familiar with the investments commonly held in these accounts. Their widespread availability has helped many individuals improve their investment knowledge. Yet, their restrictions limit access to other possible investment options and probably stunt the growth of investor financial sophistication.

During the 1980s and 1990s, the overall strength of the stock market kept most investors fairly satisfied with their returns. Retirement account values soared, and many investors became convinced that success was inevitable. Even Hollywood noticed the appeal of investing and created TV shows and movies focused on the moneyed world of Wall Street. (As an aside, when TV shows start to focus on the stock market, that's a good sign the market has gotten overheated. It's probably time to reduce the amount you have invested in stocks.)

Then, the next decade hit, and it pummeled investors with the worst 10-year performance for U.S. stocks in history. Investors, accustomed to fabulous success, experienced a terrible start to the decade with the 2000–2002 market meltdown. In 2003, however, the market roared back and grew for several more years. While the decade wasn't as strong as the 1990s, returns were looking reasonable by mid-2007. Seemingly, all was right again.

Of course, 2008 brought another major market setback with the market decline of nearly 40 percent, which devastated portfolios. Two major stock market corrections within the same decade caused many investors to question the wisdom of investing in equities at all. This seems like a natural reaction given the previous decade's terrible performance. Failure to reassess this asset class and any investment approach highly dependent on its performance would have been irresponsible. Unfortunately, during this same time period, mediocre bond returns couldn't compensate for the equity market's struggles. Overall, it was a tough decade for the standard investment model and, by extension, for most investors.

Yet, even during this terrible time span, not all investors struggled. In fact, many endowments earned excellent returns over the decade. Their success came in spite of the stock market decline and middling bond returns. In order to achieve this success, it stands to reason that they must have been doing something different than directed by the standard investment model. And they were. Their deviation from the basic MPT model enabled them to thrive when most investors failed.

These investors appeared to enjoy an almost unfair advantage. While the previous decade seemed to present constantly changing conditions to all investors, endowments used newer and more sophisticated tools to achieve their success. To use a sailing analogy, it was almost like individual investors were sailors stuck with the old Egyptian and Roman square sails and traditional hulls able to use only tailwinds to make progress while endowments were sailing with triangular sails and advanced keels capable of propelling them forward even with a headwind.

As you might expect, the success of endowments during a decade in which more traditional portfolios struggled has led to increased criticism of MPT. While the very smart money abandoned the traditional model decades ago (just as explorers abandoned more primitive sailing techniques), widespread challenges within the investment community serving individuals have been fairly muted because many advisors have been unable to offer an alternative.

Now, times are changing. Recent failures of the traditional portfolio design are forcing much greater focus on the limitations of this model. Individual investors are becoming increasingly aware that more advanced strategies are routinely employed by wealthier individuals and institutions. Fortunately, the financial services industry is evolving, albeit somewhat slowly, and alternatives to stocks and bonds are gradually becoming part of more investment plans.

Today, the criticism of using only stocks and bonds and the MPT model goes well beyond the model's unimaginative portfolio recommendations. Instead it focuses more on the relevancy of the strategy and the model. The central charge leveled against the strategy is very simple: It only includes stocks and bonds that trade on public markets in the United States. This is obviously a very limited view of today's world. The simplistic viewpoint reveals the origins of the model and assumptions about investing that are rooted in a very different time and a very different world.

The standard strategy includes no discussion of foreign equities, foreign bonds, real estate, private companies, hedge funds, commodities, limited partnerships, business development companies, managed futures, oil and gas, private debt, or any other investment that doesn't fit neatly into the category of publicly traded domestic stocks and bonds. In essence, many of today's investors are ignoring potential tools that could help them sail forward under far more types of conditions.

The obvious shortcomings of the standard interpretation of MPT have spawned a new approach to investing that I believe offers many potential benefits to individual investors. There's no reason these benefits must remain solely in the possession of institutions that have successfully employed the endowment strategy. They make no effort to keep this approach a secret or prevent other investors from employing it. Most even publish their plans before they pursue them.

This approach is widely referred to as the endowment model. In the ensuing chapters, we'll discuss what's different about this approach and how you may be able to adapt many of its most attractive characteristics. While your portfolio must differ from that of an endowment, just as all endowments differ from one another, I believe you'll see many potential benefits of applying this technique in your portfolio.

3

The Endowment Model

How did the endowment model begin? Oftentimes, accepted wisdom slowly materializes out of the fog. There's no real beginning, it just is. While MPT accelerated investors' grasp of investment concepts with stocks and bonds, the employment of these asset classes in investment portfolios had been around for centuries. Yet surprisingly, the endowment model can trace its history to a specific beginning point.

This more progressive and sophisticated investment approach has been emerging since David Swensen became the chief investment officer for Yale University in 1985. After taking over the Yale endowment, Swensen developed an investment approach for the university predictably named the "Yale model." Over time, this strategy has come to be referred to as the "endowment model" or "endowment strategy" because so many different universities' endowments and institutions have adopted it.

Endowments' recognition of the opportunity resulted partly from their tremendous intellectual capital. When you are managing billions of dollars, spending large sums on talented and trained personnel as well as on cutting-edge research makes perfect sense. An annual one-tenth of one percent improvement in a $10 billion portfolio yields $10 million in a single year. That's a lot of incentive.

At a very high level, the model took a very different approach to portfolio allocation. Rather than holding only stocks and bonds, the Yale model sought to diversify across six broadly different asset categories in roughly equal amounts in addition to many subgroups within each category. In 1989, 70 percent of Yale's endowment was committed to U.S. stocks, bonds, and cash. By contrast, 2010 targets for the same three assets totaled only 11 percent.[1]

Investments generally focused on more equity-like types of assets with minimal performance correlations between them. At the same time, the model explicitly avoided asset classes with low expected returns such as fixed income (bonds). Lastly, the model changed the assumption that liquidity is automatically desirable. Instead, liquidity was viewed as a costly characteristic of investments because investors routinely paid for liquidity with lower returns. This doesn't mean that liquidity isn't important, but instead it recognizes its cost.

Very notably, avoiding asset classes with lower expected returns while lessening the emphasis on liquidity substantially reduced fixed-income holdings from typical endowment portfolios. Yet this shouldn't be read as a casual or careless disregard for risk. Endowments face many of the same constraints as individuals. They provide income to their schools and face ongoing financial demands regardless of investment performance. And they can't tell students to come back in a year or two if their portfolio performs poorly. School operations must continue regardless of their portfolio's performance. They need to provide both short-term income and long-term returns. They aren't any more excited about risk and losses than the average investor, even if they probably understand them better.

Because bonds comprise about half of a traditional portfolio for investors near or in retirement, this directional change alone signals a major departure from past investment strategies. The same was true for endowments. Fixed income had been a major part of their portfolios. The shift away from sole dependence on fixed income for safety was a big one.

Obviously, if bonds are largely eliminated or reduced, a significant portion of the portfolio must be constructed from assets that differ from those in a traditional portfolio. Then the model goes even further by generally limiting exposure to domestic stocks to about 25 percent, with many portfolio managers reducing this percentage even further. As a result, at least 75 percent of assets in a typical endowment model usually differ from those held in traditional individual investor portfolios. While this is a significant departure from past approaches, it isn't as radical as it seems.

The departure results from two primary changes. First, virtually no endowments restrict their equity investments to U.S. markets. This change seems simple, but it creates very different performance. Second, endowments include significant percentages of nontraditional assets, normally referred to as "alternative investments" or "alternative assets."

The difference in performance and volatility characteristics has been tremendous. While no standard endowment model similar to a standard MPT model exists, current endowments usually invest only about 25 percent to 30 percent of a portfolio in assets that typically comprise a more traditional strategy.

The focus on other types of investments naturally extends from the growth and modernization of the global economy. Just as economies have grown more diverse, so have the means to participate in global growth. Increasing financial market sophistication also provides investors greater access to participating in a greater variety of investment opportunities.

As radical as this new approach sounds, however, it's not as difficult or daunting to build and manage as it may seem. For many investors, relatively small deviations from the traditional model can provide many benefits. Even basic or less aggressive changes can improve portfolios.

For instance, the inclusion of international stocks and real assets such as real estate provide very simple means to diversify into assets with good performance histories and lower performance correlations. In addition, over the past few decades, various other investments such as private equity, hedge funds, managed futures, and commodities-linked investments have become available, which make investing in these various alternative investments both easier and more attractive. I realize that investments in these areas may be unfamiliar and possibly very intimidating to many people. Yet new developments in recent years have made them quite accessible to the average individual investor. Throughout the remaining chapters in the book, we'll address the endowment's approach to this challenge and how many individual investors are adjusting their investment approach to gain many of the same benefits enjoyed by the endowments.

The endowment model's focuses on alternative assets are easy to understand since these investors are seeking higher returns with lower risk just as small investors are. First, alternative assets have performed well historically. Given the endowment model's goal of replacing low-expected-return assets with higher-performing assets, better expected performance for the newly added assets is certainly desirable.

Possibly more significant is the second characteristic. Many alternative assets have a low or at least a lower expected correlation with domestic equity markets and with one another. The lower-performance correlations of the various assets provide probably the greatest key to the model's success and widespread adoption by sophisticated portfolio managers and investors.

After all, if a portfolio manager wanted only to increase expected return, modern portfolio theory and the resulting strategies dictate that they would simply add equities and decrease bonds. While the expected return of the portfolio would increase, however, so would the portfolio's volatility. In addition, not only does risk go up as stocks are added—as the percentage of stocks increases—the speed at which volatility increases also goes up. As a portfolio approaches 100 percent stocks, squeezing out just a bit more return requires taking on a much greater amount of risk than it does if the portfolio only holds 50 percent stocks.

The reason that a typical retiree portfolio is composed of about a 50/50 stock/bond mix is that with this approximate mix it's believed that the optimum amount of return can be gotten for a given level of risk. It's sound strategy for these portfolios. As the amount of equities moves higher, risk rises faster than return, especially as equity amounts move above the 60 percent level. For a typical investor, especially one approaching retirement, achieving higher returns in exchange for higher risk that grows disproportionately greater with higher levels of equity exposure is simply unacceptable.

Endowments faced the same constraints and built portfolios similar to individuals before radically changing their assumptions and resulting philosophy. Given the constraints of the traditional model, investors have taken rational action based on their choices. Unfortunately for investors, this knowledge probably offers little consolation after the last decade. However, there's good news.

The hallmark of the endowment model is that it has dramatically increased returns while reducing volatility or at least the likelihood of loss. This achievement is something that the more traditional strategies can't hope to achieve employing only stocks and bonds. The endowment model addresses the volatility challenge fundamentally different than the traditional stock-and-bond approach to investing. While the traditional approaches use the addition of bonds to decrease volatility, the endowment model incorporates multiple asset classes with lower or even negative correlations to secure upside potential without the corresponding increases in volatility.

The departure from a constrained model makes nearly all the difference. During the decade starting in 2000, if you followed a traditional portfolio strategy, you likely experienced losses even if you managed your stocks quite well. If we assume that an investor outperformed the market by 5 percent every year *and paid no investment costs*—extremely optimistic assumptions—a split stock/bond portfolio rebalanced annually would have produced returns of around 3.5 percent per year. Our brilliant investor still would have achieved lousy returns given the tremendous headwinds over this time period.

In contrast, Yale, Harvard, and Stanford did well over this time period. An investor earning only half the returns of these endowments over this same decade—a very pessimistic assumption— would have earned returns more than 50 percent greater than our brilliant stock investor. Endowments also typically generated these excellent portfolio returns while also maintaining fairly low levels of portfolio volatility. The endowment model still employs a basic premise of MPT. It seeks to reduce overall portfolio volatility by combining assets with low performance correlation. This is the same approach as MPT, but the traditional approach combines only two asset classes.

Unfortunately, half of the mix (fixed income) has a low expected return. The other half (stocks) may have a high expected return in the long term but can experience long periods of poor performance, which was painfully demonstrated during the first decade of the new millennium. In addition, the correlation between only two asset classes is highly variable. In some years, the assets are nearly perfectly correlated, but in others they will move in nearly opposite directions. Unfortunately, this means that diversification works well sometimes while at other times it's very ineffective—the years 2000 to 2010 provide too good an illustration.

In contrast, the endowment model secures diversification in a portfolio quite differently. Like the old approach, assets are included that have low or weak correlation with domestic stocks. However, there are two big differences. First, rather than including only two assets with lower levels of correlation, the endowment model includes at least six major asset classes with low expected correlation, including domestic stocks, foreign developed market stocks, emerging market stocks, real assets, private equity, and absolute return. Additional subclasses are also added. Second, nearly all the additional asset classes have high-performance expectations, unlike traditional fixed income.

The different approach forces trade-offs. Nothing really comes free. The volatility of the individual new assets can be much greater than that of bonds. This illustrates a key difference in this strategy's approach. The model accepts greater asset class volatility in exchange for potential performance and lack of correlation among the asset classes. While the individual positions may be more volatile, they perform well as a group—hopefully—because some of them do very well when others don't. The goal is acceptable portfolio volatility rather than minimal volatility of every asset class.

The key is including assets whose performances are not closely correlated to one another. While investors like high correlation when values are increasing, high levels of correlation during declines are obviously undesirable. If an asset does very well over time but performs inconsistently, as long as other assets perform well when it stumbles, overall performance of the portfolio can still be solid.

A comparison of two different basketball teams might help make this concept clearer. The traditional model is more like a basketball team with two types of players. If we assume that 40 percent of the team is composed of star players—in this case, our stocks—two of the players would be real stars. To carry the analogy further, we need to assume that our stars are identical twins who nearly always play either well or poorly on a given night, and rarely play differently from each other. The remaining players are more solid and predictable but rarely provide outstanding or inspired performances. This team may perform well when the two stars play well while the less talented players provide steady support. However, if the star players have an off night, the remaining players just don't have enough talent to win.

By contrast, the endowment model looks more like a basketball team comprised of five star players who also play well together. On the second team, not every star plays brilliantly every night, but the team with more talent is more likely to have at least a few players who perform very well more frequently because the talent pool is so much greater. As a result, the more talented team performs better more regularly, even if some of its players are not as steady as less-talented players might be. Again, the trick is making sure that at least some of the star players are having a good night if others are not.

To use another analogy, in a portfolio you want to build a dream team of assets. You might point out that doing so doesn't guarantee success, but I would add that it makes success at a very high level much more likely than if we filled a team with steady but mediocre talent.

An obvious question that can arise is, where do we find more star players? Surprisingly, the endeavor isn't as difficult as it might first appear. However, it does require looking beyond the traditional talent pool. Most of the rest of the book will cover different possible stars that can be added as well as what things they are particularly good at and when they may fall short.

An Example

In investing, much as in sports, tremendous talent exists outside of the United States. To add more talent, the most popular sports in the United States have begun recruiting actively for players outside of the country. Investors have learned this same trick. We are going to cover this section more thoroughly when we discuss stocks, but a quick overview here can show the logic.

Stocks tend to outperform bonds in most countries, not just in the United States. As a result, stocks in foreign countries provide another potential source of higher-performing assets. Because many of the factors that drive corporate growth and profits differ across countries, stock market performance across countries tends to differ both in the near term and over longer time periods. As a result, foreign stock markets offer the opportunity to add a high-performing star to the portfolio with very different abilities than another high-performance potential player on the roster: the U.S. stock market.

To be fair, stock market performance across countries can show higher degrees of correlation than some other asset classes such as stocks versus bonds. For example, the stock markets of Western Europe and the United States frequently show fairly high levels of correlation. Yet, even these markets frequently perform somewhat differently. Regardless of the higher levels of market correlation, they still provide some diversification. And many other markets can provide much greater benefits.

Interestingly, emerging markets illustrate this point. The economies of many emerging markets are growing at much more rapid rates than the U.S. economy. While much of the growth within emerging markets is a result of trade with the West, increasingly, emerging market growth comes through increased trade with each other. As a result, the correlation of emerging market performance with U.S. markets has been decreasing and is expected to lessen even more in the future. In addition, the more rapid economic growth in emerging markets frequently translates into greater stock market growth.

The combination of decreased correlation and greater growth potential can make emerging markets particularly attractive in a portfolio because they add to overall portfolio performance and increase diversification. It's like adding a star player to a team who rarely seems to be affected by issues that affect other players. For example, when everyone else is distracted by the hostile crowd and unfamiliar gym during the big road game, this player is completely unaffected and provides the star power for the night.

Greater Possibilities

Looking for talent outside of the United States provides some ability to diversify. For endowments, however, this isn't their biggest source of new star power for their portfolio. In fact, endowments find much of their new talent in nontraditional sectors outside of traditional stock markets. Their ability to successfully incorporate these alternative assets results from their willingness to accept a player under different conditions.

One of the biggest adjustments that many endowment models make is sacrificing liquidity for return and safety or stability. It's kind of like getting a star player for the same price as a lesser talent because the coach is willing to commit to keeping the player for more than a season—or in the case of a stock, more than a day. This trade-off is made purposefully. In exchange for limited or sporadic liquidity, these new asset classes often provide other desirable attributes such as high performance, stability, low correlation, or predictable income. The assets can be thought of as very angular. They do some things very well—perhaps performance and stability—but are very poor in other areas such as liquidity.

Much like building an entire portfolio of stocks makes little sense for most people, building a portfolio of high-performing illiquid holdings rarely makes sense. However, including some of these assets in a portfolio generally increases the total return while decreasing the portfolio volatility.

In addition, as more of these types of assets are added, their angular natures help them work together to form a portfolio that is greater than their individual strengths. The individual benefits of different assets compensate for the weaknesses of other positions. Some positions provide liquidity, others income, while others provide diversification to offset differing performance of other assets.

Possibly the easiest way to think of this type of portfolio is as a typical football or basketball team made up of different players with very different skills. Like the different asset classes included in an endowment model, all of the players are star players and provide great performance, but they produce it in very different ways. Obviously, a football team needs different players who excel at their individual positions; the team expects various players to have limitations in certain areas in exchange for outstanding performance in others.

On a football team, a great left tackle and a gifted wide receiver can make fabulous contributions through their unique talents. Yet expecting either to be good at all skills isn't realistic. An offensive lineman blocks big interior defensive players, and a receiver catches and runs. Similarly, certain assets provide liquidity, others provide income; some provide exposure to international markets, and yet others provide good returns during inflationary periods.

Much like any sports team, portfolio success is—or at least should be—measured by the performance of the whole, not individual assets. Using the analogy of a football team can serve to illustrate another development. At the inception of football as professional sport, players generally consisted of two types of people—faster, more athletic players and slower, less athletic players. Even specialized players weren't so special. Kickers were simply positional players who could also kick. Frequently, they were the quarterback or running back because they were usually the best athletes. The distinctions between players rarely went beyond these simple characterizations and weren't particularly pronounced. Looking again at the two types of players, they can be easily thought of as stocks and bonds. One type of player had more flash; the other was more stable.

Fast-forward to today and the evolution of the game of football and football players is remarkable. Now, virtually every position is highly specialized. There has even been a recent book and major Hollywood motion picture that chronicles the evolution of the left tackle, a position that few people, even experts, routinely notice during a football game.[2] It's laughable to think of a mountainous interior lineman who weighs over 300 pounds having the speed and agility of a lean and lanky wide receiver weighing 100 pounds less. Moreover, now every team has a kicker and a punter, and some teams actually have three kickers—one to punt, one to kick off, and another for field goals and extra points.

The differentiation of players is very similar to the evolution of investments within a portfolio in the endowment model. Decades ago, you had a couple of different investments. Today, many more possibilities exist. Sophisticated investors, like the advanced coaching staffs of today's football teams, routinely employ many different players. Similar to professional football, the differences among investment approaches are most noticeable at the highest levels of performance yet continuously trickle down to lower levels such as colleges, high school, and even peewee leagues. The benefits of correctly finding and using the right skills in the right place have become increasingly obvious at lower levels of proficiency. High school football is a totally different game than it was 30 years ago, as players have become dramatically more skilled, developed, and specialized.

Over the past several decades, the largest endowments have pioneered a different approach to investing. The success of this approach caught the attention of smaller institutions, which in turn motivated high-net-worth families and individuals to adopt the practices. Increasingly, spurred on particularly by the last decade's terrible stock market performance, individual investors are becoming motivated to incorporate the practices of wider diversification across higher-performing asset classes. If football can evolve, certainly investing can too.

4

Results

Before moving on to discuss different elements of the strategy and how to implement it, some performance measures may be helpful to better understand the potential benefits. Keep in mind several obvious facts: These numbers and measures of various levels of success are derived from the past and certainly don't guarantee future success. Possibly more relevant is that the numbers presented will be for investors; these are very different than those for individuals.

Harvard, Yale, and Stanford universities all have multibillion-dollar endowments with staffs employed solely to manage them. Few investors can claim the same. In addition, endowments have different needs and time horizons. This topic will be discussed more as we move through different investment categories, but remember that these facts are provided solely to illustrate the concept and not because you are going to be able to build the same portfolio to achieve the same results.

With all that said, the numbers are very compelling. The portfolios have performed well over time; when particular assets haven't done well, others have offset their poor performance. As a result, individual positions within the portfolio might have been volatile but the overall portfolios remained relatively stable. The endowment model essentially follows the same logic as the MPT model but utilizes far more investment categories with lower levels of correlation. In addition, the replacement of bonds with new assets with higher expected returns boosted portfolio performance.

Analyzing performance for endowments is a bit trickier than analyzing performance for many other strategies because endowments use a different calendar. To better align with the school year and their budgeting process, virtually all endowments measure performance from July 1 to June 30. So, when reviewing any of the numbers that follow, remember that they are not *calendar* year measures but instead *fiscal* year ones that start on July 1. This can create a bit of confusion, because some years that people know were great or bad may have totally different results if measured from July 1 to June 30 rather than from January 1 to December 31.

As mentioned, long-term performance by endowments is extremely compelling. Figure 4.1 shows the returns of various approaches. As you look at these numbers, remember that the

Figure 4.1 Performance of Endowments, Stocks, and Traditional Portfolios from 1999 to 2009

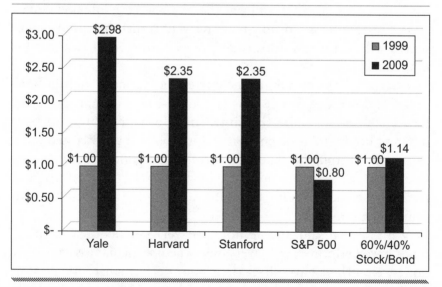

The Yale Endowment, reports for years 2000–2009; *Harvard University Financial Report 2009*, p. 10; *Report from The Stanford Management Company 2009*, p. 2; *Harvard University Financial Report, Fiscal Year 2009*, p. 10, via S&P 500/Citigroup US BIG.

numbers for the endowments are actual return numbers net of all fees (July to June, not January to December), while the numbers for the S&P 500 and the stock/bond mix are index numbers only, with no fees removed.

If we make this comparison more realistic, it looks even worse (see Figure 4.2). Few people earn market returns on stocks or bonds. In fact, most investors earn performance below the markets due to various issues (there will be more about this later). For my example, I'm going to assume modest fees of 2.0 percent for stocks and 0.5 percent for bonds. If you think these fees are high, you may be surprised to learn that these are well below average. Average mutual fund fees are significantly higher than 2.0 percent a year, and actual investor performance lags even more. There will be more on this topic in later chapters.

The difference over the 10-year period is remarkable, with all the endowments at least doubling or nearly tripling their investments

Figure 4.2 Performance After Adding 2 Percent Fees for Stocks and 0.5 Percent Fees for Bonds

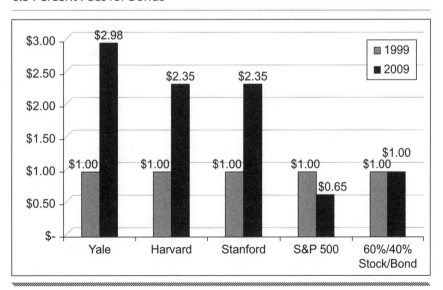

The Yale Endowment, reports for years 2000–2009; *Harvard University Financial Report 2009*, p. 10; *Report from the Stanford Management Company 2009*, p. 2; *Harvard University Financial Report, Fiscal Year 2009*, p. 10, via S&P 500/Citigroup US BIG.

while an average investor with relatively low fees has his or her investment shrink by more than a third. As we'll see later, this is a very optimistic viewpoint, as reality for individual investors as a group was significantly worse during this time period. Here, I'm simply using averages according to performance and fees of different common investments.

If we look at longer time periods, including the fabulous 1990s, the results favoring the endowment model remain compelling. Harvard's 20-year history ending June 30, 2009, generated annualized returns of 11.7 percent per year versus a 60/40 stock bond return of 7.8 percent per year.[1] Again, this is without any fees or looking at actual investor returns, which were much worse.

When compounded, the difference really stands out. Over this 20-year period, Harvard earned a return on investment of over 900 percent (11.7 percent annual return compounded) while a standard 60/40 stock/bond portfolio grew by less than 450 percent (7.8 percent annual return compounded). And, Harvard's return is net of fees while the 60/40 stock/bond portfolio assumes no fees. If we take a slightly more realistic approach and assume the same fees as above (2.0 percent stocks and 0.5 percent bonds), the 60/40 stock/bond portfolio would have grown by less than 350 percent, or barely more than a third of Harvard's gain. Again, if you are saying to yourself that these fees are high, you are probably unaware of what's really happening with your investments.

There are more interesting ways to analyze the returns. Harvard's fiscal year ending June 30, 2008, paints a more representative picture of normalcy and helps to explain why the endowments have typically fared so well. Over this one-year time period, Harvard's portfolio increased in value by 8.6 percent versus the S&P decline of nearly 15 percent without dividends.[2] Including the 7.1 percent gain of bonds over that time frame[3] would have resulted in a 50/50 stock/bond portfolio loss of about 5 to 6 percent, including all dividends, versus Harvard's gain of 8.6 percent for a spread of nearly 15 percent.

The previous year, 2007, saw a similar pattern. Harvard's fiscal year ending June 30, 2007, saw gains of 23.0 percent versus significantly lower return numbers for either stocks or bonds. A 60/40 stock/bond portfolio would have seen a total gain of around 14 percent, which obviously trails Harvard's gain by about 9 percent. All this sounds great. But all is not perfect all the time, even for endowments.

Different time periods change the numbers a bit but consistently tell the same story. Yale's endowment returned 8.9 percent per annum over the 10 years ending June 30, 2010, while stocks returned −0.7 annually. A 60/40 stock/bond portfolio would have earned just over 2 percent without fees or under 1 percent with the average fees already referenced.[4]

A Problem Year

Going back to the performance return numbers shown for the three major endowments, remember that the numbers take into account the horrible stock market decline and crash in asset values during the 2008 recession. While the big endowments still managed to perform much better than the stock market, nearly all of them suffered significant losses, which demonstrates that no model is perfect.

A survey released on December 10, 2009, conducted jointly by the National Association of College and University Business Officers and the Commonfund Institute reported that the endowment funds of major colleges and universities lost 19 percent for the year ended June 2009, outpacing the 28 percent drop in the Standard & Poor's 500 Index.[5] The same survey reported that despite some high-profile hedge fund disasters, alternative investments remained quite popular with the 435 educational institutions. The group had 51 percent of their assets invested in alternatives compared to just 19 percent invested in traditional U.S. stocks.

Given the trauma of this period and purported advantages of the endowment model, it's worth exploring this period more completely. As mentioned, the endowment's inability to excel in all markets illustrates that no model is perfect. And while the above numbers compare well with the S&P 500, probably the more relevant portfolio to analyze is a stock/bond strategy. For the year ending June 30, 2009, a 60/40 stock/bond portfolio would have lost 13.5 percent.[6] This loss is better than the 19 percent loss suffered by major colleges and universities cited in the study above. And the stock/bond portfolio looks even better when compared to the elite universities of Yale, Harvard, and Stanford, which all saw portfolio values decline around 25 percent for the fiscal year.

A letter published by Princeton University's president, Shirley M. Tilghman, on September 29, 2009, summarizes the challenge and opportunity presented by the endowment model approach:

> Last year when the sub-prime mortgage crisis sparked the near collapse of the world's financial markets and we came face-to-face with a once-in-70-year recession, that lack of correlation disappeared, and all investment classes except fixed income experienced significant losses. From this we were reminded that there is no investment approach that could fully protect an endowment against the severest of global downturns, and at the same time provide high enough returns over the long-term to enable us to preserve the purchasing power for future generations.[7]

In the face of this recent challenge, it's interesting to look more deeply into the numbers. Obviously, large institutions have very different capabilities, needs, and strategies than do individual investors. While the differences are substantial, a few are worth highlighting during any performance discussion.

First, the large endowments invest very aggressively and will even use leverage at times to increase their exposure to various asset classes. For example, Harvard attributed some of its losses in 2008 to its borrowing of 5 percent of its portfolio value in an attempt to increase returns. Effectively, Harvard held –5 percent cash. Few individual investors are so bold—for good reason.

Second, the endowments often invest in asset categories that require additional capital investments. Normally, their cash flow planning and alumni gifting enable endowments to gain exposure to investments and add funding only as needed. In 2008, however, contributions plummeted as donors were suffering through the same financial crisis as the endowments were. Many of their liquid assets also declined in value. Paying out additional funds for ongoing investments was particularly painful.

Unfortunately for the endowments, they hadn't anticipated the combined impact of a collapse in contributions, previous commitments to fund new investments, and ongoing school operational costs. As a result, many endowments and institutions were forced to sell assets at terrible times, which demonstrates that just because they usually have been smarter doesn't guarantee that they always are. Endowments learned from this mistake and adjusted their policies to lessen the likelihood of having to sell at the worst possible times.

The last major factor that possibly contributed to endowments' poor one-year performance revolves around reporting. Many of the endowments are believed to have sought out paper losses. At various private equity forums and conferences I attended during this time period, it was clearly understood—and even overtly stated at a couple of conferences—that endowments were overestimating their private equity losses in order to avoid reallocating or selling assets.

This requires additional explanation. If you are the manager of an endowment and various asset classes have declined, if they don't decline equally, you may be required to sell certain assets and buy others to bring your allocation back into alignment with your investment policy statement. During the 2008 stock market crash, public stocks fell drastically, which required many institutions and endowments to rebalance their portfolios. Holdings that hadn't fallen as much as others had to be sold to keep percentage allocations of different asset classes within guidelines.

Private equity investment values are difficult to value under the best of circumstances. During the 2008–2009 market volatility, accurate assessments of values of private companies held in private equity pools were nonexistent. Even during normal times, there's no transparent market for these investments and no public prices. They are worth what someone will pay for them, and when there are essentially no transactions, as was the case in 2008, values were based on very inexact guesstimates.

Nearly everyone benefited during this time if private equity values were understated. By assuming that private equity holdings had declined severely or at least about the same as public markets, endowments and institutions were able to avoid liquidating these holdings at very inopportune times. Private equity valuations were widely reported as severely depressed even though there was little evidence that their values had decreased as much as stated. Actually, there was very little data available at all to determine prices. While not selling at the wrong time and assuming very low valuations will likely help the long-term performance of the portfolio, it likely added significantly to endowment paper losses in 2009. In essence, the endowments had a bad year, but it probably wasn't as bad as they reported.

Moving Forward

I believe the success of endowments over any reasonable time frame mandates attention by all investors. Any sailors witnessing a boat with funny-looking sails and a different hull effortlessly moving upwind past their own boat filled with expensive oarsmen would likely work to discover the other craft's secret. The rigging may be unconventional, which requires learning and change, but the benefits could be tremendous. I believe this model presents a similar opportunity. It's different, but it offers tremendous potential. Next, we'll look at some of these key departures of the endowment model from the traditional approach.

5

Recognizing Opportunity

THE ENDOWMENT MODEL AND THE MORE TRADITIONAL investment strategies differ in several key respects. The first two differences—namely, that the endowment model has more uncorrelated, performance-oriented assets and a reduced emphasis on bonds—are quite easy to understand.

A couple of other issues aren't quite as obvious. First, endowments purposely include illiquid alternative investments, which are thought to present unique opportunities. I feel these assets can also benefit individual investors. Second, I believe endowments plan with very different assumptions than individual investors have, particularly in regard to future stock market returns. Similarly, individual investors likely would benefit from more clearly identifying their expectations for the U.S. stock market.

Illiquidity Advantage

The endowments use a key element of their mandate to their advantage. University endowments manage money for use over long and predictable time horizons. Planning horizons often exceed 50 years. The longer time frame is an integral part of their role in providing for the future betterment of the institutions they serve. Yet endowments were once slow to realize that this element of their stated purpose opened up unique possibilities.

If time horizons are very long, it follows that all of the funds in the portfolio will not all be required immediately. This is—and was—obvious. Yet, portfolio management practices often assumed that the entire portfolio must remain liquid to facilitate changes and adjustments whenever desired.

Over time, endowments also better understood the cost or price of liquidity. Liquid investments usually cost more and are worth more than similar illiquid investments because nearly all investors value liquidity. The more liquid the investment, the greater pricing premium usually associated with its value. When virtually any asset transitions from an illiquid holding to a liquid investment vehicle, the price goes up.

Liquidity premiums can only be approximated and vary across time and asset classes. As an example, a real estate holding that transitions from an illiquid structure to a readily tradable stock has historically increased in value a bit more than 10 percent. With stocks, the premium is usually much greater, oftentimes approaching or even exceeding 100 percent. People pay a premium for the ability to convert quickly to cash.

The liquidity premium also tends to be higher if liquidity is a primary benefit of a particular type of asset. Because bonds are often held specifically to provide liquidity, a lack of liquidity will likely be more severely penalized for this type of holding. Unfortunately, investors pay for the liquidity whether they need it or not because they are buying the asset after it has become liquid.

Liquidity also introduces volatility, which most investors try to avoid. Nearly any asset that can be bought and sold on a daily basis prices according to current demand. Since demand for liquid investments can change markedly and quickly, prices can as well. The greater the risk and return possibility, the greater the price variance. Nearly any liquid, high-performance potential investment routinely suffers significant pricing volatility.

For instance, cash is liquid and has no return possibility and is therefore not volatile. Bonds have more return possibility and therefore higher volatility than cash. Limited return possibilities keep volatility relatively low. For stocks, however, return possibilities are high and so is volatility. For any investment with higher return possibilities, liquidity virtually guarantees higher volatility and rapid price movements.

Many illiquid investments are also less transparent. Firms trading on public exchanges must provide standard, comprehensive information that places investors on more equal footing with one another. Illiquid investments usually disclose much less information to investors, which presents greater opportunities for more imaginative investors to find and exploit value.

The conversion of a private company to a publicly traded company through an initial public offering (IPO) illustrates these points. The value of a firm's equity increases dramatically when it becomes tradable. The availability of information on the stock and various disclosure requirements vastly increase as the company adheres to comprehensive regulatory requirements governing public companies. Also, the price becomes more volatile and transparent.

Not surprisingly, some of the first moves into illiquid investments by endowments started with investments into private firms. Endowments recognized that buying equity in private firms offered the opportunity to benefit from value increases resulting from listing through an IPO. Over time, endowments sought similar opportunities across various other illiquid investments.

Endowments also recognized that illiquid investments can offer much more diverse investment performance characteristics. Investments that trade on a stock exchange are often affected by many factors in similar ways. This tends to be true for nearly any asset viewed as a financial instrument routinely traded by many different types of professional financial managers. The inclusion of these assets in financial models and computer trading algorithms often subjects them to very similar influences, which results in correlated price movements possibly unrelated to actual asset values. For example, before the financial meltdown of 2008, the 20-year correlation of the Dow Jones Select REIT Index [one of four domestic traded real estate investment trust (REIT) benchmarks] against the broad U.S. stock market as measured by the Wilshire 5000 (an index that includes the largest 5,000 stocks trading in the United States) was usually below 50 percent and essentially never above 60 percent. By early 2011, correlation had risen to 74 percent as the asset class became more popular with managers who sought new asset classes for diversification.[1]

By contrast, illiquid assets generally escape these influences. The endowments' addition of these assets into their portfolios produced tremendous improvements in performance and much lower levels of volatility for a given level of performance. Correlation also decreased as valuations were driven more by fundamental values than by financial markets. Increased performance, lower volatility, and decreased correlation offered very welcome additions to endowments' portfolios, resulting in continued emphasis on this area.

Given the unique characteristics of these assets, they are nearly always labeled as *alternative assets*. Yet not all alternative assets are illiquid. Fully liquid foreign equities are still treated as alternative assets by many investors. Both developed and emerging markets offer attractive performance and diversification benefits. Foreign equities provide ample new investment options that are increasingly becoming a standard part of investment portfolios. The world is growing rapidly, and investment opportunities beyond the U.S. border and outside of stocks and bonds offer many attractive qualities. And, they are becoming much more accessible to all categories of investors. Thankfully, acceptance of foreign equities is moving them out of the alternative investment category and into simply another category of stocks.

Beyond foreign stocks, alternative assets usually include numerous other sectors such as nontraded real estate, private equity, venture capital, commodities, hedge funds, managed futures, oil and gas (direct investment in wells and distribution), as well as many subcategories. Wider definitions can even include rare coins, stamps, and artwork, although these items are usually considered to be investments suited only for investors with a strong personal interest or expertise in the very specific area.

Although some of these investments may be available in liquid structures that can be traded easily, endowments frequently search out direct investments that offer potential benefits ranging from less-efficient pricing to lack of correlation. When markets are less efficient, opportunities usually exist for good managers to take advantage of greater inefficiencies and create increased value.

Whether investments focus in real estate or energy, any less-standardized and less-understood assets afford potential to generate greater returns for a given risk. Of course, this also assumes that the manager you hire knows what he or she is doing. Fortunately, there are many resources available to investors to make this process easier and hopefully increase the likelihood of success.

Most alternative investments can't be valued as easily. This doesn't mean the value doesn't change, but values are usually assigned less frequently, if at all, and reporting is usually more sporadic and less standardized. In this way, these investments are just like your house. Its value may change daily, but the value you assign to it probably doesn't vary too much or too fast. And, like your house, prices for illiquid investments are usually only estimates that don't change much, which leads to much less asset value volatility.

A very common mistake made by most investors is assuming that their entire portfolio must be liquid—just as endowments had done decades earlier. For the same reason this no longer makes sense for most endowments, a completely liquid portfolio is usually undesirable for most individual investors. The reasons are simple. Performance and diversification possibilities are missed, and the flip side of liquidity for investments with strong return possibilities is virtually always volatility. If you're like most investors, you want greater performance with less volatility—just as endowments do.

Actively seeking and holding a higher percentage of illiquid assets result from a simple assumption and associated investment practice. Endowments assume that their management time horizons are fairly long and therefore they don't need to maintain liquidity across all assets they hold.

A typical endowment will assume an investment time frame that lasts at least 50 years. Most people manage their portfolios for much shorter time frames. Yet, surprisingly, the time frames of endowments and personal portfolios usually don't differ as much as was often assumed. The average couple who retires at age 65 should plan for at least a 25-year investment time frame, and 30 years is probably more realistic. Younger investors or people who plan across generations may even possess time horizons fairly similar to endowments. Fortunately, once time frames exceed 10 years, and even 5 years in some cases, many alternative investments combined intelligently in an appropriate strategy can still work well in meeting an individual investor's needs.

Few alternative investments have life spans beyond 10 years, and most offer either partial or complete liquidity over much shorter time frames. While tying up funds for several years may seem restrictive for an investor accustomed to complete portfolio liquidity, the potential advantages of performance and noncorrelation can make these investments highly attractive even for someone with much shorter investment time frames. Part of the trick is to focus on the whole portfolio, not the individual pieces.

A quick illustration makes this point. As of this writing, my father is 78. His health is great, and he takes no medication. Various tables and statistics suggest a life span lasting about another 15 years. Both his parents lived to their early 90s. What life span do we assume for him in his planning? Although it's easy to assume that long-term planning no longer applies to people approaching 80, this thinking may be shortsighted. Like all of us, he may not make it to tomorrow. But, he'll probably live at least another 10 years, if not 20. How about the average couple entering retirement at age 65? Statistically, at least one of them will live more than 25 years.

Going back to my dad, if we plan for a lifespan of 15 years and he's hit by a bus tomorrow, he has a major problem—but it's not financial. If we plan for only 5 years, however, and he lives for 20, we could be creating financial challenges that could have been avoided. Very simply, most individuals must plan for longer time horizons while also creating income for short-term needs. Many alternatives can provide excellent portfolio benefits if we eliminate the need for immediate liquidity. Moreover, assuming more realistic time frames exceeding 5, 10, or even 15 years can open up very interesting and beneficial possibilities.

Because most individuals realistically possess investment time horizons approaching decades rather than months, I believe a modified endowment strategy can provide average individual investors with many of the benefits of the endowment model while still meeting their needs for liquidity and risk management. Adjustments may be required, but they are usually fairly easy to make. The recent decade also appears to demonstrate that a strategy developed to better recognize and leverage current opportunities to meet modern needs is a very good idea. I also believe this concept will grow in importance as global economic growth shifts. Taking advantage of the many new and improving illiquid investment possibilities presents individual investors with a wonderful means to incorporate a critical part of the endowment model strategy.

Readjusting Assumptions

Beyond incorporating less traditional illiquid investments, a good investment strategy should also make realistic assumptions about likely returns of different assets. While exact return assumptions used by endowments vary, expectations for stock returns (the assumed driver of future returns for most individuals) are declining. As much as I like stocks and believe that they should be included in most portfolios (after all, my day job is managing stocks), I agree with endowments. It appears likely that future stock returns will not match averages of historical returns. If your investment forecasts assume return numbers similar to those generated over the past 60 to 75 years, you may be disappointed going forward.

Most statistics that analyze stocks begin in 1926 because of the creation of a common index that morphed over time into the now commonly recognized S&P 500. Nearly all stock market analyses cover time periods since then. The United States is hardly the developing economy it was 100 or even 75 years ago. And, after World War I and World War II, the United States, as well as Australia and Switzerland, benefited tremendously from the lack of physical and property damage domestically during the wars, unlike that suffered by many other countries. The U.S. economy grew tremendously, and corporate America enjoyed unprecedented success. Fundamentally, the long-run performance of equity investments is linked to corporate earnings growth, and our past growth has been enviable.

We're unlikely, however, to enjoy similar growth levels in the future. Theoretical and empirical research generally predicts that long-run growth in gross domestic product (GDP) exceeding 3 percent is unlikely in developed economies. While growth under 3 percent would be lower than past levels, it wouldn't be surprising, given that the United States is no longer a developing economy. Even so, the United States is a very unique country. Three percent growth and greater is certainly possible under the right economic conditions.

Unfortunately, the United States has various structural issues such as substantial sovereign debt, massive social spending obligations, and costly overregulation that are likely to dampen growth. Our government has acted as though we're still alone in the world and can ignore global competition. Obviously, that's not reality. The rest of the world has bought into capitalism, and many are now playing the game much better than we are.

Historically, real stock returns have averaged about 6 percent. Future projections reduce this number. Linking past GDP growth, corporate earnings growth, projected population growth, and various other economic trends suggests that investors should anticipate real U.S. common stock returns to average no more than 4 to 5 percent in real terms.[2] If you add in inflation of 3 percent, this puts stock returns at 7 to 8 percent. Even if you assume a historically high inflation level of 4 percent, U.S. stock returns could still average only about 8 to 9 percent. While predictions of analysts and experts vary, few anticipate long-term U.S. stock market returns significantly above 10 percent at reasonable inflation levels. Assuming that annual growth will be larger would appear to be unwise.

In addition, as common stocks have become more assessable, expected returns have declined. As a result, wealthier individuals and institutions are drifting away from complete dependence on these investments in the belief that other opportunities offer attractive substitutes within a portfolio.

Savvy stock investment strategies may be able to increase equity returns, but total returns will likely be affected by a slower growing market just as a swimmer in a river is influenced by the current. Future stock market gains probably won't average levels enjoyed during the past 50 years. Projections that we're going to return to the wonderful bull market of the 1990s with average returns approaching or exceeding 15 percent appear to be highly optimistic by nearly any measure.

These predictions aren't meant to chase anyone away from the market. Real returns of about 4 to 5 percent remain attractive for a fully liquid asset. Given current interest rates, projected low bond returns will also probably keep stock returns well ahead of bond gains (more on this in Chapter 13, "Fixed Income"). The greater point is that stock returns are not likely to match past levels. Like endowments, wise investors will probably benefit from a decreased emphasis on stocks, although those investments will likely remain a core asset category. Almost certainly, diversifying away from U.S. stocks as the sole performance asset in a portfolio will be wise.

In building a better portfolio and seeking to emulate the success of endowments, recognizing the potential benefits of illiquid alternative positions and projecting more conservative returns for stocks are probably smart moves. Early steps by endowments decades ago stemmed from both assumptions, and individual investors will likely benefit from similar moves.

As we seek to understand how best to incorporate endowment model strategies into an individual investor's portfolio, I'm going to start by looking more closely at specific investor needs. Obviously, investors can't all be lumped together. We are all far too different. Yet several generalities apply, and many common assumptions are incorrect or simply unclear. Many investors use strategies handed down from parents and grandparents that might have been appropriate in very different eras but now no longer serve modern concepts of finances and retirement goals. And many people simply act out of habit with little thought given to actual investment needs. Better identification of real needs versus assumed ones should help us better mold the endowment model applied by institutions to the needs of individual investors.

6

Investor Needs

MOST INVESTORS DON'T SPEND A LOT OF TIME REALLY PONDER-ing their possible investments. Publicly available investment material usually focuses on stocks, and most investment newsletters promise investment success through increasing equity returns. Occasionally bonds are mentioned, but they are rarely very popular and don't get too much attention; they are thought to be too boring and arcane. In addition, most investors don't clearly define their financial needs and their corresponding investment performance requirements. As a result, they fail to develop a realistic understanding of potential investments.

To construct the best portfolio for any individual investor, one needs to identify that person's true needs and then build a portfolio that satisfies his or her individual requirements. While this approach seems obvious, for many people it can signal a major departure from long-standing investment assumptions or needs that have been assumed for them by outdated portfolio software models.

Most investors need some combination of growth, liquidity, safety, income (if they are in retirement), and satisfactory tax efficiency. While this list isn't new, the interpretation of some of the terms is different. Liquidity doesn't mean that the entire portfolio is liquid but rather that enough of the portfolio is liquid to satisfy current and future needs. Safety doesn't mean that half the portfolio must be invested in assets with very little volatility; instead, the whole portfolio must possess an acceptable level of volatility. Even income may be generated by means other than regular dividends. Unfortunately, while taxes are rarely the driving force behind investments, they also need to be taken into consideration. And their importance could easily grow in future years as the U.S. government seeks ways to shore up its revenue shortfalls.

Let's define these issues further.

Growth

Most investors don't have the luxury of putting all their assets into guaranteed investments that provide little nominal growth and usually negative real (i.e., net of inflation) after-tax growth. Instead, people are living longer, more active lives, and they require more from their finances. Expectations for retirement have changed dramatically during the last 50 years.

Many investors' grandparents and even parents had very modest financial plans for retirement. Life-span expectations were not very high, and even just a couple of generations ago few people planned on living more than a few years past retirement, if they made it that far. Life expectancy when social security was instituted was only 62. If you were 65, you were only expected to last another three years. Government felt quite safe promising a benefit few were expected to use. In addition, during those few years of retirement, lifestyles were expected to be relatively modest.

Fast-forward to today, and most people expect to live very active lifestyles throughout a much longer retirement. As mentioned earlier, estimates for a nonsmoking couple retiring at age 62 project that at least one of the two will live to age 92. Most people now expect those years to be active and filled with travel and other upscale hobbies. Simple math tells us that life spans are now 30 years longer than they used to be, which presents not only a wonderful blessing but also a much greater financial challenge. For most people, nearly all of the additional 30 years of life will be financed through investments rather than a regular paycheck.

Adding to this challenge will likely be a very real but silent thief—inflation. A 3.5 percent rate of inflation doubles the costs of living every 20 years. If we assume a 5.5 percent inflation rate, costs triple in 20 years. While we can't know the future inflation rate, vast increases in government debt are creating widespread expectations that we will see significant inflation in the future. We can all hope to avoid a repeat of the highly inflationary 1970s when CD rates topped 15 percent, but today's investors must account for future inflation. For our 62-year-old retiree couple, a very optimistic projection will see costs double, and more realistic estimates approach or exceed 200 percent cost increases over their lifetime. And this is before factoring in vastly increased healthcare costs.

So, in spite of a very rough investment decade starting in 2000, most people don't have the option of sitting on the sidelines. Growth will be required to maintain purchasing power, and that requires staying in the investment game.

Liquidity

Few investors need complete portfolio liquidity; however, even for an investor with no liquidity or income needs, some portfolio liquidity is desirable in case of emergencies, changes in lifestyle, or even the possibility of better investments arising in the future. Nevertheless, requiring 100 percent portfolio liquidity often necessitates avoiding excellent investment possibilities.

Most investors, when considering liquidity, should focus on income needs and potential emergency needs. Many illiquid investments produce significant income, which can further ease the need for liquidity. The topic of income is a big one, so I'm going to defer it to the next section. Instead, I'll focus on liquidity required to possibly address an emergency.

Usually, the very definition of an emergency means we don't know when it's coming or what its nature will be; however, most people vastly overestimate the potential impact of an emergency on their portfolio. For instance, if you have a $500,000 portfolio, do you really need all of it to be liquid? Are you really going to have a $500,000 emergency that requires accessing all your money with absolutely no notice? For a portfolio of just about any size, the answer will almost always be no.

Instead, it's more likely that you could face a $20,000 or $40,000 emergency because you need a new roof or the car breaks down. Realistically, if you require $40,000 with no warning to buy a car, you've created a self-induced restriction because you could either buy a nice car for a lot less, you could buy a used car, or you could finance a car. Big expenditures with no notice simply aren't very common. Some people worry about a healthcare crisis. Obviously, medical problems can occur, but they rarely require an immediate $50,000 or $100,000 payment. Severe medical problems may be expensive, but payment is rarely required all at once without warning; instead, it is needed over time. Moreover, if a medical need arises, additional returns generated likely become even more important, not less. In nearly all cases, when larger sums are needed, there's usually at least some prior notice. More commonly, people want a larger portion of their portfolio available to pursue a new opportunity or to liquidate during some type of market panic.

Even so, the numbers involved are rarely more than a small percentage of an investor's total portfolio. This is not to say that the average investor would be well served by tying up 90 percent of his or her assets. Even the endowments usually don't go above 60 percent or 70 percent.

Rather, it's likely that a significant percentage of a portfolio, possibly even up to 40 to 50 percent, may be prudently invested in assets that have limited or unpredictable liquidity. If we again assume a $500,000 portfolio, many investors could easily remain very comfortable and meet any unexpected emergencies if $250,000 to $300,000 of the portfolio were available within a couple of days. Although this percentage may be too high and may not be prudent for many investors, the recognition that even 20 percent of a portfolio could be invested in illiquid assets can open up tremendous opportunities to improve various characteristics of a portfolio. Furthermore, even illiquid assets often have means to convert to cash with a bit of notice, although there may be penalties or inconveniences associated with liquidations.

One quick note on portfolio liquidity and alternative investments: Although I believe that the average person can benefit greatly from increasing exposure to less liquid assets, this concept is still relatively new to regulators accustomed to working with old models. Strong assumptions still permeate the industry that emphasize constant, real-time liquidity and pricing. Liquid markets have been the standard for years, and their excessive regulation usually leads to high levels of understanding and trust by regulators. Alternative investments frequently face different regulation—sometimes more onerous than that faced by standard investments—but their differences and more recent arrival usually results in lower levels of understanding and confidence by regulators. As a result, investors routinely face greater barriers in accessing these alternative investments, whether going it alone or with the help of a financial advisor.

The unique nature of these investments makes a thorough understanding and documentation of them prudent, and most financial professionals will be required to more thoroughly document your understanding of the investment as well as its appropriateness to your investment needs. Although the last decade has offered ample evidence on the wisdom of adding these types of positions, the industry has been slow to shift. Of course, I strongly believe that these types of investment provide much greater opportunity to those willing to explore the less familiar, but you'll likely have to accommodate a somewhat less hospitable investment process.

Income

For many investors who are building up their portfolios, income is not an issue. These investors have greater flexibility in designing and managing their portfolio, because there are no immediate requirements for either production of income or liquidity.

For other investors, particularly retirees, adequate income production is the single most important characteristic of their portfolio. Normally, when income is required, it must be available regardless of what is happening to underlying asset values, the economy, or total portfolio value. Furthermore, no investor ever wants to sell an asset to provide income after an asset value has dropped. Since you often can't know when asset values will suddenly drop or the economy will falter, the portfolio must be structured so that it produces sufficient income in any circumstance and provides various safety measures that prevent the possibility of a forced sale of a depressed asset to meet immediate income needs.

Furthermore, a portfolio must be designed so that income is indexed for inflation. Costs will go up over time, and income generation must keep up.

There are various ways to produce income and increase it over time. Holding assets that produce income obviously can help a portfolio generate funds. This has been the role of bonds for decades. A typical withdrawal rate from a portfolio may start at 5 percent of a portfolio at the beginning of retirement with the percentage rising through retirement. It's unlikely, however, that dividends alone will produce the equivalent of 5 percent of a portfolio on an annual basis.

For simplicity's sake, I'm going to revert back to the traditional model. If bonds paying 5 percent interest comprise 50 percent of a portfolio, bond interest payments will equal 2.5 percent of the total portfolio value. Although stocks may generate some additional income, it's very unlikely that they would average the 5 percent dividend rate needed for the portfolio to produce 5 percent from interest and dividends. The result would be an income shortfall. This can create a problem. So, how do we generate enough income?

This is a common challenge. While many books and strategies detail various means to most efficiently derive income for a portfolio, nearly all the strategies boil down to one simple practice or concept: Sell whatever has gone up the most or down the least. Taken a bit further, an even better portfolio design removes the possibility of ever having to sell an asset at a loss in order to provide necessary income. Most income generation practices simply try to maximize this strategy.

Dividend income is usually desirable because of its predictability and lack of impact on principal. Where additional income is needed, selling whatever has gone up the most or down the least works well to rebalance a portfolio and support ongoing portfolio management. As mentioned, a better strategy creates a portfolio where there's no possibility of selling at a loss or at least greatly minimizes this risk. A well-diversified portfolio should provide this benefit.

In a stock/bond portfolio, income beyond bond and stock dividends would normally be produced by selling stocks when they have gone up or liquidating bonds if the stocks have gone down. Of course, bond values can also change, but since they usually are not as volatile as stocks, the choices about what to do are usually quite simple.

The advantage of the modified endowment model is that you have more assets from which to choose. In addition, some of the assets may produce greater income than either bonds or stocks. Holding more assets provides more options to supplement dividend income. Of course, some of the new assets may also be more restrictive and provide little or no income and liquidity. As mentioned, all the pieces have to work together. As we explore different types of assets and portfolio strategies, we'll look at more specific means by which to generate income or portfolio value that can be tapped to generate income.

Another advantage of the endowment strategy is that most of the income-producing holdings also have some form of inflation hedge or growth component that can increase the principal over time. If the yields stay relatively constant, a growing base will produce a growing income stream. While this may have little impact over just a few years, the difference over the average retirement can be substantial, easily doubling income versus less-sophisticated strategies.

Safety or Lack of Volatility

For most people, portfolio volatility is highly undesirable. Institutions and endowments feel the same way, and they actively work to create more predictable returns over time. As mentioned, one of the primary goals and historical strengths of the endowment model is providing strong returns while also limiting volatility.

Nearly everyone assumes that investors with a very long time horizon and no need for income can likely better weather higher levels of portfolio volatility, particularly if they have a temperament better suited to risk. While this is probably true, adjustments will still need to be made to account for individual comfort levels. After all, no matter how good a portfolio design may be, if the investor cannot stay on course over time and avoid temptations to act against her or his own best interests during inevitable challenges, it will not be successful. A solid portfolio design not only addresses growth, income, and risk possibilities, it also considers investor emotions and facilitates the ability to sleep at night.

Yet certain types of portfolio predictability can be more valuable than others. For example, many investors who require income can withstand a much higher level of portfolio volatility if their income is highly predictable. Sufficient income to pay all the bills goes a long way toward generating confidence in a portfolio, even if the asset values fluctuate. Moreover, acceptance of some asset value volatility removes a major design constraint, since a variety of portfolio designs can provide adequate income. With greater design flexibility, it's easier to create a portfolio likely to create future growth while also meeting current income needs.

In addition, the portfolio can be designed to provide predictable income through liquidation of other portfolio assets to meet any income shortfalls. The only absolute requirement for these assets is liquidity, or more simply the ability to turn them into cash to generate income. However, it's possible that a liquid asset, such as stocks, may have decreased in value right at the time additional income is needed. A forced liquidation of a depressed asset is always a bad idea. In fact, it produces the opposite effect of dollar cost averaging. Rather than buying more of an asset for less money, when you sell any asset at a depressed value, you are forced to sell more of the asset to produce a given level of income. A well-designed portfolio should always be constructed to avoid or greatly minimize this possibility.

Numerous approaches work. If the income generated from a portfolio doesn't meet projected income or future cash needs, additional cash availability can be easily designed into a modified endowment strategy portfolio in various ways. The simplest and most aggressive approach is to hope that one of the several higher-performing liquid asset classes held in the portfolio has increased in value so that it can be sold to meet cash needs. This approach has tended to be a common one used by institutions, partly because they can often depend on alumni contributions to offset many of their cash needs. This dependability limits their likelihood of needing to raise significant cash. But because there are numerous different asset classes to choose from, it is highly likely that any need for cash, even if unexpected, could be easily met by selling assets that had increased in value.

Although some people are comfortable using more aggressive assumptions and can easily adjust to less favorable circumstances, I've found that others are more comfortable with a more conservative approach. Even if the long-term outcome from a more aggressive approach may be superior, the emotional trauma possibly resulting from less certainty or more volatility may not be worth the incremental performance improvement. To increase the safety margin and make emotional stress less likely, a more aggressive portfolio can be modified easily by setting aside a small amount of very stable assets, such as cash or high-quality bonds, that can be tapped if all the other assets have decreased in value. This can be like adding a safety valve to prevent a more serious problem. The strategy is simple, and it can be very effective.

A quick example can illustrate this. Obviously, the numbers can be adjusted easily up or down. Assume that an individual needs $50,000 a year of income from a $1 million portfolio. In this case, assume the portfolio only produces a predictable and dependable income of $40,000, which leaves a shortfall of $10,000. This situation is very common in a stock/bond portfolio. The difference between a more traditional portfolio and the modified endowment portfolio is the flexibility to meet the shortfall. In a traditional portfolio, you would sell either stocks or bonds to address the shortfall. If stocks have gone up, you sell stocks. If not, you sell the bonds.

In an endowment model portfolio, you may be able to create a higher level of income and avoid the issue altogether. Or different choices may result in less income. Regardless, to meet an income shortfall, a more diversified portfolio would provide additional asset classes to choose from, such as foreign equities, real estate, traded commodities, hedge funds, managed futures, private equity, or debt offerings. Given more asset class choices, there's a greater likelihood that one of them will have increased in value when income is needed. In addition, even if stocks have gone up, another asset class may have increased even more, providing a better selling opportunity.

Even with many additional asset classes, however, it's still possible for all of them to go down in value. Although this has historically been unlikely, in 2008 nearly all asset classes declined in value at the same time. (Some alternatives excelled during the meltdown. For example, according to the Altegris 40 Index, managed futures returned an average of 15.47 percent in 2008.)[1] To meet this type of potential need, it can be prudent to keep a small amount of a portfolio invested in a safer asset class such as government bonds (they have been safe historically, but government debt downgrades may change even this thinking), cash, or even something that nearly always goes up when everything else goes down, such as gold.

In the previous example, if $40,000 of the $1 million portfolio had been invested in conservative bonds or another very safe asset, the $10,000 income shortfall could have been met through selling bonds, thereby avoiding a forced sale of more aggressive assets that may have lost value. In addition, holding only 4 percent of the total portfolio in this safer asset would also provide three additional years of time during which other assets could (hopefully) recover. Asset volatility declines appreciably over longer time frames. For instance, the stock market historically increases in value over a single year about two out of every three years. But if the time frame is increased to a rolling three-year period, market returns are positive 80 percent of the time from 1970 through 2010, a time period that includes two terrible decades of the 1970s and 2000s. More stable assets tend to offer even better three-year rolling average returns. Volatile assets become more predictable as their returns are measured over longer terms.

Through employment of more stable bonds, predictable income is generated while the investor is shielded from potential portfolio volatility, and more aggressive assets are given time to recover their value. In addition, the portfolio design includes a larger number of assets with higher longer-term performance expectations that still provide significant income protection during nearly any market or economic cycle. The end effect is a portfolio that meets present income needs while also providing greater growth potential.

Obviously, these numbers and allocations can be adjusted easily to suit particular investor needs and preferences. But the concept stays the same. Most investors want either maximum growth with acceptable volatility or solid longer-term growth while current income needs are met. A smarter design can more effectively produce all of these outcomes.

Before jumping into more specific components of modified endowment portfolio design, one more issue deserves attention because of its effects on planning and decisions.

Inflation

If inflation didn't exist, investment management and portfolio design would be so much simpler—and my job would be a lot easier! Future growth needs would be smaller, and future income needs would be easy to predict. But in any modern economy, long-term inflation is nearly as certain as death and taxes and so it must be taken into account in any portfolio planning.

Inflation also fundamentally alters the goal of any portfolio. Unfortunately, most people identify risk solely as the risk of losing their principal. While this is obviously important, loss of purchasing power is the real risk, not loss of principal. A stamp cost 3 cents in 1946. The same service now (it depends on when you read this) costs 45 cents. Five-cent cups of coffee and penny candy are long gone. In the late 1990s, gas was under $1 a gallon, but it soared to over $4 a gallon within the next decade. Since the demise of the gold standard in 1973, the value of the dollar has declined to an estimated $0.18 of its original value.

Inflation's impact can be devastating on multiple levels, especially for investors. Not only must an investment return outpace inflation to generate a real return, it also must incorporate tax impacts into return calculations, which forces the need for even greater returns just to break even. Inflation's constant upward pressure on future expenses makes financial planning that much more complex. One of the most common mistakes that investors make is underestimating future financial needs. An emphasis on maintaining principal, rather than purchasing power, usually leads to very inappropriate and shortsighted planning and investment strategies.

Further complicating the issue, inflation is unpredictable, and future fluctuations are inevitable. There is no chart telling us inflation rates for the next decade. Given the current budget deficits of nearly every developed economy in the world, future increases in inflation rates are assumed by nearly all economists. Debate centers more on the questions of when the increases will occur and how high inflation rates might reach.

Any well-designed portfolio must account for future declines in purchasing power. While conceptually simple, successfully planning for inflation can be complex. Inflation from 1913 through 2009 averaged 3.21 percent per year.[2] Purchasing power from 1933 to 2009 decreased 94 percent.[3] This masks, however, some significant shorter-term trends.[4]

The 1970s and early 1980s highlight a recent example of the challenges created by inflation. U.S. inflation topped out at 13.3 percent in 1979 and averaged 7.09 percent for the decade. The prime rate hit 21.5 percent in December 1980, the highest level in U.S. history.[5] If you had bought a house in the mid-1960s, 20 years later, its value had skyrocketed simply because of inflation. Investments in stocks, however, actually lost purchasing power as they trailed annual inflation rates. And the 1970s and 1980s weren't the only periods of high inflation. From 1913 to 1919, inflation averaged a whopping 8.70 percent per year.

More recently, inflation has been subdued. From 1990 through 2009, inflation has averaged just over 2.91 percent per year, which suggests that inflation may be problem of the past. Current debt levels, however, will likely increase future inflation, possibly significantly. For evidence of a likely decline in the purchasing power of a dollar, all one has to do is look at our currency's decline versus nearly every other currency backed by even a minimally respectable economy over the past 20 years.

Some inflation tends to be seen as desirable. Today, most mainstream economists favor a low and steady rate of inflation.[6] Low rather than zero or negative inflation may reduce the severity of recessions by enabling the labor market to adjust more quickly in a downturn, thereby reducing the risk that stimulating the economy through monetary policy won't work.[7]

Historically, throughout the world, governments also find that inflation tends to be a great ally, and they have explicitly created inflation either purposefully or as a result of inadequate discipline of printing presses. When a government prints money to add to circulation, it reduces purchasing power for anyone who holds that currency or assets based on the currency. In this way, printing money taxes all citizens, because the value of their money goes down by the amount of money the government printed.

If you are the government, this provides benefits on multiple levels. First, it gives you more money to spend. All governments like

this. Second, printing presses don't vote or even protest, so immediate political costs are minimal. Third, inflation decreases all government debt through devaluation. Much like a homeowner with a
30-year fixed mortgage sees his mortgage decrease as a percentage
of household income during periods of higher inflation, governments experience the same phenomenon. Their debts simply shrink
with inflation. Fourth, many entitlement programs are allocated
fixed budgets. While U.S. social security and Medicare programs
contain built-in cost-of-living increases, many other government programs don't. Therefore, a government can reduce subsidies to various
groups by simply allowing inflation to erode the value of the government funds provided.

Nearly all governments understand the benefits of printing
money and allowing some inflation. It's no surprise that nearly every
country routinely experiences it. But many governments have gotten
carried away with using their printing presses, which leads to monetary chaos through runaway inflation. Inflation that's too high
usually causes problems, the most notable and common of which is
the overthrow of the existing government. Virtually no government
anywhere in the world that allows double-digit inflation for more
than a few years stays in power. How violently that change occurs
usually depends on the strength of the country's political systems.
Even levels of inflation that get much above 5 percent tend to result
in significant political instability, so most countries work to keep
inflation at acceptable levels.

Throughout history, higher inflation levels tend to be much more
likely when government debt levels increase. Growing financial obligations and increasingly limited options often push governments to
print money and create higher inflation levels than a more stable
financial situation might allow. While this complex discussion is
beyond the scope of this book, history is littered with numerous
examples of governments that used inflation to dig out—or try to
dig out—from high debt levels. One of the best examples is that of
post–World War I Germany. Its government printed so much money
that people needed wheelbarrows full of cash to buy a loaf of bread.

The continual rise and recent acceleration of U.S. and developed
Western European debt levels combined with the massive recent
influx of liquidity into the monetary supply creates an environment

that almost guarantees higher future inflation. Obviously, nothing is ever certain, but history and government fiscal challenges suggest that inflation will be a larger issue in the coming years than it has been in the past several decades. Any wise investment strategy must take this into account.

As an aside, the rapid rise in government debt combined with the decline of the dollar has led to many doomsayers' proclamations. One of my favorites is claiming the dollar will disappear and gold must take its place. While anything is possible, replacing the dollar with bars of gold seems a bit ludicrous. Will we pay for gas by shaving off a bit of our current bar? How will anyone fit their bar into the Visa machine? Inflation seems the obvious—if much less sensational—alternative. In my lifetime, $1,000 bills will probably become common. It sounds crazy, but travels across the globe highlight example after example of countries with common paper currency containing five, six, and even seven zeroes. Five hundred pennies for a cup of coffee would have sounded crazy in 1960.

In this environment, any portfolio strategy must incorporate assets that will excel during inflationary periods, or at the very least will minimize damage. Unfortunately for the traditional portfolio design, periods of rising interest rates usually affect bonds adversely and can also affect stocks detrimentally, at least in the short term. Stocks usually act as a good inflation hedge on a longer-term basis, although near-term reactions are more mixed as rising raw material costs and more expensive capital can adversely affect profits while companies adjust.

Conventional wisdom holds that stocks fare poorly under high inflation, as they did in the 1970s. But actual data shown in Figure 6.1 contradicts this belief and illustrates that the long-run inflation risk of stocks is actually quite small.[8]

Long-term real rates of return are actually greatest when purchased at highest average inflation rates. One key to the argument—and data—is the time frame. Much shorter time frames would paint a different picture. Yet the data in Figure 6.1 illustrate the value of stocks in a portfolio as an inflation hedge.

Bond reactions are simpler than stocks, as they simply don't perform well when interest rates are rising. Bonds struggle because they get hit twice. First, if you're holding a bond with a lower interest

Figure 6.1   10-Year Real Rates of Return When Stocks Are Purchased at
Alternative Initial Annual Inflation Rates, 1871–2011

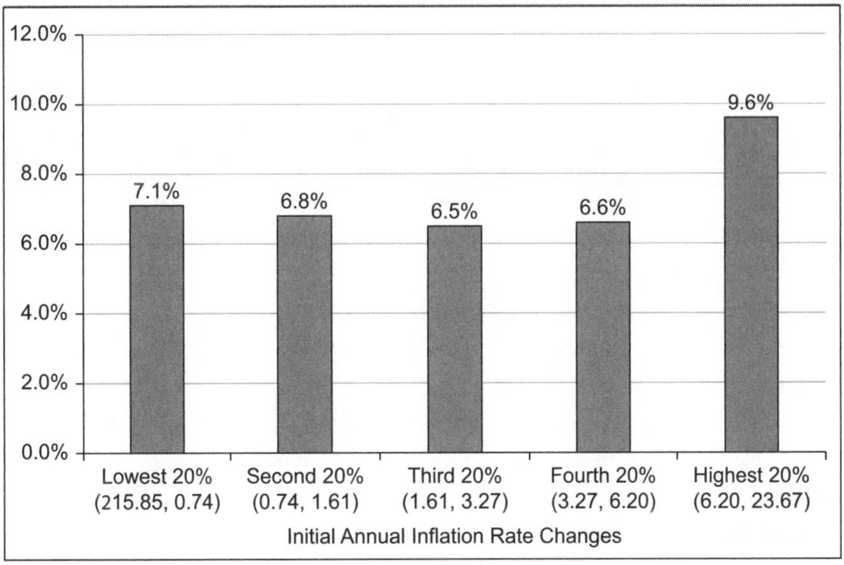

rate and inflation increases, your interest payment declines in real
terms. Second, if you try to sell the bond, the lower interest rate relative to newly increased interest rates makes your bond less attractive,
which leaves the only option to sell at a discount. As a result, there
are clear-cut trends going back over a century that clearly demonstrate both good and bad times to own bonds. Very simply, bonds
are more attractive when interest rates are high and decreasing, and
less attractive when interest rates are low and increasing.

If you put time frames to these concepts, bond returns were quite
good from the early 1980s through 2011. Interest rates started very
high and then decreased steadily. This situation provided investors
with dividend income that was increasing over time relative to
inflation and increases in bond values if they chose to sell holdings.
Conversely, when interest rates started low and progressed higher,
as they did from about 1940 to 1982, bond returns were quite poor.
Today's interest rates are low and expected to move higher strongly,
which suggests that bond returns for the next few decades will be
anemic just as they were in the 1940–1982 period.

While bonds had already been targeted for reduction in the endowment model given their historically lower rates of return, the introduction of inflation and likely future rate increases further reinforces the potential weaknesses of bonds.

In contrast to bonds, which tend to perform poorly as inflation is increasing, real or hard assets are generally deemed most desirable during periods of higher inflation. Real assets are exactly what they sound like: physical, tangible assets such as real estate and commodities. Real asset values increase during times of inflation because their relative value remains unchanged, but the actual amount of currency it takes to acquire them goes up.

For example, if five people all have $10 and one is willing to use all her money to buy a book, the book is priced at $10, or one-fifth of the total amount of currency available. If instead, the currency inflates so that everyone has $100 and the same person is willing to spend all her money to buy the same book, the book price goes up to $100 but the cost is still one-fifth of the total amount of currency in circulation. The worth of the book didn't change because one person was still willing to use all her assets to buy it. The price, however, is quite different.

The value of real estate is probably the easiest for people to quickly understand because most investors already have substantial experience in this area through the process of acquiring and owning their own home. While recent house values have been quite unpredictable, this shouldn't be a huge surprise. Inflation levels have been very low, and housing values in general had been inflated by the housing bubble that resulted from an unprecedented 10-plus years of increases in home values in every major housing market in the United States.

Anyone who bought a house in the 1960s or 1970s clearly understands the impact of inflation on real asset values. For instance, even with the recent downturn in real estate, my parents' house increased about 50 times the price they paid for it 40 years earlier. In case you're doing the math, a fiftyfold increase is a 5,000 percent increase (actually, 4,900 percent, as the first 100 percent was already there). As great as that sounds, however, it's still slightly less than a 10 percent gain compounded annually, and inflation in the 1970s was running well above 10 percent. While some of the increase in my parents' house price is due to increased desirability of the location, most of it resulted from inflation that increased the acquisition cost of the land and the replacement value for the house.

Other assets can offer similar benefits during inflation. As we move forward through different investment options, the expected performance of various assets during inflationary periods will be very relevant. While designing all parts of a portfolio to perform well during all types of inflationary periods would seem to be impossible, some good decisions can help limit the effects of inflation and even possibly position parts of the portfolio to benefit from it.

Investment Options

While there is no single definitive endowment strategy, most endowments diversify their assets across multiple different asset classes that offer high expected returns. In addition, many endowments routinely adjust their allocations as their needs change or as they believe opportunities warrant. So, remember that exact percentages are less important than the general approach. Table 6.1 outlines a potential allocation.

While the percentages in Table 6.1 may be typical for many endowments, Yale's actual percentages usually depart from this model in several areas (see Table 6.2). While some of the departure may have been strategic, some of it was also likely a result of lack of flexibility that resulted from the terrible equity market performance of the previous year. The primary differences are less money

Table 6.1   Model Endowment Strategy

Asset Class	Percentage Allocation
Domestic stocks	25%
Developed market stocks	12%
Emerging market stocks	13%
Real assets	25%
Private equity/venture capital	10%
Absolute return	10%
Fixed income/cash	5%

Table 6.2 Yale June 2010 Allocation Targets

Asset Class	Percentage Allocation
Domestic stocks	7%
Foreign stocks	9%
Real assets	28%
Private equity	33%
Absolute return	19%
Fixed Income/cash	4%

The Yale Endowment 2010 Report, p. 8.

targeted toward stocks and much more targeted toward absolute return holdings.

By contrast, Harvard's June 2010 target allocation was higher in stocks with a 33 percent allocation and much lower in absolute return with only a 16 percent allocation (see Table 6.3). Not surprisingly, both Yale and Harvard place a high emphasis on real assets with a 28 percent and 23 percent targeted allocation, respectively. Both management companies have stated plans to increase allocations to this asset class in the future.

Table 6.3 Harvard June 2010 Allocation Targets (unchanged for 2011)

Asset Class	Percentage Allocation
Domestic stocks	11%
Foreign stocks	22%
Real assets	23%
Private equity	13%
Absolute return	16%
Domestic, foreign, and inflation indexed fixed income	13%
Cash	2%

Harvard Management Company Endowment Report Updated Message from the CEO, Harvard Management Company, October 2010, p. 6.

Adaptations to the endowment strategy for an individual investor can be made fairly easily. Domestic equities are already a part of most portfolios of individual investors. Exposure to foreign developed market equities can be achieved easily in many ways. In addition, there are many existing and developing ways to invest in emerging market equities. The various equity classes can easily be combined to make up about half an individual's portfolio.

Beyond portfolio allocations to public equity markets, the remaining portion of a portfolio usually presents more of a challenge to the average investor. Yet options have increased tremendously over the past few years. An investor with an open mind can easily gain exposure to most of the remaining asset classes or find excellent substitutes that may work better.

The following is a list of the assets that will be reviewed in the coming chapters. A few of the topics addressed may be new to some investors, particularly those with no experience in venturing away from the standard stocks and bonds. However, I highlight them now so future discussions aren't a surprise. Remember that *all these investments are being used very successfully by investors across the globe*, particularly those with substantial money to invest and very sophisticated portfolio strategies. But of course, you should only invest in assets with which you are comfortable.

Assets that will be covered include:

- Domestic stocks
- Foreign developed market stocks
- Emerging market stocks
- Real estate investment trusts (REITs)
- Traded commodities
- Nontraded real estate investment trusts
- Oil and gas drilling, distribution and royalty programs
- Private equity and venture capital
- Managed futures
- Hedge funds
- Equipment leasing
- Structured notes/products
- Domestic and foreign fixed income, preferred stocks

This list looks long and possibly a bit daunting. You may even be thinking that you have no interest in becoming an expert in all these areas, and developing necessary knowledge to make all the right choices simply will not be possible. I agree. The purpose isn't to make you an expert. Even people in the financial services industry are rarely experts in all these areas. Rather, my purpose is to introduce you to these concepts and provide enough information to help you determine areas of interest.

Realistically, many of these investments are difficult to access without the assistance of a financial professional of some sort. If you pursue a strategy closely aligned with the endowment model employed by universities, you'll probably need to work with a financial professional to gain access to some of the investment options, particularly many of the nontraditional asset classes. Endowments and wealthier individuals nearly always work with experts, either internally or externally, because they recognize the potential value specialized knowledge can bring. Like most areas of modern life, investing has grown much more complicated, and relevant expertise can be invaluable. Nearly anyone who seeks higher levels of proficiency in anything—whether it's playing the piano or golfing—benefits from a coach. Investing is no different.

Yet, if you choose to go it alone, a significant portion of the strategy can be implemented using off-the-shelf products available directly to investors. As mentioned, the biggest exceptions will be with the alternatives such as real estate, private equity, absolute return, and more complex debt investments that are difficult or impossible to access without a financial professional. Not coincidentally, these areas can be the areas of greatest potential benefit because of their performance and diversification benefits.

Regardless of whether or not you choose to use a financial professional, my aim is to help you understand how the alternative investments might be able to help you improve your portfolio or why they may be completely inappropriate. Whether you choose to work with someone or go it alone, you should be much better prepared to favorably position your portfolio to meet your future financial needs.

7

Domestic Equities

ALTHOUGH MOST INVESTORS ARE FAMILIAR WITH EQUITIES, PARTIC-
ularly U.S. equities, seemingly so few of them enjoy strong success
with equities in the short or long term. Practice for most investors
hasn't made perfect or even pretty good. Rather, most individual
investors routinely employ amazingly destructive stock investment
strategies. Unfortunately, there is overwhelming evidence and
research that demonstrates this painful truth.

Investor mistakes can generally be divided into two categories.
The first common mistake investors make is trying to time the
market, which often results in investors missing the ups and suffering through the downs. The second mistake is usually some
version of poor implementation. This can range from following a
bad strategy to making poor investment vehicle selections to failing
to understand fees.

The first mistake is illustrated in Figure 7.1. During this 20-year
period ending in 2008, the S&P 500 and U.S. Long Bond Index
vastly outperformed the average investor.[1] Unfortunately, individual
investor performance isn't even close to relevant benchmarks. If the
performance numbers differed by only a few percentage points, fees
could be blamed. The performance shortfalls, however, are much
greater, which signifies a more fundamental problem.

In case you are wondering about the dates and time frame, Dalbar has completed this study and others like it many times over the past several decades. The results are very consistent regardless of duration, beginning date, or end date. In fact, I used these results because they are less dramatic and more believable. Other studies show even greater disparities. Unfortunately, investors are often their own worst enemies.

As bad as these numbers look, minimal analysis shows they are even worse than they appear. For instance, while the bars in Figure 7.1 suggest that stock investors earned only about a quarter of the returns generated by the S&P 500, when compounded the differences grow to an eightfold higher return for the S&P 500 over this time period. Using numbers, $1 invested in the S&P 500 would have grown over 400 percent while the average stock investor earned only a 50 percent total return. A 60/40 stock/bond portfolio shows even more striking investor underperformance. The 60/40 combination of indexes outperformed the average 60/40 stock/bond investor nearly elevenfold with a 368 percent return versus only 34 percent for the average investor. Ouch!

Figure 7.1   2009 Dalbar QAIB Study, 20 Years Ending December 31, 2008

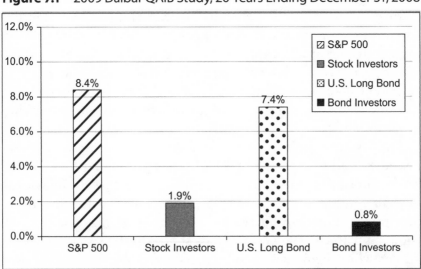

While bad strategy and/or fees can explain some underperformance, the root problem for too many investors is their failed attempts to time the market. In practice, market timing often shows up when investors jump out of the market when conditions look bad and then jump back in after conditions look better. Unfortunately, when conditions appear near their worst, the market is usually already down and an investor who sells liquidates at or near the bottom. Once conditions look better, the market has already gone up, reflecting a more optimistic outlook. Investor reentry into the market at this point misses the market run-up, which is often disproportionately large at the beginning of a rally. Many investors are very knowledgeable but act self-destructively and turn good investments into bad ones when they try to outsmart the market.

A short example makes the point strongly. Between 1998 and 2001, the Firsthand Technology Value mutual fund produced an impressive annualized return of 16 percent. This is the number most prospective investors would consider when reviewing this fund. Yet the average individual investor in this fund lost 31.6 percent over this time.[2] The fund illustrates classic investor mismanagement. When the fund went down, they sold, and when it went up, they bought. Since investors bought when the fund was high, they were in the fund when it went down. After they sold because the market declined, they were out of the fund when it later recovered, and they failed to enjoy the ride back up. Unfortunately, many other examples and studies illustrate this problem.

Within the money management industry, it's a common assumption that the best time to invest is when individuals start heading for the exits. Similarly, the market is likely topping out when small investors start piling in. Mutual fund inflows and outflows illustrate this point all too well. Mutual fund inflows hit record highs in late 1999 and early 2000 just before the dot-com crash when the S&P 500 fell nearly 40 percent. Conversely, mutual fund outflows hit record levels in October 2008 shortly before the U.S. stock market started its strongest bull market run in history.

While most financial professionals have much personal experience with investors acting as their own worst enemy, various studies provide more specifics on how investors generate the poor returns noted previously. Quotes from a paper titled "Dumb Money" by professors from the University of Chicago and Yale University are enlightening. While the paper's subject is mutual fund investors and was written for academics, the message is very relevant to individual investors. The blunt language makes the point a bit strong, even if it's less than tactful. Here are several quotes:

> On average, retail investors [individual investors vs. institutional or professional investors] direct their money to funds which invest in stocks that have low future returns. To achieve high returns, it is best to do the opposite of these investors. We calculate that mutual fund investors experience total returns that are significantly lower due to their reallocations. Therefore, mutual fund investors are dumb in the sense that their reallocations reduce their wealth on average. We call this predictability the "dumb money" effect.[3]

> This dumb money effect is sizable: stocks with high FLOW as a result of the active reallocation across funds over the past six months to five years underperform low FLOW stocks by between 36 and 85 basis points (0.36 percent and 0.85 percent) per month or approximately between 4.3 percent and 10 percent per year, depending upon the horizon of the past flow.[4]

> Thus investors hurt themselves by reallocating across mutual funds for two reasons. First, they hurt themselves by over-weighting growth stocks. Second, controlling for market-book, they hurt themselves by overweighting stocks that underperform their category benchmarks, and in particular, they pick growth stocks that do especially poorly.[5]

> It turns out that, at any horizon, individual retail investors are reducing their wealth by engaging in active reallocation across mutual funds.[6]

> By doing the opposite of individuals, one can construct a port-folio with high returns. Individuals hurt themselves by their decisions, and we calculate that an aggregate mutual fund investor could raise his Sharpe ratio [a measure of performance for a given risk] . . . simply by refraining from destructive behavior.[7]

While harsh, these strong words are accurate according to any study I have read and all anecdotal evidence I have encountered. If you doubt these statistics, just perform an Internet search on Dalbar or Dalbar studies. The web offers lots of information regarding the woeful underperformance of individual investors versus nearly any other benchmark.

The herd mentality we are all born with as part of our survival instinct works against us when investing. When everyone's getting out, the market is probably cheap because there's so much selling pressure. Conversely, when everyone's piling in, prices have already been forced up and it's likely a poor time to buy. It's not natural to go against the crowd. Most of history has taught us that when everyone else is running from something, it probably is a good idea to join the crowd. Similarly, when everyone is running toward something, experience has taught us that joining in, or even trying to get ahead, is usually wise.

Most of us learned these practices as kids. When hiking in the woods, playing in the park, or walking down the street, if everyone was running one way, you joined in and then figured out later why you were running. One personal experience is very memorable to me. When I was about age 10, several of us were exploring some woods a couple of miles from our house. We'd never been this far up this particular trail. We heard a very guttural sound coming from up ahead, and all of us started running in the other direction as fast as we could. None of us wanted to be the first to figure out what might be there. After about a hundred yards, the adrenaline wore off a bit, and we all stopped to listen. Since we didn't hear anything, we all slowly started back up the trail, very tightly bunched together. After making it nearly back to our original take-off point, we saw a large pit bull and Doberman pinscher at the ends of their chains. Without realizing it, we had wandered into the back of an old junkyard and met the decidedly unfriendly security guards.

In this case, we were well served by running and then figuring out why. And we all did this without thinking. We all simply sensed danger or noticed someone else's fear, the adrenaline kicked in, and we took off. Some of us in the back of the pack didn't even know why we were running. We only knew that everyone else was. Following the actions of the group has served us well as humans for thousands of years. Unfortunately, investing punishes this behavior rather than rewarding it.

Possible dangers in the investment field are rarely as obvious or as easy to see as guard dogs. Most people don't know how to recognize real danger and have little idea of what to do when they see it. For instance, few people see the top of a 20-year bull market with high equity valuations and think: danger. Rather, most people see everyone else getting into the market and all the reasons why the market has gone up, and think they should join in as well.

Most people develop fears only after prices have gone down dramatically, or more simply, because everyone else is running for the door. Admittedly, selling out during a downturn might save you some future losses if the markets continue declining in the near term. More commonly, however, short-term savings are lost by missing subsequent recoveries, and overall performance suffers because investors wait until after the recovery has progressed past their original exit point, and they buy back in at even higher prices. In fact, in investing you generally are best served by doing the exact opposite of the average person: buying more when there's uncertainty and trimming holdings when everything looks great. As Warren Buffett says, "Be fearful when others are greedy and greedy when others are fearful."

In this case, a well-structured portfolio strategy can be very helpful. Rather than looking only at the short term and succumbing to temptations to sell or buy because of the actions of everyone else or press coverage that feeds on fear and greed, you should have a solid portfolio strategy, which can be invaluable as an anchor that prevents panic or overzealousness. In addition, if U.S. stocks are a smaller percentage of your portfolio because of better diversification, domestic market movements will have less impact on your portfolio.

Investment Implementation

The second major reason people underperform the markets derives from poor investment strategy. While this blanket statement can cover a host of topics, I'm going to focus on two major errors. Most other errors are related to these two. The first is using the wrong vehicle to gain exposure to the stock market. Often, fees are a big part of this problem, but other shortcomings also often add to expense issues. The second is failing to take advantage of basic market trends and opportunities.

Various investment products and associated fees can present problems. Recognize that investment into any stock market, U.S. or foreign, will require the payment of some type of fee or cost. There's simply no way to avoid this. The challenge is securing high value in return for the fees that you pay. This doesn't mean that the goal is simply to minimize fees. Some are well worth their costs; others simply are not. Many fall in the middle, providing value for some investors but not for all. For any investor, the goal should be to determine what services are needed and who or what offers the highest value services that meet those specific needs.

Because most investors are familiar with mutual funds, I'll use them as an example of how these can make sense or be your worst choice. Mutual funds generally carry fairly substantial fees—much more than most people realize. In addition, most mutual funds don't perform as well as most investors believe.

Because the reasons for this are not obvious and are a bit arcane, most people are unaware of the issues. However, they are very easy to understand. Here, I'm going to highlight only the major issues.

While most people are aware of management fees and possibly other fees like 12b-1 fees, which are fees paid to firms as a marketing allowance, few people are aware that mutual funds report neither their trading costs nor soft dollar costs. Frequently, these costs are the largest fees borne by mutual fund investors. Neither of these fees are reported in prospectuses, and they rarely show up in any reports because they can't be known in advance.

Obviously, mutual fund companies trade securities in hopes of increasing returns. In some instances, mutual funds also overpay trading costs in order to provide additional compensation to firms that distribute their products. Conveniently, none of these fees show up anywhere, not even in a Morningstar report.

Soft dollar costs are fees that mutual fund companies may pay to other firms to help them market their product. They are usually paid in the form of complimentary research or technology. While one could argue that the investor wins through a better-educated or better-equipped financial professional, the investor definitely experiences lower returns when these costs are paid by the fund company.

Unfortunately, the fees are there, yet few investors know that they exist and affect the performance of the fund.

Beyond fees, other tracking issues present problems. If a mutual fund has been underperforming for many years, what does a firm do with it? A poor-performing fund is difficult to market. The simple answer is that poor-performing funds are closed. This is natural and a positive part of a competitive market. However, it also introduces a bias into the system. When investors look at mutual fund performance figures, they see only the performance of the winners. The losers no longer exist; their performance magically disappears. There's even a name for this: survivorship bias.

Here is an example from my first book:

> In 1986, the existing 586 stock funds yielded a return of 13.4 percent. If we fast forward 10 years to 1996, this number had magically become 14.7 percent. How did these funds enhance their return 1.4 percent after their history had supposedly been written? Out of the existing funds, 24 percent disappeared.[8] The funds that remained were the better-performing funds thus raising the average stock fund performance. Various studies have found that mutual fund returns as an average decrease about 10 percent if survivorship bias is included.[9]

Mutual fund companies are very aware that selling poor-performing funds is difficult.

Beyond fees and survivor bias, there are other issues that impact performance as well. Creation bias illustrates a seedier side of the mutual fund industry. Some mutual fund companies start many similar funds at the same time with similar objectives, but completely different holdings. Usually, the portfolios hold positions that are more volatile and likely to move strongly either up or down. While some of the funds will likely perform poorly given their aggressive holdings, it's likely that at least one fund will perform exceptionally well. Once an excellent track record has been established in one fund, the rest are folded into it, and a single high-performing mutual fund emerges. Holdings are adjusted to produce more predictable returns, and the fund begins life with an excellent performance history that likely has little to do with its probable future performance.

Various other issues can plague mutual funds, ranging from inefficient tax treatment to sales loads. However, a basic statistic provides probably the easiest evidence of problems with mutual funds.

David Swensen, the originator of the endowment model, is fond of referencing Robert Arnott, chairman of Research Affiliates, LLC. Arnott has become quite notable for his excellent research on various aspects of the equity markets. In a September 6, 2005, *Wall Street Journal* interview, David Swensen spent considerable time discussing the high costs and relative poor performance of mutual funds. In that article, Swensen referenced Arnott's data that showed that 10-year after-tax return of mutual funds trail the returns you would have earned in an index fund by 4.5 percent per year.[10] He cites various issues for these performance differences, particularly fees, taxes, and survivorship bias.

While this percentage seems amazingly high, similar numbers have been found by other studies and researchers. Some investors are aware of issues with mutual funds and turn to Morningstar's ratings to guide them. While this may seem prudent, Morningstar has very incomplete data, as many fees aren't listed. In addition, use of Morningstar rankings—at least in the manner that most investors employ the data—leads to even poorer investment decisions.

When it comes to past performance, the standard industry disclaimer that past performance does not guarantee future success is particularly true with mutual funds. Starting on December 31, 1999, the Burns Advisory Group analyzed the subsequent 10-year performance of mutual funds rated five stars, which is the highest possible rating given by Morningstar. The results are disappointing. The 218 domestic stock funds with five-star ratings typically lagged behind their category averages over the period. And not only did they lag behind their category benchmarks, they also trailed the other mutual funds in the group. The stars turned into dogs.[11] Similar studies routinely demonstrate similar patterns.

While I have cited some basic evidence regarding the deficiencies of mutual funds, there's far more that I haven't bothered to address, such as management turnover, style drift, and category shifts. With all that said, it sounds like I think that mutual funds are a terrible investment vehicle that should be avoided at all costs. As with many topics, the issue isn't that simple. Surprisingly, I still believe that mutual funds can make sense for certain investors under specific circumstances.

When to Use Mutual Funds

Mutual funds were designed to provide small investors access to equity and bond markets. For many people, they perform this service well. Mutual funds often charge little or nothing for incremental investments and facilitate very small purchases. Under various circumstances and in nearly all 401(k) accounts, there's no fee to add money to a mutual fund account. This can be a great advantage, particularly when smaller amounts are invested on a regular basis. For example, an investor contributing $100 per month to a mutual fund would be far better served buying mutual fund shares with no trading costs than paying even very low trading fees to purchase more efficient investments.

In addition to having low transaction costs, mutual funds frequently provide access to a large support and informational system that can help investors learn and establish themselves. Easy access and a good support system can make this investment option very appropriate for smaller accounts. While high annual percentage fees may seem exorbitant, they still may be preferable to fees and charges that may result from other forms of investment. In addition, there is the hope that the advice and expertise make the fees worthwhile.

Most experts today still recommend mutual funds for people with less than $50,000 to invest. And if you have a 401(k), your only option is mutual funds. At this point, you are simply best off hoping that you have good mutual funds for your choices.

Of course, there's also another basic issue. Not all mutual funds actually trail their respective index by 4.5 percent nor incur average fees. There are funds and fund families that charge less, which can make them a more attractive option to larger investors. If you have a greater amount of money to invest, however, there usually are better vehicles available to you.

Trends and Opportunities

As mentioned, many investors fail to take advantage of trends and opportunities. One clear trend for larger investors is to move away from mutual funds, which often fail to provide good value. There are various ways to do this. Obviously, you can invest directly in stocks or other vehicles and manage your money on your own. You would only pay trading and custody fees. This is a viable option for some people.

Most individual investors, however, when left on their own, horribly underperform the market, as discussed earlier. More simply, while an investor may be able to eliminate some fees by going direct, for most people the result is a savings of a few cents on fees but a loss of big return dollars through ignorance, poor implementation, and lack of discipline.

It's no accident that higher-net-worth investors are far more likely to work with an advisor than are less financially successful investors. As wealth increases, the propensity to work with an advisor increases dramatically. Wealthier people understand the value of expertise and are willing to pay for it. They also buy intelligently. They hire advisors who employ more sophisticated strategies rather than simply put their money into overpriced mutual funds.

The better trends and opportunities pursued more frequently by professionals and sophisticated investors usually focus on two areas. First, they choose investment vehicles that carry fewer fees and provide good value for fees charged. In addition, the fees are generally much more transparent. Second, strategies purposely seek to take advantage of known market trends such as avoiding overpriced growth stocks mentioned in the "Dumb Money" article. Chasing the latest fad is not the emphasis.

Getting Good Value

With the minimization of fees and maximization of value for money spent, probably the two most common trends of the last decade have been the growing emergence of separately managed accounts

(SMAs) and the use of exchange-traded funds (ETFs). Sometimes accounts combine the two trends by holding ETFs in SMAs—keep up with the lingo!

A bit of explanation is in order. Exchange-traded funds trade like stocks but actually are pools of investor funds managed passively to mimic specific indexes such as the S&P 500 or a particular sector index. Investor interest in ETFs—and, as a result, the amount of investor monies invested in them—has skyrocketed because they provide a very targeted investment at a low cost.

Separately managed accounts are stock accounts in which individual positions (i.e., stocks) are held directly by the investor. This is very different from a mutual fund in which individual investor funds are all lumped together with other investors. SMAs may hold individual stocks or ETFs. In some cases, mutual funds are used, but this is becoming much less common because of the higher fees and other disadvantages of mutual funds. When holding the assets directly, the investor can see all transactions, fees (except mutual fund fees, if used), and tax liabilities. In many cases, the investor's specific tax issues can even be managed.

As you might imagine, this individualized attention doesn't come free. In fact, 20 years ago, most separately managed accounts carried minimums of over $5 million per account. Today, thanks largely to ever-advancing technology, you often can get the same service for account values under $100,000. Fortunately, the remarkable reduction in account size hasn't been offset by fee increases. In most cases, fees have stayed largely the same, making SMAs generally much less expensive than mutual funds. Costs for some SMAs are less than half the costs cited earlier for mutual funds.

Low fees alone don't make SMAs a good choice. These investment accounts also carry other advantages. All positions are owned directly by the investors, who can see exactly what they have, including all potential tax liabilities. Because the securities are all purchased in the account for a specific investor, there is no additional tax liability assumed at the original purchase. This situation differs significantly from mutual fund investments in which all original purchases assume the current and completely unknown tax liabilities of the mutual fund. Some SMAs also facilitate individual tax management. Fees are also completely transparent. You know exactly how much you are paying. Depending on a person's tax situation, the fees may even be deductible as a professional service.

In spite of these advantages, SMAs are not for everyone. Because investors can see their exact positions, this can make them a less desirable vehicle for some. A portfolio is a bit like sausage—sometimes it's better to simply enjoy the end product without knowing everything that's inside. In looking at an SMA account, inevitably some positions will not do well, and some people struggle with too much knowledge and can't look past the individual pieces.

In addition, SMAs are not free. Some people may find other approaches more appropriate to their needs. Overall, however, there is a reason SMAs have enjoyed such rapid growth during the last decade, particularly among larger investors. They are another example of investment services originally offered to very wealthy investors that have trickled down to a much wider investor base.

Investment Strategy

Lastly, the specific investment style deserves attention. It's been known for many years that certain sectors of the market outperform others over time. But most of these strategies are less sexy than many common choices. For instance, most small investors invest in small-capitalization (small-cap) growth stocks if they are trying to be very aggressive. Ironically, this category is the single poorest performer over time.

Some basic information highlights the intelligence of following or overemphasizing exposure to particular markets. The assumption by the majority that small-cap stocks do better than large-cap stocks is correct. Most people, however, wrongly assume that growth stocks outperform value stocks. While definitions vary, growth stocks are usually categorized as securities expected to experience high future growth. Value stocks are securities that offer higher value through some measure of price-to-earnings or book value. More bluntly stated, value stocks usually have prices that are lower because the market believes the firm has some problems.

Table 7.1 shows the growth of $1 from 1927 through 2010.[12] While it represents a very broad range of securities that would be virtually impossible to replicate in an individual portfolio, the numbers

Table 7.1 Value Versus Growth, 1927–2010

Category	Value of $1	Annual Compound Return
Small-cap growth	$1,205	8.81%
Large-cap growth	$1,723	9.28%
Large-cap value	$10,747	11.68%
Small-cap value	$119,471	14.93%

clearly illustrate a value performance premium. It also shows the power of compounding and the value of seemingly small increases in annual returns.

Going back to the study titled "Dumb Money," the authors made another interesting observation: "Using various issuance mechanisms, the corporate sector [i.e., industry professionals] tends to sell growth stocks and buy value stocks."[13] Essentially, professional investors have this figured out and have practices in place to help them buy value and sell growth stocks. Conversely, "individuals, using mutual funds, tend to buy growth stocks and sell value stocks."[14]

Value stock outperformance is not the only well-known investment trend that can be used for profit. Another is dividends. Various research suggests that stock management strategies that emphasize higher-dividend paying stocks have historically outperformed in many different economic and market environments. A study going back to 1970 was completed in 2002 by a couple of finance professors, Kathleen Fuller of the University of Georgia and Michael Goldstein of Babson College. They compared total monthly returns for dividend-paying stocks and non-dividend-paying stocks on the S&P 500. According to their results, dividend-paying stocks produced monthly returns of 1.4 percent, while stocks that paid no dividends lagged at only 0.9 percent per month. On an annual basis, this equates to about a 6 percent difference. Moreover, in their conclusions, Fuller and Goldstein maintain that their results are generally true, no matter if the data is taken from December 2000 or December 1970.[15] A more recent study completed in 2011 by the Wellington group confirmed outperformance for dividend-paying stocks and added that the trend was particularly apparent during periods of uncertainty. [16]

Obviously, buying a stock that pays a dividend or a value stock is no guarantee of outperformance or even good performance. However, it appears to tip the odds favorably. Regardless, the concept is simple. Stocks that have dividends usually provide better performance. It's also no coincidence that stocks that pay higher dividends and value stocks are often the same stocks. Because the price of value stocks has often been forced down while their dividend has remained constant, the dividend yield tends to be higher. The higher yield obviously contributes to return performance and essentially gives these stocks an immediate return advantage.

If we pull all this information together, we see several themes that can be fairly easily summarized:

1. **Don't try to time to the market.** While market timing sounds wonderful, the strategy is nearly impossible to execute successfully.
2. **Choose a good investment vehicle.** This probably means avoiding mutual funds in favor of less expensive and more transparent approaches such as separately managed accounts. Obviously, other approaches also exist, but there are several good reasons SMAs have been growing so rapidly in recent years.
3. **Follow a sound strategy.** This can mean focusing on more value-oriented stocks or dividend stocks. Minimally for most people, it likely means avoiding small-cap growth stocks.

The previous list is obviously brief and could certainly be expanded. Simply stated, the core of equity investing is finding a good strategy and then sticking to it. There's not one golden strategy. There are many. The issue for most people is the lack of discipline to consistently follow any intelligent strategy.

Not surprisingly, most endowments don't strategically plan to outperform in equity investing. While they welcome outperformance and strive for it, they recognize that efficient exposure to the asset class is the greater goal. They work very hard to avoid underperforming, and they employ disciplined approaches to minimize obvious mistakes. Endowments are very realistic and don't chase the latest fad, newsletter promise, or hot tip. Instead, they employ a disciplined strategy to gain effective market exposure and emphasize long-term performance.

Fees Revisited

As mentioned, you want to maximize the value you get from fees while also keeping fees to a minimum. For some investors, this can mean doing everything themselves. However, the research against this approach is overwhelming. Few people have the time, talent, and inclination to be effective. Individual investors are virtually always their own worst enemy. There are always exceptions, but not many.

Rather, most people receive tremendous benefit from paying for expert advice, even if the primary value of the advice is keeping them from panicking during inevitable market downturns. Hopefully, a good financial professional provides more than hand-holding services, but for many if not most investors, panic prevention alone justifies all of an advisor's fees.

In addition, most advisors understand the financial system far better than individual investors. While their expertise can provide numerous investor advantages, one easily understood benefit is that they frequently save their clients product expenses and fees, which more than offsets the fees these advisors charge. Effectively, the professional advice is free.

A recent study by Envestnet, a sizable money management firm, provides insight from an interesting source: individual investors themselves. Envestnet simply asked investors what they thought. The results, published June 30, 2010, reported that despite the market's previous volatility and poor performance, 79 percent of investors with advisors said that these professionals' professional advice is worth more than it costs.[17] Given the previous horrible decade for the stock market and the particularly rough three years preceding this study, four out of five investors voicing confidence in professional advice seems amazingly high.

Many individuals have no real experience working with financial professionals and assume the worst about their utility based on lack of knowledge or bad publicity about rogue advisors. Fortunately, reality differs, as wealthier people understand well. In fact, a 2011 study from Cerulli Associates shows that wealthier households are seeking advice more than ever. Of households with investable assets between $2 and $5 million, 33 percent use multiple financial advisors. The percentage grows to 58 percent for households with more than $5 million in investable assets. Wealthy households with $10 million or more in investable assets work with four or more advisors 64 percent of the time.[18] By contrast, in 2008 barely 16 percent of the top category used four or more advisors. Part of motivation for the move to more advisors is believed to be a desire to incorporate more strategies than simply investing in the U.S. stock market. Regardless, a good financial professional should be well worth his or her fees, even in an area as straightforward as equity management.

Now that we have addressed equities—the single most common holding for investors—let's move into areas of less familiarity. We'll begin with international equities.

8

International Equities

AMAZINGLY, EVEN AS RECENTLY AS 10 YEARS AGO, INVESTING IN
international equities was seen as exotic and unusually risky. Because
the United States has such a large economy and its equity market is
so much bigger than any other country's, the average U.S. investor
could easily afford to ignore markets outside the country's borders.
In addition, the 20-year U.S. stock market history preceding the
year 2000 was excellent and richly rewarded investors focused solely
on the United States.

In spite of the success of U.S. markets, endowments recognized
the possible performance and diversification benefits of markets
overseas. In 2000, Yale already targeted an international market
allocation of 40 percent of its total public equity investments.
This decision looks pretty easy in retrospect. U.S. stock valuations
were sky-high after the run-up in U.S. stocks tied to the Internet bubble. Concurrently, the developing world was starting
to become more of a global economic force. Yet few individual
investors followed a similar route, and only more forward-thinking
institutions moved strongly into international holdings. Today, the
story has changed.

Developed Markets

If we start with a simplistic view of the last 10 years, adding only developed markets as defined by the MSCI EAFE Index (Morgan Stanley Capital International, Europe, Australasia, and Far East) didn't help that much. For simplicity, the following analysis uses more common calendar year returns rather than midyear returns employed by endowments.

The decade from 2000 to 2009 was terrible for both U.S. and non-U.S. developed markets. The U.S. stock market lost nearly 10 percent over this time, and non-U.S. developed markets saw growth of just over 12 percent. While the disparity of 22 percent seems fairly large, if we compare the S&P 500 to a 60 percent domestic/40 percent MSCI EAFE portfolio, we only raise the return from –1.0 percent per year to 0.0 percent per year. It helps, but not much. In addition, adding in developed international markets would have actually raised the overall equity volatility by about 10 percent because international stocks were more volatile during this decade because they had more up years. This compares unfavorably to the previous decade in which the addition of international developed market stocks would have decreased volatility by about the same 10 percent.

Long term, the addition of international developed markets has a solid history of giving a bit more stability to portfolios and helping with performance. As the time frame is lengthened, foreign developed markets usually become less of a performance factor, as their long-term performance tends to be quite similar to the United States. Their inclusion in a portfolio, however, still provides diversification benefits. For this reason, endowments and most sophisticated investors have maintained strong international exposure for many years.

More exact numbers on correlation illustrate some of the potential benefits. As mentioned, correlation measures the statistical relationship between any two variables. Values range between –1.00 and +1.00. A correlation of 1.00 indicates perfect correlation between variables. If two assets are perfectly correlated, their movements will be exactly related to each other. A correlation of –1.00 denotes the exact opposite. A correlation of 0.00 means there is no correlation.

Developed markets correlation (defined by the EAFE Index) with large-cap U.S. stocks was 0.92 from December 31, 2000, to December 31, 2010. Correlation with small caps was lower at 0.86.[1] Since anything less than 1.00 (i.e., perfect correlation) is helpful, the addition of developed markets would have benefited a portfolio. However, to have a major impact, correlations under 0.80 are desirable, and obviously these numbers fall a bit short. The addition of the developed markets would have added diversification, but relatively high correlations would have lessened the impact.

Emerging Markets

The more interesting discussion revolves around emerging markets. Most people in the United States are becoming increasingly aware of the growing strength of emerging economies. Unless you have failed to buy anything in the United States in the past 20 years, you are no doubt aware that China is developing rapidly. Most investors have grown more interested in benefiting from the growth of a market like this.

I lived in Hong Kong from 1993 to 1996 and had the pleasure of working in 14 different Asian countries over that time frame. I saw firsthand the explosive growth of Asian markets that ranged from China to Malaysia to India. Today, some of these economies hardly resemble emerging markets. In fact, Singapore now has a higher gross domestic product (GDP) per capita than the United States, and even Shanghai residents enjoy a higher per capita income than that of the average Italian. Various other countries are producing phenomenal wealth that is transforming societies.

The evidence of this growth is overwhelming, so I'll just note a few specifics. Since 1990, emerging markets have accounted for over half of global growth. They now account for over 40 percent of the global economic activity measured at purchasing power parity, or 30 percent at market exchange rates.[2] Other more recent sources place these numbers even higher, with emerging economies now at more than half of the world GDP at purchasing power parity as of mid-2010.[3]

Possibly as important from an investment standpoint, these economies have become much more stable and appear poised for predictable, long-term growth. In the late 1980s, many developing economies were plagued by hyperinflation and various basic economic challenges. During this period, inflation in Argentina was 3,500 percent; Brazil, 1,200 percent; and Peru, 2,500 percent.[4] In the 1990s, developed countries steadily introduced strong fiscal and monetary discipline. Now, inflation in Brazil and Peru is fairly close to U.S. standards, and even Argentina's inflation rate is a fraction of earlier levels despite recent government missteps.

By various other standards, emerging markets are adopting a more disciplined form of capitalism and government than the United States. Emerging market sovereign debt levels, fiscal discipline, regulatory regimes, and increasingly, even legal structures are superior to the Unites States, or at least rapidly improving relative to the United States. The United States still holds a great hand in the global economic poker game, but emerging markets are increasingly outplaying us. Emerging markets now hold more than 75 percent of world currency reserves. Goldman Sachs predicts that by 2040 the five emerging markets of China, India, Brazil, Russia, and Mexico will have larger combined economies than the traditional economic powerhouse G-7 nations that have dominated global economics for centuries.[5]

The strength of emerging markets can be seen in their recent stock market performance. While the S&P 500 declined 10 percent from 2000 to 2009 and non-U.S. developed markets grew only 12 percent, the MSCI Emerging Market Index grew over 155 percent during the same time period, nearly 10 percent per year.

Predictions for future growth are also promising. In 2009, emerging markets' GPD growth averaged 2.0 percent versus developed markets contracting by 3.4 percent. Over the two-year period from 2010 to 2012, forecasts estimate cumulative growth for emerging markets of 30 percent versus only 5 percent for developed markets.[6]

The list of major economies that completely escaped the 2008 recession includes only 11 countries; all of them emerging markets.[7] Annual growth of emerging markets over the medium term is projected for all regions of the world between 4.0 and 7.5 percent, rates that most of the developed world hasn't seen in decades.[8]

Most likely, the major global economic story for the remainder of our lives will be the ongoing development of emerging markets. As we start to take a more comprehensive view of international markets, it quickly becomes apparent that emerging markets demand attention. Given the expected growth of these markets, exposure to them in a portfolio should be a given.

If we assume an investment approach in line with the endowment model already mentioned, about half a portfolio's equity exposure would be in international markets and about half of the international portion would be in emerging markets. This would result in a 50/25/25 allocation of domestic/developed market/emerging market equities. If this had been the allocation from 2000 to 2010, the equity portion of the portfolio would have grown by nearly 29 percent rather than shrinking by 10 percent. While these numbers still aren't great, given the horrible drag of U.S. markets during this time, a spread of nearly 40 percent through the inclusion of international markets, and in particular emerging markets, certainly would have helped any portfolio.

There can be another factor to consider. As emerging markets grow and increase trade with other emerging markets, they are becoming increasingly independent of developed markets.[9] The decoupling, as it's widely referred to, has raised hopes of economists and investors that another factor less dependent on the United States and other non-U.S. developed markets can smooth economic cycles while providing more diverse investment opportunities.

In some cases, the lack of correlation has been helpful, as the emerging markets' equity performance has behaved very differently than that of U.S. markets. For instance, in 2007, the MSCI Emerging Markets Index increased 34.56 percent versus the S&P 500's 5.49 percent increase. And in 2002, the same index lost only 6.17 percent versus the S&P 500's 22.10 percent decline.

Emerging market holdings, however, don't always help portfolios. When the world panicked in 2008, emerging markets were trounced and suffered losses nearly a third greater than the S&P 500. But in the following year, the same emerging market index tripled S&P 500 returns to provide a cumulative two-year outperformance advantage of 40 percent.

A 10-year correlation history reveals the diversification benefits resulting from emerging markets inclusion. The Emerging Market Equity Index (EME) correlation versus U.S. large caps from December 31, 2000 to December 31, 2010 was 0.87, and correlation with small caps was 0.83 over the same period.[10] While the numbers fall short of the desired 0.80 level, they are closer, and emerging markets secured a greater diversification benefit over this 10-year time period while adding tremendous performance.

While emerging markets help diversify a portfolio, their smoothing effect is erratic, as the relatively high correlation limits diversification benefits. The liquidity of global markets combined with rapid flows of capital result in higher correlation of equity markets worldwide. It's notable, however, that even with the interconnectedness of global markets, sizeable diversification benefits still exist.

Yet, along with their potential outperformance, the higher volatility of emerging markets must be accounted for. From 2000 to 2010, emerging markets returns were more than 50 percent more volatile, as measured by their standard deviation, than the S&P 500's returns. Of course, part of this resulted from the simple fact that emerging markets had positive total returns versus the S&P 500's backward march. In some years, emerging markets helped offset losses or contributed to gains, but in other years, such as 2008, they made them worse. The net effect was an increased volatility of about 20 percent, which isn't bad considering that nearly all the gains were generated by this sector.

Part of the volatility results from the smaller size of these countries' economies and stock market capitalization. A county such as Chile with fewer than 20 million people is likely to be affected more by capital flows than is the United States.

Older data show more desirable results regarding volatility as well as returns; however, I believe this data should be severely discounted, as emerging markets are very different today than they were even 15 years ago. It was just over 20 years ago, in 1989, that the Berlin Wall fell. Deng Xiaoping, the Chinese leader that spearheaded the major economic rebirth of China, supposedly spoke his famous words "To get rich is glorious" in 1992, which unleashed the astounding wave of entrepreneurship that continues to this day.

The largest economies of South America were still mired in hyper-inflation up to the early 1990s. Today, economies from India to Brazil are completely different. Analyzing and extrapolating economic data from very different time periods likely leads to erroneous conclusions.

Now, the picture looks very different. Capitalism is no longer questioned as the economic system that produces the most prosperity for a nation. While there are still a few outliers and the occasional rogue state, solid future growth seems very likely from economies highly motivated and recently freed to better themselves. In short, while investing in emerging markets requires a bit more faith, as there is less historical data, the recent and, I believe, more relevant data strongly suggest that these markets will continue to grow rapidly, if less predictably. Portfolios are likely to benefit from inclusion of these markets.

Implementation

Once you have decided to invest in international markets, you will need to determine your preferred method of doing so. Investing internationally is not quite as simple as investing in U.S. equity markets. Greater difficulty in adding this sector to portfolios has contributed to lower international equity allocations. Yet increasingly integrated and sophisticated financial markets have made international investing much easier than it was just a few years ago. There is no longer any reasonable excuse to avoid this category other than a specific belief, which I believe would be mistaken, that monies are better allocated elsewhere.

In addition to the usual issues facing individual investors in U.S. equity markets, international investing presents several new ones. Country-specific practices, regulatory requirements, accounting standards, investment vehicle options, and even legal access to markets often vary tremendously from their U.S. counterparts. The simple issues of where and how to invest are much more complex questions. A domestic investment automatically assumes an investment in the United States, whereas an international investment determines only that monies will be sent to another country. Deciding where to invest isn't obvious. Moreover, the means of investment may differ dramatically. How do you invest in Indian stocks given that Americans aren't allowed to buy shares on the Indian exchange?

For a domestic equity investment, I advocated using a separately managed account, or SMA, comprised of individual stocks. But this same approach presents numerous challenges outside of the United States. How do you obtain, process, and track relevant information on international securities?

When my wife and I lived in Hong Kong, our equity portfolio consisted mostly of Asian stocks. We routinely worked with sector, country, and regional data as well as easily accessible company information, and we understood it all from an up-to-date and local viewpoint. When we moved back to the United States, we found it very difficult to manage these equities due to lack of information and our increasingly out-of-touch perspective on the region. As a result, we eventually liquidated all our local holdings, fortunately for us just before the Asian markets crashed in 1998.

Access to international investments also differs by country and region. Investing in Canada or Germany is straightforward. You can buy stocks, mutual funds, and ETFs that all trade on U.S. exchanges, or you can buy international stocks directly on these foreign exchanges. Data is widely available, and accounting standards are similar, which facilitates straightforward stock analyses.

On the other hand, many other countries, in particular emerging markets, often present a very different picture. Accounting and disclosure standards may diverge dramatically from those in the United States, making standard stock analysis difficult or even impossible. Many of the vehicles commonly available in some developed markets, such as ETFs, mutual funds, and sector-focused investments, don't exist in overseas markets or can't be accessed by U.S. citizens. And investors can even face legal obstacles stemming from policies concerning their citizenship.

In addition, costs on international exchanges are usually high. Trading and custody fees can seem outrageous by U.S. standards. Fees are often greatest in emerging markets with less-developed financial markets. Expected additional regulatory requirements in the United States will probably further add to these costs.

Moreover, building a diversified international portfolio from individual stocks is much more challenging. Although you can build a diversified U.S. stock portfolio with only about 15 to 20 stocks, this becomes mathematically problematic across multiple countries. For instance, if you want good exposure to various economies, even if you keep your holdings to only 10 positions per country, you may be forced to buy hundreds of stocks to secure adequate country diversification. Since less than 25 percent of your portfolio will likely be devoted to this sector, this approach could result in a complex and confusing international stock allocation filled with hundreds of tiny positions. Not only would the selection and management of these different positions be difficult for nearly anyone, trading costs alone could be prohibitive.

For these reasons and more, I believe most individual investors should avoid using individual stocks to secure international exposure. It's simply too challenging. Not surprisingly, it's also very difficult to find financial professionals or organizations offering SMA solutions for international equities. Existing offerings nearly always focus on larger foreign markets, and the solution isn't comprehensive enough to provide individual investors with adequate foreign market exposure.

Instead, I recommend using ETFs focused on specific regions, countries, or sectors of stocks. The increasingly comprehensive availability of international ETFs makes creating various types of international portfolios easier every year, and many options exist to target specific countries and various sectors. Costs are low, and competition continues to drive them lower. The ETFs are also tax-efficient. Vehicles such as SMAs can successfully employ ETFs to provide an investment approach that combines excellent strategies, effective investment vehicles, low overall fees, and professional management.

Some ETFs focus on broad regions, for example, the Morgan Stanley Country Index, Europe, Asia, Far East (MSCI EAFE) or the Morgan Stanley Country Index, Emerging Markets (MSCI EM). Or, just as there are ETFs that mimic the S&P 500 in the United States, there are ETFs that mimic the major indexes of most major markets in the world, including major emerging markets. There are also international ETFs that mirror different international sectors or investment styles, such as energy, small cap, or value investing.

Strategies can be very simple, such as using one ETF to secure exposure to developed markets and using another to gain exposure to emerging markets. Or strategies may target individual countries or industries. I like the latter approach if one has enough funds to diversify because many trends can be identified that likely make overweighting certain countries, regions, or even sectors more attractive.

Yet for all their pluses, ETFs aren't perfect. No investment ever is. By design, when ETFs are used, foreign market exposure is secured only through buying representation of an index. You are not going to outperform the index because you are buying an approximation of the index.

While trends and inefficiencies present opportunities in any market, most financial professionals believe greater opportunities to exploit market inefficiencies exist in many foreign markets, particularly in emerging markets because of their lower sophistication and limited access to information. These markets may enable a savvy stock picker to add value—something that can't be done with an ETF that mechanically copies an index. (Technically you can outperform a country index through employing sector-based ETFs within the country, if they exist. But few employ this approach on an international basis because it's too granular for most investors, and ETFs rarely exist in emerging markets that would facilitate the approach.)

As a result, some financial professionals claim that a significant opportunity has been missed if ETFs are used, because a manager hasn't been empowered to find hidden value. Other professionals argue that investing only in ETFs that represent a country's stock market secures a more solid proxy for the country's stock market performance while essentially removing potential underperformance that could result from higher fees or bad management. Both arguments may be correct, depending on the country and specific circumstance.

The lack of ETFs that target particular sectors of the world economy or specific countries presents another issue. If you are an endowment fund with billions to invest, you can probably develop investment strategies that target specific types of investments such as technology companies in Israel or mineral companies in Peru. If you are an individual investor and want to add a targeted investment in Ghana with ETFs, you are out of luck as of this writing.

In this case, ETFs are almost a victim of their own success. Their absence from many developing markets and specific sectors is conspicuous. While the number of offerings has grown rapidly, if you want to use ETFs in some countries or for many specific international sectors, you'll simply have to wait. While it can easily be argued that most countries lacking targeted ETFs might not be developed enough to warrant attention, claims that some of the lesser-developed and rapidly growing economies represent some of the best opportunity may be legitimate. Risks are frequently higher, but greater potential returns and lower correlation may be worth it.

To summarize, while ETFs have limitations, they enable construction of excellent, cost-effective international portfolios that target various combinations of developed and emerging markets. If you choose professional management, I believe SMAs using ETFs usually present the best approach for the widest number of investors.

Alternative Implementation Strategies

If for some reason ETFs aren't acceptable, there are still a few different ways to access international stock markets. Many international stocks trade on U.S. exchanges through American depositary receipts (ADRs). In addition, it's relatively easy to buy international shares directly on many developed market foreign exchanges throughout the world. As mentioned, this approach can rapidly become quite complicated and will almost certainly force the exclusion of multiple attractive emerging market securities and even whole economies.

Beyond individual stocks, certain elements of international investing lend themselves well to a previously maligned product: mutual funds. Why bring them up again, especially since many of the issues that plague mutual funds in general can be even more problematic in international mutual funds?

In spite of some obvious drawbacks, within particular countries or regions mutual funds may offer performance or diversification characteristics perceived as superior to other strategies. Overseas, market trends and opportunities often differ significantly from those in the United States, and a local presence may help managers better identify and profit from market inefficiencies. International mutual funds offer one of the best means for a good manager to excel.

Mutual funds may also offer access to regions, styles, or sectors often unavailable through ETFs. A more targeted or simply different approach internationally may work best for a particular investor, and mutual funds may offer this.

All that said, I still believe common cost and structure disadvantages of mutual funds frequently position them poorly, which necessitates truly outstanding performance to overcome their deficiencies. So while the opportunities available at an international level may position some mutual funds to flourish, others seem to have a much greater likelihood of delivering weak relative performance—even internationally. If you decide this makes sense for you, be sure you understand your reasons for choosing this vehicle.

The key points from the international section are:

1. Invest internationally for both diversification and potential performance reasons.
2. Pay special attention to the more rapidly growing emerging market economies. Their stock markets are likely to offer higher growth potential. Still, keep in mind that their lower level of development and smaller size will also probably result in higher volatility.
3. Choosing a good investment vehicle is important in this sector as well. ETFs likely represent a good option given their flexibility, low fees, and easy access. Mutual funds can also present an attractive option, but they may still possess cost and performance limitations associated with the domestic version of this investment. International individual stock accounts are probably too impractical for nearly every individual investor.

As before, the list is brief and could be more comprehensive. However, the key points are straightforward.

Before we finish up with equities in general, let's revisit the original allocation of 50 percent in U.S. equities, 25 percent in developed international markets, and 25 percent in emerging markets. These general percentages are often followed for a couple of reasons. First, over the past several decades they have approximated the general percentages of global stock market valuations. Before the rapid growth of emerging markets over the last couple of decades, the United States made up about half of the world's market capitalization, with Europe comprising somewhat more than half of the remainder. Emerging markets were simply what was left. It was therefore very logical to spread out exposure to global equities approximately according to their relative percentage of equity markets.

The second reason is less cerebral. This allocation is easy. Split the equities in half, and then split the international allocation in half between emerging and developed markets. Even though it's easy, the allocation works well by providing broad exposure to different markets as well as solid diversification. Since there is no set standard like there has been for a stock/bond portfolio, an easy and understandable allocation is better than an unnecessarily complicated approach.

In today's rapidly evolving global economy, does this allocation still make sense? To determine an answer, it might be helpful to look at current global economic activity. As mentioned earlier, emerging markets now account for over 40 percent of the global economic activity measured at purchasing power parity or 30 percent at market exchange rates.[11] Anyone following the value of the dollar over the past few decades has also seen the growing strength of just about everyone's currency relative to that of the United States. If this trend continues, as it is widely expected to do, increases in foreign currency valuations alone will result in tremendous emerging market growth.

Market capitalization percentages also reveal some very interesting changes in world markets. Although the numbers are constantly changing and are certainly inexact, strong trends stand out. As recently as 2004, the United States made up about 44 percent of total global market capitalization. By mid-2008, the U.S. market represented only 29.9 percent in spite of the fact that the U.S. market performed very well relative to global markets during the financial meltdown.[12] The U.S. market is still the world's dominant market with nearly four times the market capitalization of Japan's 8.8 percent and about 5[1/2] times China's fourth-place market capital of 5.4 percent.[13] However, its dominant position is obviously lessening.

Other country trends are telling. In 2004, Japan's market capitalization was over six times the size of China's.[14] By early 2008,

China's market capitalization was higher than Japan's for several weeks before starting a temporary slide. But, by mid-July, China's market capitalization had overtaken Japan's before again dropping temporarily. Regardless of temporary ups and downs, China seems almost certain to permanently pass Japan and assume second place behind the United States.

Emerging markets in general are probably the most important investment consideration, with longer-term trends appearing to be fairly straightforward. By mid-2008, emerging market capitalization represented around 25 percent or more of total market capitalization—up over 100 percent since only 2004. Over the last decade, nearly every emerging market has increased its relative market capitalization percentage quite significantly. While temporary pullbacks and leaps forward are inevitable, recent and expected trends strongly suggest continued growth of emerging markets, at least on a relative basis.

Market capitalization percentages resemble the relative percentages of global economic activity, with foreign developed countries representing about 40 percent of market capitalization, with the United States comprising about 30 percent. Simple math suggests emerging markets make up the remaining 30 percent. Again, the exact numbers are less important than the general trend, as the numbers change constantly.

Most investors, even the most sophisticated investors, don't follow an exact market capitalization weighting, which would be around 30 percent U.S. markets, 40 percent foreign developed markets, and 30 percent emerging markets if we used the previous numbers. They frequently set different allocations for a number of reasons. First, the numbers change constantly. Second, most developed markets simply haven't grown as fast as the United States, and overweighting foreign developed markets has historically been a poor strategy. Third, most U.S. investors' liabilities are in the United States, and most people are more comfortable more closely matching assets to their liabilities. There can be numerous other reasons as well.

I would argue that it makes sense to weight emerging markets at least as heavily as nondeveloped U.S. markets given their expected future growth. Not only are these economies growing more rapidly, future currency fluctuations will likely favor emerging markets. Most likely, higher emerging market emphasis will increase portfolio volatility. The increasing decoupling of economies, however, will likely offset this somewhat.

Very easily, using more current market capitalization weightings combined with a common desire to maintain a higher exposure to a home market could easily bring any investor back to the original 50 percent domestic/25 percent developed/25 percent emerging markets allocation.

With a bit more information, however, adjusting the allocation to 40/30/30 or even 33/33/34 could be easily justified. I believe the increased allocation toward emerging markets makes a great deal of sense, but not all investors will be comfortable with the potential increased volatility. And of course, there's no magic in any of these numbers. The most important step is the first one. Start by diversifying some of the portfolio internationally, and then go from there. Many smaller investors begin by allocating 20 percent of their equity allocation internationally.

There's one last issue that can be important. If the equity allocation of a portfolio includes significant international exposure, which is highly recommended, performance is likely to differ from U.S. equity markets, perhaps significantly. While this can be very desirable, it can take some reorientation to recognize that good or bad news regarding "the market" is likely referring to a different set of equities than you may hold in your more diversified portfolio.

I've found that most investors tend to dismiss or fail to notice better performance of foreign markets during bad times for U.S. markets and overemphasize inevitable U.S. outperformance. Investors feel badly when they shouldn't and then don't feel good when they believe they should. Some investors struggle to make this adjustment. The portfolio adjustment should be well worth it, but for some people, it takes some discipline, or just a little bit of remembering, to make the jump.

By now, hopefully the potential value of including international investments is very clear. Endowments have been practicing this for decades, and it's helped them weather storms in the equity markets while also securing better portfolio performance.

Exact international allocations are a more individual decision. Obviously, individual considerations should weigh into any decision. The previous information should provide solid information to help determine a course forward.

Getting back to the broader topic of the entire portfolio, if we follow a more standard endowment allocation, domestic and foreign equities will comprise around half of a typical portfolio. Because a typical portfolio equity allocation may be higher or lower than 50 percent, much if not the majority of the portfolio will be invested in something other than equities. Earlier, I stated that bonds are not going to make up the other half of an endowment portfolio. So, now we will move into more unique types of investments that can create a more diversified and higher-performing portfolio.

9

Real Assets

ENDOWMENTS OFTEN ALLOCATE THE LARGEST PERCENTAGE OF their portfolio other than stocks to real, tangible assets, otherwise knows as "hard assets." In fact, if domestic and foreign market equities count as individual categories, real assets are often an endowment's largest single asset category. Yale's fiscal year 2010 (June 2009 release date) target allocation for real assets increased to 37 percent from the previous year's 32 percent.[1] It missed its target, only reaching 27.5 percent, but increased its target for the 2011 year to 28 percent.[2] Harvard's target was lower but still significant at 23 percent.[3] Given that most investors completely lack real assets in their portfolios, the allocations of endowments strikingly differentiate them from that of individuals.

In the words of David Swensen, Yale's portfolio manager:

> The real assets portfolio plays a meaningful role in the Endowment as a powerful diversifying tool and a generator of strong returns. Pricing inefficiencies in the asset class and opportunities to add value allow superior managers to generate excess returns over a market cycle.[4]

My focus has been on strategies employed by endowments, given their higher profile, but nearly all institutional investors emphasize

101

real assets to some extent. Many, if not most, of the buildings in commercial districts throughout the United States are owned by an institutional investor rather than by the company occupying the building or an individual investor. But real assets include more than real estate. Endowments may spread their hard asset allocations across holdings as diverse real estate, oil and gas, precious metals, industrial metals, agricultural products, timberland, and other commodities.

Real assets are frequently emphasized in institutional portfolios for several reasons. Because of their perceived strong historical performance, real assets satisfy the endowment requirement of strong long-term performance. Just as importantly, economic ups and downs effect real assets differently than stocks or bonds. The resulting performance differences can secure excellent diversification in portfolios. While it's always possible that there may be some correlation across any real asset and the stock market, the correlation tends to be limited, and in many cases is actually negative.[5] For instance, ETFs for the commodities index and U.S. large-cap stocks show an inverse correlation of −0.58.[6] While this relationship isn't quite as simple as it may seem, as we will see later, generally low correlation of real assets with other investments remains consistent and can be invaluable in building a more stable portfolio.

The stock market tends to anticipate economic trends as seen by usual patterns of stock market movements. Stocks tend to fall well before the economy actually registers a recession. Similarly, the stock market usually starts rising about four to six months before a recession ends. In contrast, real estate values normally lag the economy. Rents and prices tend to stay quite strong even well into a recession because firms can't simply decide to pay less rent or break their leases. Valuations may also be much less affected by economic changes given the "stickiness" of property cash flows or longer-term nature of future value projections. If real estate values decline, prices usually hit bottom after a recession has ended by which time the stock market has usually completed a strong recovery.

In addition to diversification, real assets add another very desirable characteristic to portfolios. They are normally an excellent hedge against inflation. Unlike many other assets that suffer when inflation hits—think bonds—typically most hard assets increase in price during times of inflation, often tracking inflation very closely.[7]

As mentioned earlier, an investment's ability to offer an inflation hedge makes it attractive, especially in light of the government's debt levels and recent spending in the United States. Just as the topic of inflation can be quite complicated, the relationship between real assets and inflation can be as well. Various issues from employment levels to energy costs can cause inflation, while other real assets, such as real estate, tend to follow inflation. Moreover, the causes and effects of inflation change frequently over time.

Nevertheless, one benefit of real assets is their positive correlation with inflation whether they directly cause it or are affected by it. There is wide agreement that an increase in commodity prices (e.g., oil and building materials) can quickly cause inflation. If commodity prices increase and cause inflation, obviously holding or having exposure to the increasingly expensive asset that is acting as the root cause of inflation is likely to be good for a portfolio.

Even if commodity price increases cause inflation, however, you don't need to hold commodities to benefit from their price increases. As money declines in value, purchasing power declines, and it takes more money to purchase the same amount of real assets.

In the case of real estate, if commodity price increases are the primary cause of inflation, real estate will also increase in price as replacement costs increase and price levels rise. Inflation results in more money in circulation, which causes price increases for all goods. If demand stays the same for real estate, prices will simply increase to reflect the same demand but lower purchasing power for the currency. This is normally what happens.

The topic of inflation can get complicated. In the previous example, I made the assumption that demand stays the same, which may or may not be true. Obviously, demand can go up or down.

If high employment causes inflation through wage increases, demand for real estate will likely increase, resulting in both demand and decreased purchasing power pushing prices up. In this case, two major factors pushing real estate prices higher will likely raise those prices more than the inflation rate.

But the opposite can also happen. If inflation caused by increased prices of commodities causes a slowdown in the economy, demand for real estate, due to an increase in unemployment, may decrease. Rising replacement costs and decreased purchasing power would push prices up while demand could be forcing prices down. In this case, the results would likely be less clear. Real estate would still likely increase in cost to keep pace with inflation, but it might take longer or require a future rise of demand back to previous levels.

As one can easily imagine, this topic can be a very big, complex one. The concept, however, tends to be very simple. Real assets are of limited supply. The value, not price, of real assets tends to stay relatively constant or increase over time as demand for various assets increases over time. If purchasing power goes down, prices will go up. The same trend generally applies to virtually all real assets, whether they are real estate, timberland, oil and gas, or commodities.

But even these seemingly straightforward assumptions can be violated. Longer-term trends can affect these prices. For instance, we have gotten better at finding some types of commodities such as aluminum and copper, so in some cases inflation-adjusted prices have decreased. At one time, aluminum was considered a rare metal even though it's the most abundant metal in the earth's crust. The problem was the high cost of refining the metal. Once new technologies and processes were developed, aluminum became inexpensive and widely available. Yet, this hasn't happened to most other metals. It still takes about the same amount of gold to pay for one year at Yale University as it did when the school opened, although tuition has obviously increased dramatically in dollar terms since then.

Price increases will not affect all real assets equally. With real estate this is very easy to see, as price increases can vary dramatically by location. It will also be true across various real assets categories. During the highly inflationary period from 1970 to 1981, oil prices increased 1,100 percent while Canadian farmland prices increased 550 percent.[8] Part of this disparity resulted from oil's pivotal role in causing inflation during that time as the Organization of Petroleum Exporting Countries (OPEC) worked aggressively to increase the global price of oil.

And to further complicate the discussion, there is also evidence that rises in commodity prices may cause inflation in the short term but may also be adversely impacted by longer-term inflationary periods, unlike real estate. While commodity prices are often highly correlated with short-term inflation, longer-term inflation can actually negatively impact commodity prices as demand for commodities slows or drops.[9] As a result, commodities often require a different approach, and they may not even be appropriate for many investors. As different means to gain exposure to various real assets are covered, we will look at the pluses and minuses of different types of assets. All these patterns and correlations may sound quite complicated, but fortunately investment strategies can be much simpler.

Moving Forward

The combination of performance, diversification through lack of or inverse correlation, and inflation protection all make real assets a very desirable component of most portfolios. Although this may be true in theory, for many investors, taking the plunge to add hard assets can be a bit daunting.

Access to real assets has historically been difficult for most individual investors, which has resulted in negligible portfolio allocations for most of them. Some real assets also lack liquidity, which creates planning and management issues. For example, if you buy a stock and decide the next day to do something different, you can sell your holding and quickly change directions. Doing that isn't so easy with many real assets.

Furthermore, even liquid assets such as commodities can strike fear in the heart of the average investor, as commodities can be hard to understand, unexpectedly volatile, and management intensive. As we move forward, we are going to explore various means by which investors can add exposure to real assets in ways that are manageable and comfortable. Fortunately, the investment industry has greatly expanded the accessibility of real assets through various new or enhanced investment products. As with international investing, adding positions in real assets has gotten much easier.

Real Estate

Given its pivotal role in many endowment portfolios and its familiarity to investors, I'm going to start with real estate and cover the topic thoroughly. Keep in mind that many real estate characteristics are common to other types of alternative assets. The more familiar topic provides a great basis to introduce concepts applicable to other areas.

The various desirable characteristics of real estate frequently make it the largest single allocation within the real assets category. Sometimes even an endowment's or institution's entire real asset portfolio will be comprised of real estate. The sector is relatively easy to understand, as most people have a natural feel for the category given their personal experience.

Like any distinct category, real estate reacts somewhat uniquely to inflation. In the short term, inflation usually increases the value of land and structures. The land value increases because there is now a greater supply of money chasing the same amount of land. Structures go up in value because replacement costs increase as materials become more expensive and building labor costs rise. Rent increases, however, nearly always lag cost increases because existing leases must expire before higher rates can be renegotiated.

In nearly all cases, the end effect is appreciation for real estate during times of inflation. The inflationary effects are usually fairly dependable because the primary factors affecting real estate prices are all positively correlated with inflation.

The benefits of real estate in a portfolio have been recognized for a long time by institutions. And real estate's potential portfolio contributions have been respected within the academic community for many decades.

During my graduate school days in the early 1990s, I remember very clearly an academic paper arguing that investment real estate should comprise approximately 20 percent of an individual investor's portfolio excluding a person's primary residence. I remember the percentage clearly because the claim clashed with the common assumptions of the time. At that time, the U.S. equities bull market had been raging for years, making the stock market particularly sexy, and I had just spent three years on Wall Street where stocks were the answer to everything.

Moreover, investment courses always focused on equity markets. Real estate seemed so dull and old-fashioned. While I don't have that reference material anymore, and can't tell you why the research produced that number, I still find it interesting that academic studies were suggesting significant real estate allocations more than two decades ago. Obviously, much has changed since then. A 20 percent allocation may or may not make sense, but having *some* real estate allocation probably does.

Investors can add real estate to a portfolio in various ways. The most familiar investment vehicles to most investors are real estate investment trusts (REITs). To qualify as a REIT, a company is required by the Internal Revenue Service (IRS) to invest at least 75 percent of its assets in real estate, derive at least 75 percent of its income from rent or mortgage interest, and distribute at least 90 percent of its taxable income to shareholders. In exchange, profits are not taxed at the corporate level but only at the investor level.

REITs are usually companies that hold and operate real estate. Some REITs, however, may be mortgage or timber companies operating legally as REITs because of the more attractive tax structure. For discussion purposes, I'll be referring exclusively to the much more common real estate-focused REITs.

There are various types of REITs, including publicly traded REITs, nontraded public REITs, and private REITs. Probably the most familiar form is the publicly traded REIT that trades on an exchange just as IBM or Coca-Cola do. When you buy the stock, you buy shares in a company that owns and operates real estate—hopefully, for a profit.

Traded REITs

Although publicly traded REITs represent an investment in a company that invests in real estate, this is not the type of asset that I'm actually discussing. This type of holding is simply another stock sector, like the technology or utility category. I believe real estate can be a very good sector to include in a stock portfolio given its long-term performance and somewhat lower correlation with the overall stock market. The National Association of Real Estate Investment Trusts (NAREIT) is formed largely to help people better understand and incorporate traded REITs into their investment strategies.

A good stock strategy should already include this type of asset, or at least consider it, as already discussed. Correlation is lower than various other categories at 0.71 from December 31, 2000, to December 31, 2010.[10] The lower correlation versus most other categories of tradable stocks can make the category a desirable part of a portfolio. Even though the investment is originally based on real estate, the performance tends to be more correlated to the stock market and various other factors that primarily affect the stock market.

This data also masks a recent trend. Correlation between traded REITs and the broader stock market has markedly increased in recent years as more professional investors incorporate this asset class into their equity strategies. This likely benefits the equity portion of an investor's portfolio but limits the category's potential to contribute as a hard asset.

Other Approaches

Beyond real estate ownership through stocks, investors can own real estate the old-fashioned way: buy it directly. While I'm not really suggesting this approach for individual investors, as it's too complicated and inefficient, endowments and institutions may employ some version of it.

Looking back at historical performance between two common indexes quickly reveals why. The NAREIT U.S. Real Estate Index tracks traded REITs while the NCREIF Property Index measures performance for institutional, directly held real estate. Comparing the standard deviations of the two illustrate dramatic differences in the investments. On a quarterly basis from 1978 to 2010, publicly traded REITs have a standard deviation of 9.18 percent versus the private, nontraded institution real estate of only 2.27 percent.[11] This makes the traded REIT standard deviation four times that of the nontraded. On an annual basis, standard deviations are 18.79 percent for the private real estate versus 8.21 percent for the nontraded real estate.[12]

Not surprisingly, the standard deviation of the traded REITs and the stock market over the same time period are very similar, producing levels within 10 percent of each other for both the quarterly and annual return variations. Equities available through traded REITs are really financial instruments and should be treated as such. This is just one reason that endowments invest directly in real estate or some type of vehicle that provides them direct ownership of real estate rather than a financial instrument.

An obvious advantage enjoyed by endowments versus individual investors is their size. A few billion dollars commands attention. Not only does their size give them a potential advantage during negotiations, they can spread their costs over larger amount of investments, which provides them scale advantages. As a result, the size of endowments has historically enabled them to find and structure deals that have been completely inaccessible to the individual investor.

It's been very difficult, if not impossible, to invest directly into real estate without becoming a real estate expert or even a Realtor. Even if someone had the time and expertise to facilitate direct investment, developing a diversified portfolio would have been nearly impossible, and most commercial properties were inaccessible.

Fortunately, during the past couple of decades and particularly over the last 10 years a major trend within the investment world has vastly increased the investment options available to individuals seeking to invest directly into real estate. The trend is a direct result of the declines of pension funds and the rise of individual retirement accounts, primarily the 401(k), which became available in 1980. While there are obviously still many pension funds in the United States, the number of people covered by them has plummeted over the past several decades. Because rapidly increasing amounts of people's future retirement are now managed directly by individuals, the providers of real estate investments have been forced to follow the money.

For investors, this trend is creating new opportunities. Companies that only worked with pension funds decades ago now routinely provide investment opportunities directly to individuals. And the increasing amount of wealth managed by individuals has created demand for additional investment choices.

The companies that provide investment options directly to individual investors seem to have a favorite tag line: "Institutional quality real estate for individual investors." This jingle is repeated ad nauseam within this sector probably because it clearly and succinctly summarizes the value proposition.

Nontraded Real Estate

While there are various means to invest directly into real estate, the largest and most common vehicle facilitates direct investments in real estate through a vehicle called a nontraded REIT. As you might expect, a nontraded REIT is very different from a traded REIT.

When you buy shares in a traded REIT, you are buying shares from another shareholder on a secondary market. The value of the shares is determined by supply and demand for the shares. If a company is out of favor, you might be able to buy the shares cheaply. If sentiment changes, the share prices may go up, which is good or bad, depending on whether you are a seller or buyer. Price changes may or may not have any relation to the underlying value of the real estate. It could be that the stock market is fluctuating, or perhaps various other factors that influence stock pricing are affecting market sentiment. This is simply the nature of a publicly traded stock.

Nontraded REITs are very different. When you make an investment into a nontraded REIT, you are giving a company funds to purchase commercial real estate directly. More simply, you are hiring a company to buy and manage a real estate portfolio for you. When you hire this company, you are making several decisions that all have different ramifications.

Nontraded real estate will vary according to the type of real estate targeted, management approach, return targets, initial and likely future dividends, likely tax treatment, and planned exit strategy. As you might expect there is no right answer for everyone, although some categories tend to be more popular than others. Because most investors lack expertise in this area, I'm going to address several of the specific characteristics of nontraded real estate a bit more thoroughly.

It's notable that even though nontraded REITs don't trade on an exchange, at least not yet, they are still highly regulated, answering to FINRA (Financial Industry Regulatory Authority), the SEC (Securities and Exchange Commission), and every state (NASAA, North American Securities Administrators Association) in which they are sold. All their financials are public and filed with the SEC. Even the burdensome Sarbanes-Oxley rules apply. *Nontraded* does not mean *nonregulated*.

Real Estate Sectors

The major sectors of real estate are generally thought of as Office, Retail, Multifamily (e.g., apartments), and Industrial (e.g., warehouses). Other sectors exist, such as Hospitality (hotels), Healthcare, Public storage, Specialty, and so on. Some companies may even choose strategies that emphasize locations or a particular use of real estate. To differentiate themselves, companies nearly always declare a particular strategy that can range from targeting specific sectors to specifically building a diversified portfolio through buying various types of properties. Since there are various offerings from different companies, you should choose the strategy or strategies that you most like.

Management Style

As you might expect, company managements also differ. Competencies and emphases can vary dramatically and lead to very different results. Even companies that focus on office properties may employ very different strategies that range from a focus on location in prime spots to an emphasis on cost-efficient building management. In my experience, there is not one style that works the best. Rather, the firms that manage to excel across the most areas of significance usually achieve the greatest success.

Return Targets

Most investors want the greatest return; however, most also want to minimize risk. Real estate provides ample opportunity to move along the risk/reward scale.

Commercial office properties provide a straightforward example. This sector, like most others, is commonly divided into three categories: core, value-added, and opportunistic. Core real estate is generally made up of high-quality buildings filled mostly with rent-paying tenants. Yields and value will likely increase with inflation and possibly through various management actions, but opportunities to make major improvements in the property and increases in rental yield are limited. Because the property is stable and viewed as less risky, initial valuations—and purchase prices—are higher.

The lower risk likely decreases potential returns. These investments, however, still tend to be a favorite of various investors, including institutions, because the risk/reward ratio is seen as desirable. Returns are often good, with a significant percentage coming through constant and fairly predictable cash flow. The immediate cash flow can easily reach or even exceed 5 to 8 percent per year. Future return potential through inflation or other factors can further add to the total growth numbers. Obviously, numbers will differ and will be greatly affected by the quality of the management team.

Value-added real estate is often similar to core, but some type of problem with the real estate provides opportunity for significant improvement and possible increases in future value. Initial yields tend to be lower either because vacancy rates are higher or cash is needed for improvements to raise occupancy rates and improve the property. Successful improvements will likely increase returns, but that is not guaranteed. Even successful changes may fail to enhance value for any number of reasons ranging from new market demands to unexpected competition. Usually, investors also exchange greater potential value increases at a later date for lower up-front income.

Opportunistic real estate targets larger increases in value through some type of more significant improvement. The range of property types in this category is very diverse and can include everything from raw land to structures needing significant renovation. Usually, properties in this category don't provide any income and may even require further investment. In return, if improvements are successful, returns can be much higher.

Most nontraded REITs focus on the first category, core, because it seems to provide the most desirable attributes to the widest number of investors. Yields are often quite good at around 5 to 7 percent, and they often increase over time. In addition, some future share price appreciation is normally expected, with increases usually matching or exceeding the inflation rate. It's worth stating again, however, that these are investments in real estate, not supercharged, guaranteed CDs.

Because various attributes will differentiate one nontraded REIT from another, most investors will also want to invest in at least a couple of different offerings to further enhance the diversification of their portfolio.

Dividends

As previously mentioned, most nontraded real estate focuses on the core category of real estate, which provides a fairly significant dividend, usually greater than 5 percent. As of December 31, 2009, the average distribution yield for nontraded real estate was 6.52 percent, according to Advisorbiz.com. Blue Vault Partners calculated the average yield paid by nontraded real estate at the end of 2010 to be nearly the same, at 6.5 percent. The dividend is the income net of expenses that the property is producing. Ninety percent of this income must be paid out to shareholders in order for the REIT to maintain its preferred tax status. Many people like nontraded real estate because the income is usually generous and normally quite predictable. Management companies work very hard to pay a good dividend immediately when investors provide them with funding and then try to slowly raise it over time.

A note of caution is warranted regarding dividends, as they can be misleading. During the early stages of raising capital, managers often carry large cash balances while negotiating future property purchases. As a result, they are frequently paying dividends on their entire investment portfolio even though substantial funds may be generating little income. Up-front dividends are paid to attract new investors. Where does the money come from? Very simply, the dividends are paid out of raised capital.

For the investment to be successful, managers must balance excess dividends paid out against future dividend projections and expected value increases. While the practice is common, dividend coverage, or lack thereof, often provides a good point of analysis in determining the potential success of the investment. This is fairly obvious. If a manager continues to pay a dividend that isn't covered through cash flow, this arrangement eventually resembles a Ponzi scheme and investors will suffer. Also just because a dividend starts higher doesn't mean the investment is better, since there's no requirement that the dividend be fully covered by cash flow.

In addition, dividend increases and the dividend itself are not guaranteed. During the financial meltdown of 2008 and 2009, some companies were forced to reduce their dividends because of increased vacancy rates, drops in rent rates, and/or increased expenses incurred to attract new tenants.

Yet, as a business, they can adjust and capitalize on opportunity. During the economic slowdown, other companies continued to raise their dividends as their management successfully operated their properties or bought advantageously while property prices were depressed. The greater point is that dividend yields are usually an attractive attribute of nontraded REITs, but they can change without warning at management's discretion.

Tax Treatment

The corporate structure of nontraded REITs enables all investors to reap many of the benefits of directly owning real estate. In most cases, this results in some fairly significant tax savings. The most basic and obvious tax advantage is the ability to defer any tax payment on a percentage of the dividend received. While this percentage is usually around half the dividend, some nontraded REITs provide all their income as tax deferred due to specific tax treatment. In most cases, the tax deferral lowers your original cost basis so that when you eventually sell your shares you will be forced to pay taxes on the income, but it will be at a long-term capital gains rate rather than an ordinary income rate. Even in real estate, the government doesn't give you a free tax pass.

Volatility

The general lack of volatility, or movement, of the nontraded REIT share price ranks as one of the more attractive characteristics of nontraded real estate for many investors. Virtually all nontraded REITs set an initial share price of $10 to keep the math simple. When you make an investment, the number of shares you own is simply your investment divided by 10. While the management company is raising funds, the share price remains at $10 per share.

The pricing stability can be a great influence on a portfolio, because the value of your investment on your statement never moves. During market turbulence, this can be wonderful. However, it's also rarely perfectly accurate. If you purchased shares one year and then you purchased them on the same day the following year, can you assume that the average value of all the holdings in the portfolio is exactly the same? Probably not.

Ongoing new investments into the nontraded REIT during the offering period allow managers to dollar cost average properties into the portfolio. Some purchased properties will ultimately produce better results than others. The best properties may be the first ones purchased or the last added. On average, all investor commitments are treated the same regardless of when they were added. And the argument is often made that the fairly steady fund-raising of the funds produces an overall value that will be fairly close to the original share price while minimizing price volatility.

In 2009, the regulators made a change that they hope will provide a bit more transparency to the potential value of the real estate. At least every 18 months after fund-raising ends, the value of the shares must be updated according to an independent appraisal of the properties. After the first revaluation of the properties, future revaluations are normally done around the end of the year because of regulatory requirements in retirement accounts.

While the appraisals provide at least some pricing information during the life of the investment, the practice is marginally helpful at best. You can't really know the exact value of the real estate until someone else buys it. As anyone with a house can understand, appraisals serve as guesstimates only. Moreover, finding comparables for the only 60-story office tower in the most desirable location within a unique city can be realistically impossible. Numerous factors can affect price, ranging from corporate strategy to property prestige to buyer/seller ego. Many valuations use some version of discounted cash flow to estimate value. This is the same method generally used to value stocks, which isn't very comforting given the pricing inefficiencies common with equities.

Another dynamic that valuations fail to consider further complicates this process. Many valuations of the portfolio properties consider only the values of the individual properties. A significant contributor to the value of a nontraded REIT is the aggregated character of the portfolio. Private equity firms, traded REITs, and other investors usually pay a considerable premium for real estate if it is part of a larger portfolio of properties with specific characteristics and known, predictable cash flow. The purchasing company doesn't have to find properties, complete due diligence, purchase the building, install management, and possibly improve the building. Nearly any liquid investment will command a premium over its illiquid counterpart. While there's no exact aggregate premium value, it's generally assumed to be about 10 percent, but ranges can vary considerably.

Realistically, investors need to realize that they will really only know two things about the value of this investment: what they bought their shares for and what they eventually sell them for. In between, they will likely collect a nice dividend that usually increases a bit over time, but it could stay the same or even decrease. In most cases, the underlying asset value will remain at its original level until 18 months after fund-raising closes, assuming the investment isn't liquidated before then. Throughout the holding period, the investment value will rarely change and will likely offer only a rough approximation of the eventual sales price of the assets.

Time Frame of Exit: "Going Full Cycle"

Certainly one of the biggest characteristics that separates nontraded REITs from traded REITs is their lack of liquidity. If you buy a traded REIT, you can sell it immediately. By contrast, if you buy a nontraded REIT, you have made a commitment that will likely last for several years. In addition, you don't control the timing of the sale because you have delegated the liquidation of your real estate to your professional managers.

The length of time of holdings will vary. Most nontraded REITs target a hold time of around six to eight years, although experts in the field reference other statistics that show that the average deal only lasts three to six years. In recent years, providers are increasingly emphasizing shorter hold times due to investor preferences.

These time frames, however, mask tremendous differences between programs as well as the individual investors in the programs. Some nontraded REITs may raise capital for up to four and even six years, although competitive pressures are pushing time frames closer to a two- or three-year average. In many cases, nontraded REITs target a liquidation date before the 18-month revaluation requirement deadline. If the nontraded REIT raised capital for six years and then liquidated one year after closing the fund, the earliest investors would have held the investment for seven years versus the latest investor's one-year hold period. In this case, the average may be three and a half years, but individual experiences vary widely. As you might expect, this often impacts average return numbers dramatically.

As the previous example illustrates, investment selection can greatly affect the duration of the investment. Most nontraded REITs announce the closing of their funding programs around six to nine months in advance of the official date, although exact time frames will vary. In this instance, strategy can affect your flexibility and also your returns. If you invest in nontraded REITs shortly before they close, obviously the duration of your investment will be less than any investor preceding you.

In addition, by waiting to invest until just before an offering closes, you will have a much better idea of what the property port-folio looks like. Specifics such as modified funds from operations (MFFO), a measure of total portfolio cash flow, will be quite clear as will other factors, including dividend coverage and debt structure. While you may have little interest in or understanding of these issues, a good financial professional will be able to decipher this information and use it to estimate the quality of a potential investment.

Investing later in the offering's fund-raising period also offers the potential to increase your annual rate of return. Investors can have many reasons for investing in a nontraded REIT early in its fund-raising cycle, such as the desire for income or the usual 5 percent share discount on dividend reinvestment. Also, remember that the asset value is very stable, remaining at $10 per share.

A different investor who purchases shares five years later, however, will buy her shares at the same price. If the offering liquidates two years later and share prices increase by 20 percent, the original investor will have earned the dividend for seven years and then realized a gain of 20 percent. The later investor will realize the same gain but over the much shorter time period of two years.

In the case just mentioned, if we assume a fairly standard re-investment discount of 5 percent and a constant dividend of 6.5 percent (which is a bit simplified, but not far from realistic), the first investor will realize a 9.84 percent return per year. Because the second investor earned the 20 percent capital appreciation gains over only two years rather than seven, the second investor's annualized gain will be 17.23 percent. An investor with a time frame of 4.5 years, exactly at the midpoint of these two investors', would have earned an annual return of 11.44 percent. Obviously, compressing the capital gains into a much shorter time period significantly increases annual returns. As you might have guessed, investing immediately before the closing deadline is a strategy that is frequently employed.

In addition to the final exit strategy, virtually all nontraded REITs offer a potential early exit. Most will repurchase shares at full value if the original investor dies. Most also offer some type of early exit net of a liquidation penalty. The most common terms are to disallow exit during year 1, and then charge 7.5 percent, 5 percent, and 2.5 percent as exit fees in years 2, 3, and 4. After four years, the investor can simply redeem his shares for the original purchase price. The firms offer these programs because they usually believe that it doesn't hurt current shareholders—and may even help them because the investment may have increased in value above the repurchase price. The purpose is to provide some flexibility to shareholders who need additional flexibility.

But there's a catch, and it can be a big one. These programs are available only if less than a certain percentage of shareholders take advantage of them or, in some cases, only if the board of directors chooses to leave them open. For this simple reason, the redemption programs are something that I believe investors should assume don't exist. If for some reason an investor really needs to liquidate and the program is open, that's great, but don't count on that being the case.

The year 2008 provided a great example of potential problems. During this year the stock market declined 37 percent, and most investors suffered even greater losses in their stock portfolios. The option of liquidating nontraded real estate at full value or very near to full value after earning a nice dividend for years became very attractive if one needed cash or simply wanted out of any risk-based asset.

During the few years following the 2008 decline, many of the nontraded REITs experienced large increases in redemption requests. While some nontraded REITs honored all redemption requests either immediately or over a couple of quarters, others completely closed their programs. Given the potentially unpredictable nature of redemption programs, it's simply best to assume that the investment will be held until future liquidation.

So how and when do you get your money back? As mentioned, the time from inception to complete liquidation is often around six to eight years, and most funds provide a target date or a date of maximum latest liquidation. But you will not know the exact exit date until it happens.

This lack of certainty is significant. Endowments and institutions accept the illiquidity of these types of investments in exchange for return potential, diversification, and stability. While the same characteristics will usually be attractive to some, and investors may be willing to make the same trade-off, individuals may not have the flexibility to accept longer and unpredictable time frames.

Just as you have delegated the authority of all other aspects of nontraded REIT management, you also delegate authority to your management team to get the most from your investment through an advantageous sale. For many investors, this can be one of the most valuable services provided—maximizing a sales price through recognition of the best time to sell. Most managers are far better able to maximize sales prices than are individual investors. And they are less likely than panic-prone individuals to sell at the wrong time.

Most firms use one of three possible means to return your investment, although one is most commonly used. First, firms can liquidate all the properties and send your money back. This strategy tends to be very uncommon because it removes the premium usually created through building a portfolio of properties that can be sold as a group. Managers focused on more opportunistic properties are more likely to use this exit strategy, as they can predictably sell holdings immediately after major improvements are completed.

Second, a nontraded REIT can go public, thereby becoming a traded REIT. Investors' shares transition from a stable $10-per-share holding to a stock that is marked to market on an exchange every second. After the nontraded real estate becomes a public stock, most original shareholders liquidate their holdings fairly quickly, which causes downward pricing pressure on the stock. To guard against too many immediate sales, selling groups usually organize public offerings and provide a floor to the stock price during the initial months of trading. This option is growing in popularity, but the uncertainty around publicly traded share prices and the inherent desire by most original shareholders to avoid holding a stock can make this exit strategy less attractive.

The most common method of liquidation has been selling the whole portfolio to another entity. While many different groups may buy the portfolio, the most common purchasers are traded REITs and private equity groups. In these cases, original investors will either receive cash for their shares or possibly a combination of cash and shares if the purchaser is a nontraded REIT. Regardless, the investment will be liquid, and investors can quickly and easily convert their holdings to cash, if they want to.

Performance

Endowments like real estate because of the good long-term performance of the asset class combined with the diversification benefits and inflation hedge. Yet for all the purported performance of nontraded REITs, finding reliable numbers presents a challenge. No common index exists, and firms don't report numbers based on a common system. In addition, because the securities don't trade, true correlation and performance data relative to indexes don't exist. There are simply no regular daily/monthly/quarterly/annual valuation benchmarks for nontraded REITs from which to derive total return data. In addition, because investors enter the investment continuously over a multiyear period, the assumed beginning date of investment for comparison purposes will dramatically affect results, as we have already seen.

To get a general idea of the sector's performance, we can look in a few different places. The National Council of Real Estate Investment Fiduciaries (NCREIF), the not-for-profit trade association, calculates the NCREIF Property Index (NPI), a commercial real estate data and performance measurement. NCREIF compiles the most complete total rate of return measure of investment performance of a very large pool of individual commercial real estate properties acquired in the private market for investment purposes only.

This is *not* the same as the nontraded REIT market; rather, all the properties in the NPI have been acquired, at least in part, on behalf of tax-exempt institutional investors, with the great majority being pension funds. This index assumes that the included real estate carries no leverage. In reality, virtually all real estate purchased by endowments, institutions, and nontraded REITs is partially financed to increase returns. If funds can be borrowed from a bank at 5 percent while the underlying asset earns 10 percent, the equity holders (buyers) increase their profits through the spread. None of this profit potential is included in the NPI. The lack of leverage also results in understating the properties' real volatility. Just as expected returns would be higher, so would any price swings.

In addition, as a group, these investors are viewed as quite conservative. Their numbers will likely represent fairly conservative deals. There is also no distinction between very low risk deals or higher-risk deals, as all data is lumped into one number. Regardless, it's reasonable to assume that these investors have a good idea of what they are doing. At least they have a lot of money.

From the starting date of collection in the first quarter of 1978 through the end of 2010, the index has averaged 8.90 percent per year net of all fees. Had we analyzed the data only through the end of 2007, the numbers would have looked better, with a 10.30 percent annual return. During the financial meltdown, the losses in this sector differed markedly from the stock market's. Losses and subsequent gains were not as wild, and the timing was quite different. This real estate index declined only 6.46 percent in 2008 versus the S&P 500's loss of 37.0 percent. Real estate's lagging nature showed up in 2009 as real estate declined 16.86 percent while the market bounced back 26.5 percent. The year 2010 saw both indexes earn positive returns, with real estate up 16.65 percent while the market increased 15.1 percent. Over the three-year time period, the real estate index and the S&P 500 both lost about 10 percent, but real estate's standard deviation was about half of the S&P 500's. As usual, property income helped steady real estate returns. Had these two assets with very different yearly return numbers been combined in a portfolio, overall performance would have been much less volatile. These numbers shed some light on returns and volatility, but they really only apply to a select group of institutional investors.[13]

More relevant data regarding only nontraded REITs is a bit harder to find. Probably the best data available are provided by the firm Robert A. Stanger & Company, one of the most respected consulting firms that serves the nontraded real estate community. It calculated returns for the many deals that liquidated in 2007, which represented a substantial portion of the funds raised late in the 1990s and early in the 2000s. For the programs that did liquidate, the internal rates of returns averaged 12.5 percent per year without dividend reinvestment and 13.6 percent with dividend reinvestment. These numbers assume investments were made in the middle of the offering period. The range of returns among the individual nontraded REITs was 7.3 percent to 16.6 percent without reinvestment and 7.4 percent to 18.1 percent with reinvestment. The lack of losing deals is encouraging, even if it guarantees nothing.[14]

These performance data demonstrate the potential benefit of hiring experts to manage your real estate investment *and* time its sale. Rightly so, most of the managers of nontraded REITs believed that valuations were very good in 2007 and chose that year as a liquidation date. It's easy to argue that their judgment contributed significantly to attractive overall return numbers.

In addition, these numbers are likely understated. Had you invested later in the fund-raising cycle, your annualized returns increased, in many cases very substantially. Many investors understand this, and it's very common that nontraded REITs raise a disproportionate amount of their funds in late stages of their fund-raising cycle, often experiencing a large influx of investment funds very near the investment cut-off date. The previous return calculation numbers simply assume an average investment date midway through the fund-raising period. This is extremely unlikely. As an aside, the industry is working to generate more uniform performance benchmarks to help investors better assess past performance.

Correlation numbers are even harder to find. For nontraded REITs, at various conferences and due diligence meetings I have attended, correlations for nontraded REITs ranging around 0.00 to 0.10 have been frequently cited. The claim of zero correlation stems from their lack of mark-to-market pricing. This seems highly inaccurate given that nontraded real estate normally pays a positive dividend of about 6 percent while the market has historically produced average returns of about 6 to 7 percent above inflation over time. There has got to be some correlation somewhere in there. I suspect claims of no correlation are based as much on lack of information and fuzzy definitions as on applicable and relevant history. Many correlation claims are probably unreliable and overstated. As these investments move more into the mainstream and valuations become more frequent, better data will become available, and correlations will almost certainly be shown to be above zero. Yet I believe that more accurate data will still reveal correlations well under 0.50. All my anecdotal information suggests low correlations. Numbers this low would verify substantial diversification benefits that these assets are widely believed to offer.

After covering a lot of different data, a quick summary of a potential means to invest in real estate is in order.

1. Traded REITs versus nontraded REITs are very different investments, with traded REITs more closely resembling a stock market investment while nontraded REITs provide a means to invest directly in real estate.
2. Different types of nontraded REITs can facilitate investment in different properties with various management styles and return targets.
3. Dividends usually average around 5 to 7 percent, and a significant percentage of the dividend, or even all of it, may be tax deferred.
4. Prices of the shares tend to be very stable, with prices usually remaining at $10 per share until around 18 months after the fund-raising period ends, at which time a revaluation of properties will usually be completed around year-end. (Note: Because this is a regulatory requirement, this could change at any time.)
5. The timing of the sale of the investment is controlled exclusively by the managers and directors of the nontraded REIT, and time frames can vary from very short (possibly under a year) for late investors to very long for early investors in longer-lasting offerings (possibly up to 10 years).
6. Performance appears to have been quite good, but exact performance data may vary considerably across investor time frames. In addition, performance numbers are a bit sparse, and their lack of comprehensiveness could be misleading.

Positives Versus Negatives

So, what are the positives and negatives of nontraded REITs? Looking at the positives, I believe nontraded REITs offer a very attractive combination of performance, diversification, price stability, inflation hedge, income (if desired), and preferable tax treatment. The negatives are pretty straightforward: potential lack of liquidity and lack of mark-to-market pricing. For some, the negatives outweigh all the positives. For others, portfolio liquidity provided by other investments makes this potential drawback a nonissue.

Non-traded REITs have generated some criticism. Any investment rapidly attracting new capital from other investments seems to invariably generate bad press as competing interests fight change and loss of capital flows. Having experienced explosive growth over the past decade, nontraded REITs fall into the same pattern and have been targeted by critics. By far, the most accurate criticism of nontraded REITs is their lack of liquidity, including only a vague target for future liquidation. It's a definite potential drawback that any investor needs to consider carefully before moving forward.

Other charges are usually much less accurate or are often simply wrong. Fees are sometimes highlighted. Obviously, there are costs incurred in creating, managing, buying, and selling real estate. There are also fees associated with selling the investment to investors. In a nontraded REIT, you can clearly see these fees in a prospectus, but in other real estate investments, including traded REITs, they are often much more difficult to find. Although high fees will always hurt investment performance, the mandated transparency in fees for nontraded REITs helps keep their fees in line across the industry and within acceptable ranges. In cost comparisons with traded REITs, non-traded REITs tend to position quite favorably on such issues as fund-raising, management, and asset disposition.

Possibly the most emotionally charged accusation regarding nontraded REITs is that any financial professional who recommends investing in them must be motivated by a desire for commissions. This is an especially potent charge given some of the more infamous recent scandals. True, financial professionals *are* paid a commission to sell nontraded REITs—as they are with all brokerage products, including items as banal as mutual funds. (As an aside, in rare cases, financial professionals can charge a fee rather than a commission, but this is currently a very difficult thing to do from a regulatory perspective. This situation may change in the future with ever-changing products and regulations.) But this charge seems relatively toothless given a few basic facts. On an annual basis, there are many other products that are much more profitable to recommend than nontraded REITs. And fees paid to the financial professional, when annualized, tend to be lower than or commensurate with annual fees earned by fee-only advisors and various other financial professionals. If financial professionals really want to maximize their own income, there are many better alternatives. These charges tend to be made by either people not licensed to sell nontraded REITs or professionals whose firms will not allow nontraded REIT sales because they are not profitable enough for the firm to carry them on their investment platform.

Investor Requirements

Regulations about who can and cannot purchase nontraded REITs can be an issue for some people. For example, states may impose investor requirements for minimum net worth and/or net worth and income. They may require investors to have, say, either a net worth of $250,000 or a net worth of $150,000 and an annual income of $75,000.

I have never been able to get a solid answer from a regulator or product sponsor on the exact reason that these requirements exist. The best guess I've heard was from a senior manager of a nontraded REIT firm. He believed that the requirements were a holdover from the mid-1980s when some investors held an overly large percentage of their portfolio in tax shelters structured as limited partnerships that imploded when the ridiculous tax benefits were eliminated as part of the 1986 tax reform. These "investments" only made sense as long as the tax law provided massive tax benefits to otherwise worthless investments. Although current-day REITs (traded and nontraded) offer a corporate tax benefit, the tax benefit to the investment is minor and the complete repeal of the benefit would have a limited effect on the investment. In addition, a major change to the tax benefits seems highly unlikely, as similar tax treatment by various governments is growing rapidly across the globe. The U.S. REIT tax structure has become the global standard.

Additional Real Estate Opportunities

There are a couple of additional significant types of real estate investments available to high-net-worth investors. Keep in mind that the nontraded REITs that have been addressed here are large, pooled, diversified investments available to investors who meet fairly low standards of net worth or income. The funds usually target raising around $1 billion to $3 billion, although some get much bigger. For investors who meet the government's definition of an accredited investor, however, numerous additional investment opportunities become available through direct participation programs.

The original definition of *accredited investor* as defined by the Securities Act of 1933 was changed by the 2010 Wall Street Reform and Consumer Protection Act, so it's likely to remain constant for a while. For individual investors to qualify as accredited investors, they need to meet one of three requirements:

1. A person with an individual net worth or a combined joint net worth with a spouse of at least $1 million, excluding the value of a primary residence.
2. A person with individual income in excess of $200,000 in each of the two most recent years or joint income with a spouse in excess of $300,000 in each of the two most recent years and a reasonable expectation of reaching the same income level in the current year.
3. A director, executive officer, or general partner of the issuer of the securities being offered or sold, or a director, executive officer, or general partner of a general partner of that issuer. (This is likely irrelevant for most investors, but I have included it to be complete.)[15]

Investors who satisfy any of these requirements are deemed by regulators to have more capability to either fend for themselves or hire experts to act on their behalf. The law affords them less protection than investors who don't meet the accredited investor requirements, but dramatically reduced regulatory requirements result in a greatly expanded pool of potential investments.

The impact of the different regulatory framework can't be overstated. The greatly simplified filing and reporting requirements for these investments make them highly attractive to firms seeking capital. Less onerous regulations and dramatically lower costs also enable much smaller offerings. The simpler regulatory structure results in more raising of capital through this channel than through the public stock market in spite of far fewer potential investors. Of course, the lessened regulatory requirements combined with smaller offerings can result in riskier investments.

There are many different offerings in this category that may target nearly any type of entity that seeks to raise capital. Whether it's a biotechnology company, the latest Internet startup, or the local carwash, any type of company can use this channel to raise capital. Similarly, within the real estate sector, the variety of types of investments tend to be greater because the smaller offerings are usually much more targeted. An offering may buy one or only a few properties rather than hundreds. An investor can choose to invest in a single downtown property that offers higher return potential if specific property improvements are made successfully.

Offerings may be similar to nontraded REITs and have a target of a good dividend and eventual liquidation. Frequently, the smaller sizes of these offerings enable targeting of specific opportunities. Investments tend to focus more on taking advantage of a particular opportunity and frequently seek higher returns. In addition, some investments may more closely resemble bonds and offer high income with little opportunity for future capital gains. This type of income investment is usually senior to most or all other capital, as is the case with bonds.

Because of the increased complexity of these investments, they tend to be most appropriate for more sophisticated investors. In addition, the larger portfolios of accredited investors also enable them to diversify across several smaller investments and build diversification within this sector.

Like anything, these offerings can be great for some investors but a poor fit for others. Most investors who pursue this type of investment are a bit more comfortable with risk or like to take a somewhat more active role in their portfolio management. As always, individual considerations must be considered before moving in this direction.

1031 Exchanges

There is one other type of investment in real estate that can offer investors significant tax advantages. The investment is referred to as a 1031 exchange. Most offerings are only available to accredited investors, although exceptions exist. Anyone, however, can take advantage of the tax code. The "1031" name derives from the section of tax code that addresses the opportunity.

If you have played the game Monopoly you will be familiar with a 1031 exchange. When you trade in green houses for a red hotel, you are effectively completing a 1031 exchange. You exchange your houses for a hotel without paying taxes. Similarly, a 1031 allows you to swap one piece of real estate for another without paying capital gains taxes.

A very significant industry has evolved to meet the demands of people who seek to buy and sell real estate without paying capital gains taxes. The big catch with 1031s is that you can't take control of the money yourself but must work through an intermediary. This topic is a large one, and can't be covered at length in this book. But if this seems like something from which you could benefit, be sure to talk to an expert before you start the sales process. You could save yourself a lot of money in taxes.

There are obviously other means by which any investor can own real estate. The areas covered previously address the most common products available on the market to the widest array of investors. Endowments have emphasized the real estate sector for decades, and now individuals have much greater opportunity to do the same.

How Much to Invest in Real Estate?

Once investors understand the potential value of adding a real estate sector, a common question arises: What is the right percentage of a portfolio to target toward real estate? There is no simple or right answer to this. Exact percentages will need to be developed in concert with other portfolio demands and personal preferences.

Nevertheless, I, along with many experts, believe at least 10 percent of a portfolio should be targeted toward real estate, and possibly much higher percentages can be appropriate. Targets around 20 percent are common, although liquidity issues can become a greater factor as allocation percentages rise. Other investors may be comfortable with even larger targets when other things are factored in, such as personal liquidity issues and return targets. Because real estate can provide a significant income stream, particularly when tax benefits are included, income needs can be a significant factor in investment decisions.

Another key factor affecting real estate allocation percentages will be the portfolio allocations of other hard assets. Most likely, if an investor targets significant portfolio allocations of hard assets other than real estate, the real estate percentage may be smaller in order to keep the overall real asset allocation in line. Yet even this may not be the case. As mentioned, Yale University's endowment targeted a very large 37 percent allocation for 2010 to hard assets; apparently, it chose to increase exposure to this entire sector across the board. Since setting an exact real estate allocation will require determining potential exposure to other hard assets, let's move past real estate on to other hard assets.

Commodities

Commodities aren't as scary as some investors have come to believe. While the asset class is somewhat mysterious to many people, given its unpredictable and sometimes difficult-to-understand performance, it can act as another great performance asset in a portfolio while also providing very low correlation to other assets. Also, as mentioned, commodities can be a great hedge against inflation.

The key to success with commodities is determining a sensible means of investing. Even more so than with stocks, how you invest in commodities can drastically impact your success. Many different investment vehicles provide exposure to commodities, but because of inherent strategy limitations and internal approach shortcomings, they often fail to deliver positive results even when the targeted commodity performs well. We will address how you can successfully invest in the sector and what key strategies to avoid.

Commodities can include a wide range of different investment possibilities. By definition, commodities are goods that are priced

the same regardless of who provides them and how they are produced. For example, no matter where copper, oil, wheat, or sugar
come from, the price is the same for an equivalent good. Because all
the goods are the same, the market determines the price. Agricultural goods such as corn, wheat, and eggs are "soft" commodities;
"hard" commodities refer to anything mined. From an investment
standpoint, the distinction doesn't usually matter.

Performance

Endowments consistently seek assets with high-performance
potential. Commodities satisfy this requirement, although their
unique performance can confound investors. Commodities tend
to follow long-term trading patterns that often last decades. Longlasting bull and bear markets should be familiar to any long-term
stock investor, but the performance of commodities can lead to confusion regarding the asset class.

Figure 9.1 demonstrates—very neatly—the nearly opposite performance of stocks and commodities over the 40-year period from

Figure 9.1 Performance of the Standard & Poor's Goldman Sachs
Commodities Index versus the Standard & Poor's 500 Index, 1970–2009

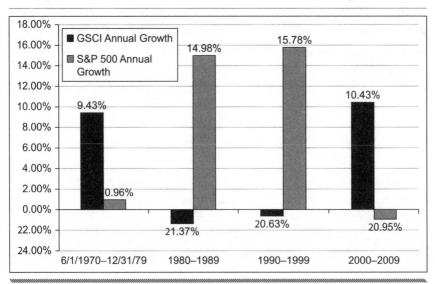

Source: http://www.standardandpoors.com/indices/gics/en/us.

1970 to 2009. (The data start on June 1, 1970, as that's the date that the Standard & Poor's Goldman Sachs Commodity Index [S&P GSCI] started.) During decades in which commodities did well, stocks struggled, and vice versa. If we look at the numbers in the figure, it appears that investors can't seem to win, since one investment seems doomed to suffer while the other thrives.

Yet a bit more analysis reveals that the second decade of the new millennium likely presents a different opportunity. Commodities tend to perform well when inflation is rising, and they excel when inflation is low and rising. The second decade of this century will probably present this combination. Equities tend to perform well when inflation is relatively low or falling. Stocks don't like high-inflation environments with inflation levels continuing up. We seem to be nowhere near this possibility, and the next decade likely presents a favorable inflationary environment for stocks and commodities.

Looking forward, endowments are emphasizing commodities as a category based on a couple of key assumptions. First, inflation is expected to increase from very low levels, and commodity prices should rise with decreased purchasing power as they historically have done. Second, emerging markets are rapidly increasing their consumption of just about everything. The combination seemingly sets up very strong pricing pressure on commodities, which makes future valuation increases likely. Many believe that the first decade of the millennium took us about halfway through a secular (long-term) bull market for commodities. It's no surprise that endowments have increased their allocation to this segment.

Lack of Correlation

Historically, commodities have offered strong diversification benefits because of their low correlation with most traditional asset classes. During the five-year period from the beginning of 2003 to the end of 2007, the correlation of the S&P GSCI Commodity Index was only 0.30 versus the Russell 3000, 0.42 versus the MSCI (Morgan Stanley Capital International) World ex-U.S. stock index, −0.06 with the Lehman Brothers Aggregate Bond Index, and 0.13 versus the NAREIT Index.[16] Longer-term trends show similar numbers. From December 31, 2000 through December 31, 2010, correlation for the

Dow Jones–UBS Commodity Index was 0.42 with U.S. large-cap stocks and only 0.33 versus small caps.[17] The S&P GSCI versus the S&P 500 for the 10-year period ending February 28, 2011 was significantly lower at 0.30.[18]

Slight deviations in time-frame measures and index comparisons reveal variances in correlation, yet the low correlation pattern is constant, remaining under 0.50. Because correlation below 0.8 provides very significant diversification benefits and anything below 0.5 is generally viewed as quite low, commodities are commonly believed to provide strong diversification benefits. The exact numbers are not really important. The greater point is their historically low correlation with broader markets.

Volatility

Another major consideration is commodity price volatility. There are different measures of commodity volatility, and seemingly all of them record high price volatility at times. Rather than defining an exact volatility measure, it's simpler and probably more meaningful to concede that an undesirable attribute of commodities for most investors is their fairly rapid and wide price swings relative to many other investments, including stocks.

Inflation Hedge

Commodities can provide an excellent inflation hedge. In the short term, commodity prices frequently cause inflation, but over longer time periods inflation may adversely affect their prices. Unfortunately, even these patterns aren't always clear or consistent. Different studies and analyses don't always agree. And the choice of time frames greatly affects the end conclusions.

The assumption that commodities provide at least some inflation-hedging benefits, particularly in the short term, seems accurate. This has been especially true when inflation begins increasing. Most research suggests that the link between commodities and inflation lessens as inflation decreases or when strong economic cycles wane. The lack of consistent patterns highlights the value of good portfolio discipline. If this asset class has done very well relative to others and its percentage allocation has increased beyond original targets, it's likely a good time to rebalance rather than pour more on the pile.

Means of Investment

To further complicate the subject, the diverse means to invest in commodities, whether traded or illiquid, introduces yet more unknowns. For instance, investors can choose from various vehicles such as futures contracts, equities, exchange-traded funds based on a broad-based commodities index, mutual funds, direct investments, and various forms of more complex derivatives. In addition, various broad sectors such as gas, oil and gas, wheat, and metals can be targeted. Of course, there will usually be substantial variations in how each of these different approaches will perform during different economic and political environments.

Although commodities possess various limitations, for many diversified investors the benefits may outweigh the drawbacks. Choosing investment types and approaches can make the sector more attractive and help investors reap the benefits while remaining comfortable with their portfolio.

Traded Commodities

There are three primary means by which individuals can invest in traded commodities and natural resources: direct ownership of physical commodities, ownership of commodities futures, and investment in companies that operate in commodities sectors. The differences among these approaches are dramatic and will likely drastically affect various performance and volatility results.

Commodities can be purchased and held by individual investors. As you can imagine, this is rarely done. Even the wealthiest and most sophisticated investors seldom have the capability to assume physical possession of oil, gas, agriculture products, or most metals. The one major exception can be precious metals. It's relatively easy to buy and physically store gold. This approach, however, introduces costs and fails to secure even minimal diversification.

More commonly, individuals invest in a vehicle that purchases and trades commodities futures contracts to gain access to commodities. A futures contract is simply a contract agreed to today between two parties to buy or sell a specific amount and type of asset at a specified future date at an agreed-upon price. Farmers and many other companies and individuals use futures contracts to lock in prices and remove future price variability. The buyers of futures contracts obtain direct exposure to commodities without taking physical possession of anything.

Few individual investors invest directly in futures contracts; instead, they choose a manager who does this for them. The contracts are complex and quite challenging for most individual investors to manage. Mistakes are more common, given their complexity, and miscues can be exceedingly costly. More than one brokerage firm has been nearly bankrupted by an unintended or unwise futures contract trade. It's surprisingly easy to buy all the oil in an oil tanker, although safeguards have grown increasingly advanced.

The buyer of a futures contract is obligated to take future delivery of the commodity. Obviously, few portfolio managers really want to accept delivery of thousands of barrels of oil or tons of orange juice. Instead, as the delivery date draws near, they sell their contract on the open market and buy a new contract for the same underlying commodity with a more distant delivery date. While different managers address this requirement differently, the basic challenge is the same. As time goes by, their futures contracts must be sold and replaced by new contracts with a delivery date farther into the future.

When commodity prices are increasing, forced sales and repurchases are costly. The value for contracts with shorter time frames is nearly always less than the price of new contracts with more distant delivery dates. The time premium associated with the greater time exposure is built into the new contract. While the price difference between the expiring contract and the more valuable contract with a distant delivery date is usually only a small percentage, paying the premium monthly can really add up. This affect is so well known within the commodities industry it's been given a name: contango. The pricing differential of new versus old contracts is known as "negative roll yield." While the words sound complex, the problem is simple, and unfortunately it is hard to eliminate.

As a result, many strategies that utilize futures contracts to gain exposure to commodities markets have dismal performance records during periods of commodities price increases. For instance, while the Goldman Sachs Commodity Index increased by 170 percent during the first decade of the millennium, many of the best-known mutual funds using this approach actually lost money over this period.[19]

ETFs new to the market seem to be following the same pattern. The *Wall Street Journal* noted the terrible performance of the largest oil ETF, the United States Oil Fund (USO), versus the West Texas Intermediate Index (WTI), the primary crude oil benchmark in the United States. From January 1, 2009, to May 11, 2011, the WTI Index was up 123 percent while the USO ETF increased only 19 percent.[20] Severe underperformance of commodity ETFs is common, which results in scathing criticism of this investment vehicle. Regrettably, many investors with the foresight and intelligence to add commodities via mutual funds or ETFs before their big decade-long run-up still missed out on commodity price increases because their investment choice performed so poorly.

Although new strategies are coming out that try to address this issue, success has been elusive. In addition, employing futures contracts possesses other problems. While investments can be made in large and common commodities, investors still face surprisingly limited options within the broader commodities markets. Currently low interest rates also reduce returns on cash holdings that managers must keep on hand as collateral for backing futures purchases. Since interest rate returns have been a very significant part of overall returns for this strategy over time, today's ultralow interest rate environment adds yet another challenge.

Possible Solution

Given the potential challenges of investing in commodities, it's very understandable that most investors simply avoid them. Lack of suitable vehicles combined with more challenging performance characteristics seems to validate decisions by many investors to just say no. Yet I believe there is a way to successfully add commodities to most portfolios. Moreover, new developments continually arise that may introduce even better possibilities in the future.

The approach I currently recommend is simple and straightforward. It secures investment in commodities through ownership of companies operating in the commodities sectors such as metals, oil and gas, and agriculture. Within the industry, this strategy is known as a "pure-play" investment. This approach offers the attractive combination of exposure to long-term commodity price trends, access to a broader range of commodities, and management and company specific value creation. And, it's easy for nearly any investor familiar with equity markets to understand.

Equity Investment Benefits

As would be expected, commodity price trends generally affect the valuations of companies operating within particular commodity sectors. As prices rise and fall, corporate profitability, the primary driver of equity prices, generally rises and falls. In addition, corporate structures may magnify or diminish the effects of price changes to the benefit of investors. Regardless, investing in companies active in various commodities sectors provides a great exposure to various commodities markets.

Investment into corporations can also provide much greater access to particular commodities than is available through futures exchanges. Commodities inaccessible via futures contracts can be readily added to a portfolio through equities.

Lastly, and I believe most importantly, equity investments in corporations provide specific exposure to managerial and company specific value creation. Firm personnel have the ability to anticipate market trends, manage capital needs, and leverage expertise. The value added through management action can add to commodity price increases or mitigate commodity price drops. Corporations also offer the potential to profit from commodities regardless of price movements, which can be very important in longer-term value creation. This is particularly true for commodities since they are non-earning assets and produce no wealth of their own.

When viewed over the longer term, I believe that positive and value-adding corporate actions enhance investor returns by adding a tailwind to commodities returns. In addition, as firms adjust to and leverage different market opportunities, natural market inefficiencies provide opportunities to identify and benefit from differing levels of corporate value creation.

This solution isn't perfect either because it's possible that significant increases in commodities may not be correspondingly reflected in the stock prices of companies operating in the sector. In addition, because these stocks trade on the stock market, they may be subject to price swings that have little or nothing to do with actual corporate or commodity values. I believe the overall benefits of this approach, however, make it the most attractive option for the majority of investors. Interestingly, some of the benchmark commodities indexes follow the same approach of tracking companies in the sectors rather than commodity prices themselves.

Because of the complexity of this subject and the lower understanding of this investment area, I recommend hiring an expert to manage your commodities investment the same way you would your stock investment. Most financial professionals feel the same way and turn management over to professionals with more specific expertise. This area is rarely an area of expertise for investment professionals, much less individual investors.

Unlike many other alternative investments, one obvious advantage of commodities, either through equities investments or futures contracts, is liquidity. These investments can be easily and readily converted to cash. Of course, the flip side to liquidity is volatility. If commodities are included in a portfolio, they may help reduce overall volatility through their lack of correlation, but it's still likely that the commodities allocation itself will be volatile.

Commodities Management

Successful commodities investments become more likely with a good relationship with a financial professional or diligent manager. Commodities can be more attractive when the global economy is expanding or inflation is rising, and their unique performance characteristics present special opportunities and challenges. Yet the timing of likely price fluctuations often differs dramatically from more traditional assets such as stocks. When they grow in relative value, many if not most investors are tempted to add to the sector to capture more growth. Yet, just as with stocks, this is rarely a good idea and attempting to time your investments usually causes more harm than good. Instead, if your commodities holdings have increased, it's often best to rebalance the portfolio by selling and locking in gains in the same way you should in your stock portfolio. Conversely, if a commodity investment's relative performance is poor, good portfolio management likely dictates making additional investments into commodities through buying low to maintain the target allocation.

While this sounds so simple, in my experience, most investors fail horribly in maintaining rebalancing discipline, especially when it requires additional investment into a depressed asset. While this is generally true even with stocks that are more familiar to most investors, commodities can present a greater challenge. Investors can very easily slip into self-doubt or overenthusiasm with a less familiar investment.

If investors lack confidence in future commodity pricing trends or aren't convinced that they can follow through on proper management of commodities, it may be better to avoid them altogether even if those investments are likely to perform well. As we have seen with stocks and various vehicles used to invest in commodities, excellent performance of the asset class does not guarantee investor success.

Direct Commodity Investments

Just as with real estate, commodities can also be added to a portfolio through direct investment. Endowments like this approach and frequently favor it. One example is direct purchases or holdings in oil, gas, and timberland. Endowments learned long ago that wise investments through less commonly employed channels frequently present excellent opportunities to enhance performance and diversification. But there is a reason that many early adopters are endowments and other institutions with ample resources. They have both money and expertise. Fortunately, direct investment into commodity-related fields is another area in which more options are quickly opening up to individual investors.

Less-liquid direct investment programs can provide a good alternative for some investors. Investors may seek to avoid the volatility of traded commodities or may seek further diversification within the sector. Professional management of direct investments, and even their lack of liquidity, can make portfolio management easier and less stressful for many investors.

This type of investment also has many advantages and disadvantages that can make it much more attractive for certain investors and less interesting or inappropriate for others. This is true whether these investments are compared to any other ones in a portfolio or to the narrower field of real assets.

The world of direct investments into commodities can provide some very unique and attractive opportunities. Unfortunately, it also offers the possibility of much less appealing outcomes. The types and structures of offerings can be much greater than those available through traded commodities. Yet the breadth of different commodity exposure will normally be much narrower.

These seemingly contradictory statements can be easily explained. Exposure to various commodities through equities and even futures contracts can be very large, ranging from metals to food to building materials. There are far fewer possibilities for direct investments, as they are generally limited to oil and gas and possibly timber. Other options can exist, but they tend to be much less common and highly speculative.

Within these narrow segments for direct investments, however, the range of offerings is substantial. Most of these offerings are available only to accredited investors. The offerings are usually smaller, which necessitates lower offering costs. Although there can be exceptions, they are not very common. Even if you don't fit into this category, you will likely find the following information interesting, as it's an asset class that affects nearly everyone in a developed society on a daily basis.

Oil and Gas

Oil and gas still account for approximately two-thirds of the energy used in the United States. Oil alone supplies about 97 percent of the energy used in U.S. transportation.[21] We all know that these fuels are key to our economy, yet most Americans have been conditioned to believe that all our oil and gas comes from foreign countries or possibly Alaska.

While we import the majority of our oil, the United States is still the world's third largest oil producer.[22] In fact, the United States actually exports oil to Canada and Japan because it's cheaper in some cases to transport it to their refineries than to domestic locations. The United States also happens to be the world's largest energy consumer, and it uses as much oil as China, India, Russia, Germany, and Japan combined.[23] As a result, we import about two-thirds of all the oil we consume.[24]

Natural gas is much more plentiful and is rapidly taking over market share from coal-fired power plants. In fact, we have so much natural gas in the United States that prices have dropped significantly and there is growing pressure to allow us to export to countries in need.[25] Natural gas is plentiful and burns much more cleanly than nearly any other fossil fuel. While we also have imported natural gas, our domestic supplies are substantial, with known reserves growing faster than consumption. Production can be easily increased and is largely limited by lower prices that keep supplies down.

Regardless of your beliefs or convictions about the future of fossil fuels, these energy sources are critical to our economy and will remain the key energy source for the foreseeable future. Currently, various green energy sources supply limited amounts of our energy, and most revolutionary technologies remain a long way from commercial viability. For now, almost no green energy sources are economically viable without significant government subsidies.

While the introduction of electric cars is an obvious sign of coming change, technology developments and mass adoption will take years. In most cases, electric cars are still not commercially viable without government support, and they still depend on various commodities as their original energy source. At this point, most of the electricity used in electric cars is a simple transfer of fossil fuel consumption from the car engine to a natural gas or coal plant far removed from sight. In addition, their batteries require lithium and various other valuable commodities that create tremendous environmental impacts in other places that are usually more politically palatable because they are beyond U.S. borders. Again, this isn't to say that we won't see major change in the future. After all, oil has been a major force for barely 100 years, and it's not likely to last as the major energy source for another 100 years. Fossil fuels, however, are going to be with us for quite a while.

I'll leave the debates on policy and environmental issues to others and instead focus on some of the investment opportunities. Our continued need for energy creates ongoing demand for finding and producing more supplies. Oil and gas wells deplete over time, while demand continually increases.

Various companies continually search for and develop new sources of energy. As you can imagine, technology has radically transformed the energy exploration and development business as it has nearly every other area of our lives. Today, many oil and gas projects use new technology to revisit drilling sites abandoned years ago because of low potential or capture challenges. Various new technologies usually create opportunities that can make production much more predictable than past efforts in which explorers drilled a hole and hoped for the best.

In addition, the United States still provides substantial tax incentives to find and produce energy. In many investments, the tax benefits can be a significant contributor to the attractiveness of the investment. This can be a bit scary since the government can always change these rules. Yet in most cases, all the tax benefit is up front, so, if the tax regulations change, modifications wouldn't affect previous investments. Over the years, there have been proposals to alter the tax treatment, but it now appears that the tax breaks will continue for the foreseeable future.

The wide range of investment possibilities and possible investment and tax benefits makes it very difficult to succinctly describe all the possible investment options. They can be, however, broadly categorized into a few common focuses.

Most, although not all, oil and gas offerings include some form of tax reduction. Many offerings allow individuals to claim a tax deduction, not a tax credit, of up to 100 percent of the initial investment in the first year. Depending on your tax bracket, this deduction can provide substantial investment incentive and greatly enhance future returns. Other offerings provide substantially lower levels of deductions and may instead focus more on total return potential.

The timing and levels of returns are also likely to vary widely. I have seen programs that have provided annual returns in excess of 50 percent per year with a complete project time frame of less than five years. Other similar time-frame programs have failed to return all of an investor's capital. Often, these types of offerings provide somewhat more limited tax benefits in exchange for greater return targets.

Another common type of deal structure focuses on drilling wells that produce oil or gas that depletes as the oil or gas is pumped from the well. Most of these types of investments provide a very large up-front tax credit near or possibly equal to the entire original investment. In the first full year of operation, a higher level of production is expected from the wells, and returns may exceed 15 to 20 percent of the original investment. In each of the following years, this percentage is expected to drop. Most of the returns are usually gained in the first decade of the well's life, but they can continue for periods up to 40 years, and perhaps more, albeit at very low levels. Obviously, these numbers are just examples, but the structure tends to be similar across this type of offering.

These investments don't tend to be as risky as is usually assumed by most investors. Dry holes are exceedingly uncommon and, in most projects, they simply don't exist. These investments are rarely the all-or-nothing deals Hollywood has fostered through old movies. Instead, risks are usually tied to current oil or gas prices, the amount produced by a well, and the length of time the well produces. Various deal structures can also affect these risks substantially.

Other common programs focus on royalties in which investors own the land and lease it back to oil drillers, producers, and/or transporters. These programs tend to focus on producing cash flow that can increase over time if more production is created. Again, there can be substantial tax advantages to the income from the properties.

Timber

Oil and gas is likely to be the most common direct investment, but others also exist. Investors can invest in timber through offerings structured as nontraded REITs. Although the actual investment vehicle may be a nontraded REIT, their success is tied to dynamics in the timber industry, not to office rents. Part of the reason that endowments and other institutions like timber is that one's investment is literally growing every year.

Demand for wood will usually drive the eventual investment value. If managers choose to wait to time the sale of the assets, the total amount of assets owned continually increases. While this certainly doesn't guarantee a good or even positive return, as there are many different factors that affect profitability, a constantly growing amount of product for sale normally increases eventual proceeds. Unfortunately, the lack of yearly cash flow in many timber deals can make ongoing management difficult, and the possible lack of a dividend often makes the offering less interesting to smaller investors. As a result, finding quality offerings in this space can be difficult or even impossible. This investment is also notable in that it may not require accredited investor status.

Liquidity of Direct Investments

As with many other direct investments, commodities direct investments usually present a liquidity limitation regardless of the investment. Even though the entire investment may be illiquid, however, many investors like some oil and gas offerings because of their high levels of expected cash flow and lack of correlation with other investments. In addition, there will usually be very different liquidity expectations across different investments with different objectives and structures.

Tax Treatment of Direct Investments

The special tax treatment of many of these deals also factors into returns, and there's tremendous variance of tax impact by investor and time frames. This doesn't take into account the potential tax benefits that may accrue to an individual who received a one-time bonus or other financial windfall while all future investment income would be earned at lower tax rates that result from different taxable income levels.

Performance of Direct Investments

Given the diversity across the offerings, it shouldn't be surprising to learn that returns numbers vary tremendously. Furthermore, there's little public data available across the multiple investments. In addition, the long time frames involved and lack of standardization of performance calculations further complicates performance assessments. Accurate and applicable performance numbers are sketchy at best and are usually limited to particular investment providers or small groups of investment providers. In these cases, firms often give details of past investments that may provide some reasonable data. Of course, their history about a previous deal guarantees nothing about a future one that you may be considering.

The benefits, however, can be very strong. This sector can provide investors exposure to many different opportunities or risks. Unlike a tradable commodity, a direct investment can provide investors exposure not only to oil and gas prices but also to operator proficiency, oil and gas field yields, and technology improvements.

Some investors like the possibility of finding and entrusting a management team to make good choices from which they will hopefully benefit. Wise choices can add to increases in underlying commodity prices or help mitigate commodity price declines. As always, poor operators or simply bad luck can also lead to poor performance. No two oil or gas fields are ever the same.

The Last Key Consideration

After all that discussion, there's probably one variable that's likely at least as important as all the issues already mentioned. It is nearly impossible for individual investors to pursue these direct investment opportunities on their own without very large sums of money and very good inside contacts. Nearly all investors must depend on a financial professional to identify and recommend appropriate opportunities. As a result, the knowledge of your financial professional is likely to have a major impact on your success in this area. It's not that he or she can ensure success. There is, however, ample opportunity to apply specialized knowledge effectively in this field to make success more likely and failure less costly.

While many excellent opportunities exist in this sector, it's also important to realize that the opportunities are there partly because so few people, including financial professionals, are knowledgeable in this area. Wise choices can be extremely beneficial in providing excellent performance and diversification benefits. A knowledgeable financial professional can provide tremendous value in pursuing these opportunities.

The variety and potential complexity of offerings, though, also means that missteps can be easier and more costly to make. If you ask your financial professional about this opportunity and you get a deer-in-headlights look in return, it's probably unwise to proceed.

You don't want to be anybody's test case. Deal structures can also result in very long-term investments, so you want to be sure you are quite comfortable with the possible benefits and risks. In addition, the firms that financial professionals are associated with can be very important in influencing the quality of the various offerings available. In short, as always, make sure the professional you are working with knows what he or she is doing.

Gold

One last case that deserves special attention is gold. While gold is a commodity, it doesn't necessarily behave like most other commodities—or any other investment at all, for that matter. Rather, it tends to act as the ultimate investment safe haven. In 2008, the stock market declined 37 percent and nearly every asset other than U.S. Treasuries declined in value. The GSCI commodity Index, which includes gold, declined nearly 50 percent. Yet gold rose 4 percent from $836.50 to $869.75 per ounce.[26]

Gold tends to be a very polarizing investment. Most people either love it or are completely indifferent. Historically, it has served as a good diversifier against disasters, but it hasn't been a very good investment most of the time. When everything else does go down, it usually goes up, but that's usually been about the only time it performs well. From 1792 to 1972, gold increased in value less than 0.0035 percent per year.[27]

The story changed, however, after the United States went off the gold standard in 1975. From the end of 1975 through 2009, gold has averaged a 5.80 percent increase per year, although nearly all of this increase came after 2002.[28] Interestingly, since the start of gold's run-up in 2002, various other assets have struggled. Hence, gold has attracted some big fans. If it reverts to past history, its performance may be quite weak, but obviously that has yet to be determined.

Moving Forward with Commodities

The first step is to determine whether or not commodities are a desirable part of your portfolio. If an investor chooses to include this asset class, a target allocation will need to be identified. Since many people simply use real estate as their entire exposure to the real asset category because of its familiarity and investment ease, targeted commodity allocations are often nonexistent. This may not be the best portfolio design or the best approximation of the endowment model approach, but it's often a more comfortable approach for individual investors. Furthermore, the smaller allocation to the investment usually means its exclusion doesn't result in an overly large departure from the endowment model.

As an asset class, I normally suggest that investors include commodities if they are either actively looking for a particular portfolio benefit or they clearly understand the potential risk/reward trade-offs. This doesn't mean that an investor has to be a commodities expert, but it's often very apparent that some investors are simply not wired for the distinctive performance characteristics of commodities. While it can be a very attractive asset class, its unique nature can make it a bit more challenging for some investors to comfortably incorporate into their portfolio. Portfolio size can also make a difference. If an investor's total investable assets are less than $500,000, avoiding the sector may be best, as there are limited investment options available for smaller portfolios.

Another option regarding commodities is to purposely select investments that are less liquid and less volatile. This obviously introduces liquidity constraints into the portfolio. It may be more appropriate for investors who are seeking greater diversification without the likely extra volatility associated with commodities investments traded on public markets.

After deciding to include commodities, the obvious next step is to choose a target allocation. As always, percentage allocations are probably best determined by very specific investor needs and comfort levels. In addition, investment availability will probably affect the allocation target. If an investor isn't accredited, most likely the only option available will be some versions of traded securities.

There's no right answer to the exact percentage to use. In my experience, most investors are generally not comfortable going much above 10 percent of their entire portfolio or over one-third to possibly one-half of their real asset allocation. Most endowments seem to target less than half of their real asset allocation to commodities, but there are always exceptions, and data on this are sparse.

A couple of examples might be helpful. If we assume a 20 percent allocation to real assets, a typical portfolio might allocate two-thirds of that figure, or approximately 13 percent, to real estate, with the remaining 7 percent going to commodities. A larger portfolio might split the commodities allocation across traded equities and direct investments; a smaller portfolio would probably be limited to traded equities.

Given future projections for inflation and commodities prices, the percentages mentioned may be low for real assets as a category and commodities within the sector. For investors comfortable with the asset class, larger allocations may be appropriate, and a higher allocation to real assets would be consistent with recent endowment practices. Most likely, Yale's 37 percent allocation represents a high upper limit.

Moving Forward with Real Assets

While there are other options available within the real assets sector, the choices already discussed represent the large majority of offerings appropriate to most individual investors. The attractiveness of these assets for reasons ranging from performance to diversity to stability have made them a major focus of endowments and institutions for decades.

Given the excellent and growing choices available to individual investors, I believe that most investors, like endowments, can positively impact their portfolios through inclusion of real assets in their portfolios. Various recent developments and increasing awareness of the attractiveness of this asset class further improve the choices and possible opportunities available to investors.

We have now covered the top four categories of the endowment model: domestic stocks, developed market stocks, emerging market stocks, and real assets. If we refer back to our potential portfolio allocation outlined in Table 6.1, their percentages add up to 75 percent of the total portfolio. While any individual's portfolio is likely to vary from this exact percentage, the overall size of the number is significant. Using very straightforward and widely available investments, we have covered approximately three-quarters of a total portfolio allocation commonly applied by large and very wealthy endowments.

While specific products available to individual investors will certainly differ from the investments utilized by endowments, the approaches already covered provide excellent means to secure solid exposure to diverse asset classes that can provide the basis of a very solid portfolio. Furthermore, these investments are widely available and generally well understood by financial professionals. Next, we will look at further means to diversify portfolios commonly used by endowments and available to individual investors.

10

Private Equity: A Stronger Move into Nontraditional Asset Classes

ONE OF THE MAJOR CONTRIBUTORS TO ENHANCED ENDOWMENT portfolio performance over the past several decades has been private equity. As with other asset classes, endowments have had much success with private equity that may not be easily replicated by individual investors.

The *Journal of Wealth Management* draws this conclusion for one very obvious reason. Some endowments, including the most famous practitioner of the model, Yale University, have achieved extraordinary success in this area. Duplication of their returns seems unfathomable.

For example, Yale's annual return on private equity investments since inception in 1973 through 2010 has averaged an astonishing 30.3 percent per year.[1] Wow! The math for this investment is amazing. An investment of $1 in the private equity portion of the portfolio would have grown to around $20,000 over this time frame. Over the same period, stocks averaged a very respectable 9.8 percent per year, and $1 grew to about $35. While stocks were good, Yale's private equity returns bettered stocks by more than 500 times.

149

The incredible performance enjoyed over this time frame by Yale and other endowments provides a strong basis for the *Journal of Wealth Management*'s conclusion. No investor should expect to hit numbers like Yale's under the best of circumstances. The category's strength and growing accessibility to investors, however, does make it potentially very attractive to many individual investors. With this in mind, I believe private equity can be a very positive addition to many investors' portfolios even if they don't have access to the same managers that Yale has.

What Is a Private Equity Investment?

A private equity investment is an investment in a private company that doesn't trade on public stock exchanges. In most cases, private equity companies are smaller than their public company counterparts, but not always. In the last decade, some of the more prominent private equity investments have been purchases of public companies by investors taking the company out of public ownership and back into private control. A few examples include Toys 'R' Us, Burger King, Elizabeth Arden, and The Gap.

Investors who convert a public company back into a private one believe that they, or their hired management, can make better operating improvements in the company without the onerous regulatory and operational requirements associated with operating as a public company. Focus shifts from quarterly results and satisfying public shareholders to longer-term strategic repositioning. Often, risks are assumed that public shareholders wouldn't accept. Decreased costs, less bureaucracy, and removal of barriers to change hopefully bring about valuable improvements. Greater focus also often results, as ownership and management are freed to focus exclusively on the organization's goals rather than the frequently competing interests of various public and institutional shareholders. After improvements are made, the company may be sold to other investors: either another company, a different private equity firm, or investors through public markets.

Although these public to private conversions are high profile and garner much attention, they are not the most common investments made by most endowments, institutions, or individuals. It's not that the investments can't be very successful, as past takeovers have demonstrated. Privatizing public companies, however, isn't usually the preferred form of private equity investment for several reasons.

Most public companies carry a liquidity premium because their shares trade on a secondary market. The standard price premium of any publicly traded entity means that problems need to be pretty severe for privatization to be attractive. In addition, private companies vastly outnumber public companies. As a result, most investors focus on the much larger and more opaque world of firms that have never been public. Probably most importantly, a smaller private company that has never traded on an exchange frequently presents greater opportunity to add value. The company and the opportunity associated with it aren't widely known, which usually results in lower valuations and greater upside potential.

Companies viewed as attractive to private equity firms nearly always possess proven concepts and clear track records. In these instances, current company ownership and potential investors believe new resources in the form of cash, management, technology, or another value-adding component will significantly impact some or many aspects of the firm. New investment aims to substantially improve the value of the company in a fairly short time, usually within five to seven years. After affecting improvements, investors will attempt to sell the more valuable firm to another buyer just as happens with the larger private equity deals. These two characteristics—a proven concept and a successful operating history—differentiate private equity from its related cousin, venture capital.

Because private equity investments usually focus on companies that already generate profits through providing a product or service to a proven market, the purpose of the investment is to somehow improve on what's already being done. Emphasis usually centers on professionalizing the operations and management of the firm.

By contrast, venture capital normally focuses on companies with unproven but interesting concepts and little operating history. Often, there is no assurance that a market for the company's product or service even exists. The investment is usually much riskier given the combination of concept, management, and operational risk. As you might expect, however, the return potential is also higher because investors are getting in before there is demonstrated value.

For numerous reasons, I strongly suggest that small investors avoid venture capital. First, relative investment returns have been poor, especially when risk levels are included. Various studies suggest that returns approximate marketable equity returns[2]; yet other studies suggest that those numbers are optimistic. Venture capital returns were only 3.1 percent for the 20 years beginning in 1985, while the S&P 500 returned 11.9 percent over the same period. Returns also varied from 721 percent to −100 percent and had a whopping standard deviation of 51.1 percent.[3] Given very poor returns versus the risk, this investment seems highly unattractive.

Yet another factor overrides almost any argument. Return numbers for venture capital firms and their partners are heavily skewed in favor of a small number of insiders. The highest quality and most respected venture capital firms, about eight in number, enjoy vastly superior deal flow. They allow preferred investors access to investments, often rationing offerings among their select list. Venture capital firms not in this select group who are willing to accept new funds are almost always also-rans and represent much poorer prospects.

Changes to vehicle structure and partner fees over the past decade that were difficult for venture capital appear to have further disadvantaged new investors. While some investors enjoyed tremendous success in the dot-com 1990s, this time period appears to have been a very special exception. Even most endowments shy away from venture capital given the difficult and highly biased playing field. If $1 billion can't get you a good seat at the table, trying to muscle in with a few thousand bucks seems unwise.

In contrast, private equity offers greater access and greater opportunity with much less emphasis on winner-take-all investments. Hence, it has enduring attractiveness to endowments, institutions, private wealth offices, and increasingly, individual investors.

Private equity investments often take advantage of different characteristics of private versus public markets. Most investors value liquidity and are willing to pay a significant premium for the flexibility provided by an investment that trades on an exchange. In addition, public companies also present investors with an up-to-the-second valuation of their investment. It may or may not be accurate, but there's always a valuation.

By contrast, private equity values are opaque. The eventual value of the investment will be what someone else is willing to pay for it at some future point. Until that happens, investors don't really know the value of their investment. There's no public market that assigns a value to the entity, and no analysts offer opinions on it. As a result, valuations for similar organizations vary considerably among private companies versus public ones. This can create tremendous opportunity for investors and managers who are experienced in valuing and buying firms.

The J Curve

While the economic outcomes of nearly every private equity fund investment take years to unfold, investments usually follow a standard valuation curve. This investment return pattern is referred to as the "J curve," which takes its name from the shape of the firm's value on a graph (see Figure 10.1). The vertical axis shows a firm's value, and the horizontal axis displays elapsed time. The J curve can apply to either a company or a private equity fund that invests in multiple private companies.

Figure 10.1 The J Curve

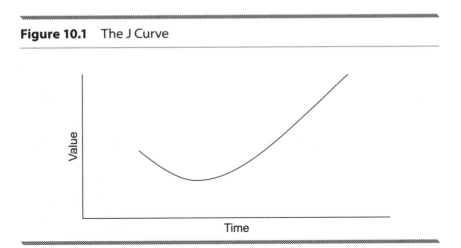

The cause for the J curve is driven by multiple events. In the early years, investments are usually valued at cost. In most cases, multiple companies are purchased in a private equity fund. If the private equity investment is a fund rather than a single company, fees are usually drawn from committed capital rather than invested capital, which leads to a higher impact of fees in the early years.

More importantly, the nature of private equity investments almost necessitates a decrease in corporate value before benefits appear. Private equity investments nearly always focus on making major changes, hopefully improvements to a firm's management and operations. Initially, these changes are disruptive and may decrease value as costs rise and profitability falls.

In addition, invested funds are easy to measure and track in accounting systems. Expenditures will be closely monitored for effectiveness, and there are benefits to write-offs. By contrast, value creation takes time, and intangible improvements may be difficult to value. There is also little incentive to accurately track an investment's value well in advance of its sale.

While investment value may decrease for months or even years, investors hope that invested funds and management resources will produce results, creating significant increase in company value in the relatively near future. The value increase is the tall side of the J, which hopefully reaches a much higher point than the original entry point of investment.[4]

Performance

Institutions and various wealth individuals have flocked to private equity investments over the past few decades because of the sector's performance. This type of investment has done very well despite a rather anemic stock market over the past decade.

As mentioned, Yale's private equity returns are incredible, with an average annual return from 1973 through 2010 of 30.3 percent per year. Harvard's returns are a bit more down-to-earth at 15.5 percent per year from 1999 to 2009.[5] Harvard's numbers include a loss of 32 percent in 2009, which was likely overstated. Stanford's performance is lower at 11.8 percent per year from 1999 through 2009.[6] While Stanford's and Harvard's numbers don't appear remarkable, the returns are still very impressive when one takes into account the losses domestic markets suffered over the same time frame.

Wider data on this subject tells a similar story. The Thomson Reuters US Private Equity Performance Index (PEPI) posted a 20-year annual return of 11.3 percent through March 30, 2010. Furthermore, all private equity outperformed public markets across 1, 3, 5, 10, and 20-year time frames (all the time frames available).[7]

According to Ibbotson, a widely respected authority on asset allocation and portfolio implementation, private equity also offers various additional benefits. Private equity improved the risk/return ratios of its assumed asset allocation model, and Ibbotson projects that private equity will become a traditional beta asset class in the near future, although the financial consulting firm doesn't specify a timeline.[8] Ibbotson's viewpoint is consistent with the sector's growing popularity and increasing acceptance by various investment professionals.

The firm also goes on to say that the lack of widely accepted benchmarks has generally prevented investors from understanding the risk, return, and correlation characteristics of private equity and hence the role of private equity in a diversified portfolio. In my experience, this statement is very accurate. Lack of understanding of this sector has slowed its acceptance. Furthermore, a lack of investment options has also made the investment category difficult to access.

There are several trends, however, that are bringing private equity into the mainstream. First, awareness of the potential benefits is increasing. It's no longer a secret that endowments have enjoyed tremendous success with private equity, and there is greater awareness that increasing numbers of other investors have attained similar results. Growing investor demand for private equity options is increasing the diversity and availability of investment options. Structures are also evolving through greater securitization of private equity options, which makes the investment more available to smaller investors.

Diversification

Lower correlation with other investments always ranks as an important attribute of any alternative investment. Not surprisingly, private equity normally adds portfolio diversification, but that is not a given. Different studies find different patterns. As circumstances change, correlation between private equities and public markets fluctuates tremendously. Because clear and consistent conclusions are hard to discern and can be easily misleading, I'll stick to a few general trends.

Because private equity exits are usually more related to the underlying company fundamentals than are stock market valuations, private equity liquidations and success are somewhat independent of the stock market. The recent decade's performance provides an illustration. The narrower business focus of these smaller companies provides a diversification benefit, as their success or failure will be more dependent on fewer variables. Various factors that affect other investments, however, can likewise affect private equity. This correlation often increases during extreme events.

General economic conditions that increase corporate profitability will likely affect the majority of private equity firms in similar ways. Unfavorable economic conditions for corporate America likely affect private equity somewhat in the same way.

Perhaps less obvious are the effects of capital and equity markets on private equity. Many private equity firms provide investor exits through sales to public companies or through public offerings. Successful exits in both areas become more likely when the stock market is doing well. By no means is a high-flying stock market required, but it helps, adding at least some private equity correlation with general markets.

Correlation is probably most observable during terrible markets. In 2008, when the stock market was cratering, successful exits of private equity companies were virtually nonexistent. This doesn't mean that the private equity values necessarily declined, although highly unfavorable business conditions generally lowered profitability. More specifically, the lack of exit opportunities as a result of lessened liquidity effectively drove cash values down. In reality, deals didn't get done and most intelligent investors simply waited out the storm. Not everyone, however, had this luxury, and even some endowments unloaded offerings to meet allocation requirements or to avoid required capital calls at inopportune times.

Capital markets can also affect private equity valuations. When interest rates are low and money is cheap, various entities, whether potential buyers or private equity firms, may have more money to spend, which drives valuations up. Alternatively, lack of funds can make sales difficult. Either case can affect valuations and deal flows, thereby increasing correlations between private equity and public markets.

Correlation differences will vary. Firms most dependent on a successful exit through a public offering most likely maintain the greatest correlation with the stock market. The category usually offers a good diversification benefit, but it varies over time and isn't a given.

Why Limit Exposure?

If the category has been so successful, why not focus all equity investments into private equity versus public markets? While the percentages devoted to this category by endowments have increased over the years, even endowments don't focus exclusively in this area. As always seems to be the case, the category has pros and cons.

The biggest advantage over time appears to be excellent return numbers. As mentioned above, the category performance has been strong, and much of the performance has been generated while public markets struggled.

The disadvantages, however, can also be significant. Unlike stocks in a public company, holdings in a private equity investment can be very illiquid. Even the most sophisticated investors with the best investments and contacts may be unable to sell their holdings quickly or, as the last downturn revealed, at all. As with nontraded real estate, the sale of private equity investments depends on various factors ranging from specific firm operational issues to strength of the public markets. Lack of liquidity creates an opportunity, yet levies a different cost.

Furthermore, smaller, less-diversified private equity companies create different risks than those that may exist with their larger counterparts, and the risks are assumed to be greater. The smaller size of these companies may help them more quickly adjust to changing conditions, but it also can make them more susceptible to adverse changes. While various studies claim different findings, with some estimating risk levels about the same as publicly traded small-cap stocks, the conclusions are imprecise and can be highly dependent on the assumptions employed.

Liquidity restrictions combined with a higher perceived risk profile usually lead to smaller private equity allocations even within the portfolios of endowments. As of December 31, 2010, dollar-weighted private equity allocations at 842 colleges and universities averaged 10.7 percent, according to the National Association of College and University Business Officers.[9] These numbers fit neatly with historical trends. Allocations are usually around 10 percent, although some endowments such as Yale frequently set higher targets. No doubt, Yale's higher private equity allocation is heavily influenced by its past success.

Past Investment Challenges

While endowments and wealthy individuals have generally included private equity in portfolios for many years, most individual investors haven't been active in this area. Endowments' continuous interest in the sector has created a thriving market for institutionally structured investments. Demand and the resulting market for smaller investors have been far more limited. Fortunately, as in the Ibbotson study mentioned previously, private equity investing continues to evolve, and investment vehicles appropriate for individuals are multiplying.

There have been three primary barriers to individuals in this asset class: investment structure, investment minimums, and accredited investor requirements. Because private equity investments originated with endowments, most investment structures assumed investors were highly sophisticated with strong capabilities to understand deal structures, timing of value creation, and unpredictable cash needs. Large investments, inflexibility, limited investor information, and commitment to fund future capital calls routinely characterized earlier offerings. Unexpected requirements that investors provide additional capital, often with little warning, often caused individuals the most heartburn while endowments understood ongoing funding demands to be a natural part of private equity investments.

Most institutional private equity includes potential or likely future capital calls as part of its structure. A capital call is just what it sounds like: a call for capital. The endowment enters into an investment with the expectation and contractual obligation to provide additional capital in the future if it is requested by the private equity managers. For endowments that expect future alumni donations and have teams of people to manage cash flow, the extra work of managing a capital call is well worth the potential returns and benefits of private equity investments. In addition, securing access to a larger eventual investment with a smaller amount of up-front cash can also improve ultimate returns.

In contrast, most individual investors don't like the possibility of an investment requiring additional funds with little warning. Individual investors also tend to view additional funding requests negatively. They quickly assume that additional funding requirements represent bad news from a struggling company. Institutions with more experience and greater understanding are generally more patient with the J-curve effect. They understand that new capital needs often result from successful growth rather than from problems.

Another barrier for many investors has been the traditionally high minimums required to gain access to quality investments. The millions of dollars that endowments can allocate to this sector gains them access to quality managers and deal flow. Whether endowments funded investments on their own or joined with other institutional investors, their investment was large enough to demand individual attention and possibly a more customized investment structure.

By contrast, the smaller funding capability of the individual investor nearly always requires pooling investment dollars to gain access to quality deal flow. A single investor in a much larger pool rarely influences the structure of the investment. You get what they offer.

Probably more importantly for most investors, even when investments are combined, minimum investments required have often been prohibitively high, with small commitments often starting at $250,000. Even an individual investor with a $2 million portfolio may balk at committing $250,000 to a single pooled fund. As a result, most individual investors have chosen to sit on the sidelines.

Lastly, most private equity investments have required that investors meet accredited investor requirements. Remember, accredited investors must have investable assets of at least $1 million or meet income requirements of either $300,000 per couple or $200,000 per individual. This eliminates a lot of people. Given the high minimums, few nonaccredited investors would really be interested anyway. But the requirements have acted as one more hurdle that makes more flexible offerings with smaller minimums largely irrelevant.

Although it could be argued that only more sophisticated individuals should be allowed to invest in private equity, the investment world is changing, and the general sophistication of investors is increasing rapidly. In addition, as the private equity world expands, structures and methods are standardizing and lessening the investment's complexity.

How to Move Forward

The 2008–2009 market crash greatly increased demand for alternative investments, including private equity. Not surprisingly, the market reacted by providing more ways for individuals to access the asset class. Moreover, just as providers of real estate investments have increasingly been forced to follow the money, sponsors of private equity offerings face the same pressures.

Some structural changes have been made to facilitate private equity investment by individuals. For instance, while private equity that is offered to endowments usually mandates capital calls, structures offered to individuals now rarely do. This partly results from a need to make the investment more palatable. It's also a change easily accommodated by a funding process that steadily provides cash infusions as new investors add to the pool.

Investment vehicles are also changing. Nearly all past private equity funds had been structured as partnerships, which mandated large investments by all participating investors. To attract more individual investors, product sponsors are now employing different investment vehicles that have been successfully used for other investments. The individual investor market appears to have reached the critical mass necessary for product development appropriate to different needs. As a result, products are now available to nonaccredited investors with minimums as low as a couple of thousand dollars.

Public markets are also offering traded versions of pooled capital that invest in private equity firms. In these instances, minimum investments are only one share that usually prices at under $100. While the publicly traded investments often lose much of the noncorrelation benefits and can be more volatile than the general market, they do provide even the smallest investors access to private equity.

Making specific investment recommendations in this sector can be challenging because of the greater number of variables involved and the current pace of change. In addition to standard considerations about performance goals, risk aversion, and liquidity needs, additional elements also influence decisions, including accredited investor status, the amount of funds available, and even income requirements.

Investment Options

While it would seem that the widespread interest in private equity by endowments and institutions would give them an overwhelming edge because of their access to the biggest equity funds, actual performance numbers reveal a different reality. The largest and most established private equity funds tend to produce inferior results.[10] A comparison of results from the largest private equity managers with smaller funds shows a strong inverse correlation between size and performance; academic research supports the same conclusion.

Smaller funds tend to focus more on investment returns, which enables the creation of new, larger funds and possibly expansion into other areas. The returns of smaller funds often result from performance fees and future opportunities. In contrast, larger funds earn much greater fee income, which can alter general partner behavior and lead to a greater emphasis on stability and safety.

Higher performance earned by smaller funds may seem to make these funds the more attractive option, but there can be a cost. Since performance is usually the greater emphasis of smaller funds, risk may also be higher, and managers' actions may also increase risk if they attempt to generate outsized returns. Targeting small funds to chase performance may work out well, but as always, any investment needs to be entered into with realistic expectations.

The success of Yale's private equity suggests that basic strategies can be successful. Yale management targets private equity funds that "place central importance on enhancing the effectiveness of corporate operations."[11] This represents a typical private equity emphasis. Of course, *simple* doesn't mean *easy*.

Yale's approach is notable for the organization's willingness to look beyond more traditional options. Fund size isn't the major focus; rather, due diligence on the manager's investment operation is. Understanding a firm's value creation plans and operational methods are critical and can help tip returns and risk favorably for investors. While you probably can't hope to emulate Yale's fabulous success, its approach of targeting smaller and more assessable funds is rather straightforward and reproducible.

The underperformance of large firms in private equity offers smaller investors greater opportunity than might be originally expected given the *Journal of Wealth Management*'s comments on private equity. Fortunately, this isn't a game where size means everything and large scale must be achieved before success is possible. As such, it's not a stacked deck like venture capital. Instead, strategy and management processes appear to be most important.

Of course, size is relative. "Smaller" funds may only have $250 million versus $1 billion–plus for the big firms. Smaller sizes, however, also provide opportunities for smaller investors. While a "small" fund isn't going to cater to very small individual investors, investment opportunities are continually becoming available to a wider array of individuals. Furthermore, drivers of success beyond size also indicate that investors with access to various types of private equity firms—even much smaller firms—can hope to achieve good performance.

Traditional Options

The most traditional and generally proven private equity investment option for individual investors remains the pooled fund, which requires fairly large investments and accredited investor status. Many quality options exist with substantial proven track records. Investors able to allocate $250,000 or more are often best served by this approach, although options are increasing with minimums as low as $50,000. The offerings usually don't require capital calls, but some do. Time frames will vary, but the usual target is a full cycle from original investment to complete liquidation within 10 years or substantially less.

Funds open to individual investors may be significantly smaller than the giant funds that target institutions, but as mentioned, this doesn't preclude success and can even make it more likely. Smaller funds, however, will tend to be more focused and may also possess higher risk. Understanding the investment type becomes more important with the greater focus of smaller funds, as does manager selection.

This structure has existed for a longer time period, and due diligence will likely be easier given more comparable and relevant data. A more standardized fund-raising process also lessens the number of variables involved with the investment. If you have the financial resources to go this route, it will likely offer the best risk-versus-reward combination.

New Structures

For the majority of investors unable or unwilling to commit very large chunks of cash to a single offering, new offerings provide increasing flexibility and sophistication. Even large investors, given greater potential to diversify their funds, may prefer the smaller investments.

Some firms have adopted a structure like REIT's through utilization of a business development company (BDC). This structure provides a pass-through entity like a REIT in which at least 90 percent of profit and capital gains must be paid to investors. More significantly for investors, the treatment of the BDCs as regulated investment companies enables them to work with much smaller investors and investment levels. Investor financial qualifications for BDCs follow the same guidelines as with nontraded REITs.

The use of this structure for private equity investments is fairly new, gaining popularity in 2010. The combination of investor acceptance and heavy regulatory scrutiny of "Regulation D" investments, the traditional structure for many private equity funds, is driving more offerings to adopt this structure and similar ones. I expect the type and number of offerings in this area to grow substantially in the near future. Professionals with various private equity firms have told me that they intend to adopt more flexible structures, and several already have offerings in registration with regulators.

Fortunately for smaller investors, many private equity managers who use newer structures have achieved success, or at least experience, in the private equity space with more traditional investment vehicles. Again, this guarantees nothing, but experience and good track records usually make managers more attractive to investors.

The types of private equity investments offered via various structures are also expanding. Some offerings nearly match their institutional cousins while others alter features in hopes of appealing to individual investors. Investments structured for individuals may provide ongoing income. Individuals often prefer this structure, as it provides more up-front return as well as portfolio income.

For example, some newer private equity offerings target high dividends that range from 5 to 10 percent. Like dividends paid by public companies, dividends from private equity are paid from cash flows. The difference in this situation is that the high-yield percentage is made possible by private companies that are highly cash-flow positive. But dividend size and timing may be unpredictable, as profitability among companies can vary.

By contrast, another newer style combines debt and equity to produce similar dividend levels. Because the dividend cash flow is provided through a clear debt payment schedule, dividend timing and size should be steadier. In exchange, total return expectations will probably be lower because the equity component is smaller. This can be easily understood in terms of the usual risk-versus-reward trade-off.

Beyond these structures, a small number of offerings already exists in the form of closed-end mutual funds. A closed-end mutual fund is simply a fund that rarely, if ever, accepts new funds from investors. When you buy shares of the fund, you are buying them from an investor who sells shares, just as you would when purchasing stocks. This situation is a very different one from a typical mutual fund's, which adds your investment to the general pool of funds already invested. This structure of the closed-end funds enables them to control their flow of new investment funds. They raise cash once or on specific dates so they know exactly how much money they are managing or will manage. These funds require very small minimums since investors can buy as little as one share.

Closed-end funds, however, have several downsides. They tend to be heavily affected by market ups and downs, which leads to high correlation with the general market. In addition, many of the strategies employed by these funds depend on the companies being taken public. While there is nothing wrong with this approach, the exit strategy tends to make these funds very dependent on market valuations. In these funds share prices are often more volatile than the general market. While the volatility may be acceptable, given the sector advantages, there may need to be adjustments to portfolio planning.

Over time, I expect continued evolution of private equity structures and offerings to meet growing individual investor appetite for various forms of private equity investments. These are just a few examples of possibilities in this area, and options should continue to expand.

Because private equity is generally an aggressive type of investment and can carry more risk than other types of investments, it's not for everyone. Endowments love the category because of its historical performance numbers and other attributes. As more offerings become available to individual investors in the coming years, I believe the sector's acceptance and use in individual investor portfolio design will rise dramatically.

Allocation

The percentage of a portfolio to target toward private equity investments will obviously vary by investor. A good target for most investors will likely range from 5 to 15 percent of a portfolio. Most endowments don't go too much above 10 percent, although Yale targeted a 26 percent allocation in 2009 and 33 percent for 2010.[12] Given its experience and success in this sector, its high targets seem reasonable. But an allocation of this size for an individual investor just delving into this sector is likely to be inappropriate. Even many of the private equity investment managers advise individual investors to limit investments in the sector to 10 percent of their portfolio.

Higher percentages could make sense given the lower expected risk of some of the debt and equity combinations.

As with oil and gas, the quality of private equity investments can vary tremendously by offering. The expertise and experience of your financial professional can be critical in achieving success in this area, and many financial professionals have been slow to develop expertise in this sector. Your advisor should be able to offer several good options along with sensible recommendations. If he or she can't do so, and you are interested in this type of investment, you are probably best off seeking someone already experienced in this area rather than serving as an experimental guinea pig for your advisor.

Private equity can offer a tremendous benefit to your portfolio, and success will be more likely when inclusion and selection of these investments is based on good research, sound planning, and intelligent implementation. It can be a great performance asset in a portfolio. Yet, success is more likely when good opportunities are available. Forcing an investment rarely works out well.

The next major category addresses a unique area that has exploded onto the investment landscape over the past couple of decades.

11

Absolute Return

THIS IS THE LAST MAJOR PERFORMANCE CATEGORY. I HAVE SAVED IT for last because it's the least defined and most rapidly evolving. It can be a great portfolio addition, but it can also be difficult for investors to access. Fortunately, at least one investment approach, managed futures, is becoming more standard. But before jumping to this option, we will address the general subject.

Absolute return investing was conceptually identified as a distinct asset class by Yale University in the 1990s.[1] The key aim was to produce equitylike returns with ultralow correlation to anything else. It's not hard to see where the name came from, although some people assume that the *absolute* part of the name assumes losses aren't possible. This misses the point entirely and is simply wrong. No risk equals no return. Rather, the original strategy sought to alter the risk taken by removing equity market risk or exposure. While any investor would welcome elimination of potential loss, this constraint is not a part of absolute return strategies. Alas, this isn't the Holy Grail of investing.

The original strategy sought to profit through exposure to stock price movement unrelated to general market ups and downs. Event-driven strategies focused on buying or selling stocks based on events such as mergers or some form of corporate finance transaction. Other events included mergers, bankruptcy exits, or division

167

restructuring. Value-driven strategies employ long and short positions to limit market exposure while waiting for assets that are mispriced to correct and generate returns. The use of hedging strategies employed by managers of the funds to manage risk gives the vehicles their common name, hedge funds.

Since their conceptual inception, the definition of hedge funds has morphed into seemingly any investment that pays fund managers a fee and a carried interest—a success fee typically around 20 percent of gains. While investment classification by compensation can obscure the real value and purpose of an investment, it's a direct result of a regulatory environment that lightly controls this type of structure while heavily regulating nearly everything else. More accurately, a hedge fund is a private investment vehicle that manages a concentrated portfolio of public or private securities and derivative securities that can invest both long (benefit when a security's value increases) and short (benefit when a security's value decreases), and can apply leverage (borrow money).

Originally, hedge funds actively sought to completely remove the market's returns from returns their funds generated. The purpose was to exploit market pricing inefficiencies and profit exclusively from a specific strategy or manager skill. Conceptually, if active management neither created nor destroyed value, no returns would be generated above a risk-free rate of return minus fees. Risk-free return is normally considered the rate of return of Treasuries. When active management creates value, prices move according to management's actions, not larger events linked to the markets.

An example of one type of hedge fund will help you understand the whole sector. A merger arbitrage strategy attempts to benefit from movements in stock prices of two companies involved in a merger. When one company buys another, the price of the acquiring firm usually decreases as it spends time and money to complete the acquisition. The price of the target firm normally increases because a premium will be paid for its stock. In this situation, the hedge fund will buy the stock of the target firm and short the stock of the acquiring firm. As the prices converge toward each other, the hedge fund earns a profit on price changes of both securities, and also earns interest on the cash that it uses to back the short position. The strategy is isolated from overall movements of the stock market since the hedge fund's exposure is to the prices of each security relative to the other, not the actual prices of either security.

The profit potential exists because many other buyers and sellers are not willing to bear the risk of the deal not completing. If the deal doesn't go through, or another buyer gets involved, the hedge fund will likely lose money since the stock prices of one or both firms probably will not move as expected. This strategy is known as *convergence trading.*

It illustrates a typical hedge fund tactic: identify a situation in which specific securities will change in value relative to each other in a predictable manner for reasons not linked to the overall market. Other strategies seek to identify pricing changes linked to other variables. Regardless, the concept is the same—identify a predictable pricing change and trade securities to profit from it.

When hedge fund strategies are executed well, they can be very profitable. But an ability to define a strategy in no way guarantees successful execution. Inconsistent returns from the sector bear this out. Moreover, as the hedge fund category has grown over the past decades, its use and purpose has morphed far outside its original goal of eliminating market correlation. Strategies now target many different types of exposure ranging from eliminating all market correlation to magnifying market movements.

In spite of relatively mediocre returns, the hedge fund industry has grown into a major component of financial markets, and it has generated substantial controversy along the way. It's now a $2 trillion–plus industry that serves not only endowments and institutions but also, increasingly, individual investors.

Over time, additional trading strategies that lack equity market correlation have developed. The most notable new subcategory is likely managed futures, although this investment's structure and performance history result in some practitioners assigning it its own category. This definitional ambiguity further illustrates the lack of exact science associated with investing. In the following discussions, I will start with hedge funds and then come back to managed futures.

Hedge Funds

Given all the hype surrounding this sector, it might seem safe to assume that the sector has provided great performance with little correlation to any other asset. While in some cases funds have done well, over many time periods they trail mutual fund performance. Moreover, correlations have been surprisingly high for an asset that targets low correlation. Performance hasn't been disastrous, but it probably falls short of expectations for many investors who have been led to believe that hedge funds must be wonderful given all the mass media fawning and derision by some politicians in Washington of the huge profits earned by hedge funds.

This doesn't mean that hedge funds don't or can't offer a valuable service. Different structures and offerings can provide meaningful diversification or dramatically limit market risk. But even more than most other investments, offering quality and purpose between different hedge fund strategies, funds companies, and individual funds vary dramatically. The hedge fund label provides investors with surprisingly limited information.

Performance

The original goals of hedge funds were equitylike returns and lack of correlation with the general markets. But in 2008, the industry suffered its worst year in its relatively short history with the average hedge fund losing 19 percent.[2]

Longer-term performance that predates these years is also revealing, especially when the data are analyzed according to actual investor returns rather than simple performance numbers. Research by Burton G. Malkiel, a professor at Princeton, and Atanu Saha, a principal at the US Analysis Group, focused on hedge fund performance beginning with 604 funds in 1996 and rising to 2,700 in 2003. The funds produced an annual average return of 9.3 percent, compared with 9.4 percent for the S&P 500 Index. This sounds pretty good. The returns accruing to investors, however, didn't show such a positive picture.

Two key differences lower investor returns with hedge funds dramatically. First, these funds carry much higher tax liability than most other investment strategies. High-frequency trading of hedge funds creates very high short-term taxable income when compared to nearly any other investment strategy. This isn't a problem for endowments, as they are tax-exempt entities, but it is a serious issue for investors who hold investments in taxable accounts.

Second, fees with hedge funds are far higher than those with nearly any other type of investment, with most funds charging 2 percent annual management fees plus 20 percent of any gains. The combined impact of taxes and fees is severe. In their study, Dr. Malkiel and Dr. Saha determined that actual investor returns would have trailed index returns by 20 percent even if the hedge funds earned almost 50 percent more than market returns.[3] This picture isn't pretty.

Other periods and problems have also highlighted shortcomings. The most notable hedge fund failure to date has been the Long-Term Capital Management (LTCM) implosion of 1998. Using various financial tools, including derivatives contracts, the firm created incredible leverage to produce excellent returns initially, netting around 40 percent per year. After losing an amazing $4.6 billion in less than four months in 1998 due to mispriced exposure to the Russian financial meltdown, the firm was bailed out by other financial institutions.

LTCM's original outsized returns and famous personalities, including the former head of bond trading at Salomon Brothers and two Nobel Prize winners in economics, made the firm's eventual failure and subsequent bailout particularly noteworthy. While $4.6 billion sounds small by recent financial mess standards, at the time there was significant concern that this one firm could bring down the entire financial system. Again, hedge funds attempt to contain or mitigate risk, but success isn't guaranteed.

Moreover, many other casual references and studies overstate the performance of hedge funds given the high impact of survivorship bias, which has been estimated at 2 to 3 percent per year.[4] Just as in the mutual fund industry, often only the winners' performance is counted. In many years, hedge funds simply underperform. This will be true of nearly any investment, but I believe the claims and hype surrounding hedge funds warrant greater scrutiny. These investments can be very good ones, but investors need to be very aware of exactly what they are getting.

Why am I mentioning the failures of absolute return and hedge fund strategies rather than all the potential benefits? It's not that I don't like the category, since it can be highly constructive, as it can provide numerous portfolio benefits. But hedge funds seem to generate an overly high level of enthusiasm given their actual performance. I believe investors need to be aware that this type of investment, like all others, can have its drawbacks. Just because big institutions have embraced the category doesn't mean it is the right one for all investors, or that all, or even most, offerings will be acceptable to discerning investors. If you find or are presented with an interesting hedge fund opportunity, that doesn't mean you should proceed.

Stories abound about the success of hedge funds. Prominent attacks on the industry by the folks in Washington, D.C., frequently stand on stated or presumed assumptions that hedge funds are making a killing at the expense of the average American. It's no longer enough to be a captain of Wall Street. True villains seem to be hedge fund managers. The press appears dedicated to maintaining an aura around hedge funds that I believe is often very inaccurate. It's more interesting to denigrate a successful villain than a mediocre minion.

Correlation

Hedge fund correlation delivered a correlation of 0.76 for the Credit Suisse/Tremont Multi-strategy Index versus large-cap U.S. stocks from December 31, 2000, to December 31, 2010.[5] The supposed purpose of generating equitylike returns without market correlation often isn't reality. Correlation below 0.8 delivers tangible diversification advantages, but results fall well short of initial zero correlation targets. They also trail several other categories, particularly real assets.

But these numbers mask a greater truth. Within the hedge fund sector, strategies and success vary tremendously. There are approximately 15 distinct hedge fund strategies. Some possess fairly high market correlation, while others frequently experience almost none. Correlation or performance numbers for the industry may bear little relation to a particular offering you may be considering. The diversity of offerings requires very specific offering due diligence. The industry performance as a whole has been weak, but quality exists and can benefit a portfolio.

Access and Fees

Possibly more important than correlation for many small investors is access. Like the private equity sector, the hedge fund industry historically hasn't presented individual investors many quality options. The two sectors' paths, however, seem to be diverging as the availability of offerings for private equity outpaces hedge fund availability.

Part of the challenge for all investors in this sector is fees. And fees tend to be an even larger issue for smaller investors. As mentioned, most funds charge a management fee of around 2 percent per year and then an additional success fee of about 20 percent of profits per year. Under this arrangement, investors surrender a large part of their success to managers in good years but suffer all the losses in bad years. Regardless of the outcome, managers usually make out quite well. While fees can vary, these numbers are pretty standard. David Swensen, Yale's chief investment officer, sums up the problem succinctly in his discussion of hedge funds: "In the absence of superior active results, investors face certain disappointment. Long/short equity managers must consistently produce better than top-quartile returns to justify the fee structure accepted by hedge fund investors. Investors unable to identify the best of the best should pursue passive investment strategies."[6]

While David Swensen's book was published in 2006 and much has happened since then, his opinion warrants consideration. Even if his perspective and incentives may be quite different from those of individual investors, he certainly understands the industry. Care needs to be exercised if venturing forth into this area.

Many hedge funds available to individual investors are also actually "fund of funds" rather than direct investment into the funds themselves. While this arrangement offers desirable diversification across funds, it adds costs, as the manager of managers also earns a fee that can easily approach and exceed 1 percent. Most hedge funds also require accredited investor status, which limits access for many individual investors.

Another potential pitfall results from the controversy surrounding the ill-defined future of hedge funds. U.S. government officials have been threatening to make major regulatory changes to the hedge fund industry. This has implications for current investors. The specter of future regulatory changes heightens uncertainty regarding the category. While this result might seem to be inevitable, the issue is significant enough to scare off errors and omissions (E&O) carriers who provide various types of insurance coverage to broker/ dealers who offer the product.

A bit of explanation is in order. Firms that sell securities are called "broker/dealers." This includes firms such as Merrill Lynch, Morgan Stanley, and the recently defunct Lehman Brothers. Nearly all broker/dealers of any substance or size carry E&O insurance, which covers various issues ranging from sales deemed inappropriate to fraudulent offerings. All the products discussed throughout this book are normally covered by E&O insurance. By contrast, hedge funds are often covered only on a case-by-case basis, if at all. The primary reason for that, according to E&O carriers, is regulatory uncertainty.

When pressed, insurers explain that fear of several possible changes is the reason. A regulatory change could force a rapid exit from the investment space, which could cause mandatory investor losses as investor funds are returned. Accounting and/or regulatory changes could dramatically alter investment returns. Punitive actions could also result in substantial losses. All these risks are over and above typical offering and investment risk, which can also be substantial. These fears had been lessening before the 2008 crash, but the recent market turmoil and threat of expanded regulation have brought many of the risks back to the forefront. Endowments and institutions work directly with hedge funds, so this issue doesn't affect them; instead, it affects individual investors who work with a financial professional affiliated with a broker/dealer.

The various issues I have already mentioned about actual returns, diversification, regulatory uncertainty, and lack of insurability have a fairly predictable result. Hedge funds are not offered very frequently to individual investors. Only about 10 percent of the top independent broker/dealers make hedge funds available to their clients through their independent financial professionals. Given the supposed benefits of the space, this percentage is amazingly low.

By now, you may be thinking that this area should just be avoided altogether. Yet even with all the issues mentioned, I believe they can make sense for certain investors who make well-educated decisions. High-quality offerings exist and can be excellent additions to individual investor portfolios. As should be very apparent, selecting the right fund or funds is much more important with hedge funds than with equity funds. While successful selection in either category is desirable, poor hedge fund selection will probably be more costly given the diversity of performance and correlation attained across this sector.

Selection

Most individual investors will be at the mercy of their financial professional. If he or she knows this area and has identified good options, adding the asset class to a portfolio can make sense. If it's not an area of expertise, the choice is easy: walk away. This bears repeating: Unless you have high confidence in any professional's ability to recommend a high-quality hedge fund, you are better off just saying no. There is no need to go against the odds.

If you do decide to go forward, how do you know if a fund is a good option? There are two fundamental questions that should be asked about every hedge fund. First, what is the objective of the hedge fund? In other words, what is the hedge fund trying to do? Second, what is the investment process of the hedge fund manager? Essentially, this asks how the hedge fund manager plans to achieve success. Is the process based on a system or strategy that can be explained and predictably replicated, or is it based on a single brilliant manager who goes with his gut? If it's the latter, all the expertise could walk out the door one day, leaving no meaningful strategy in place.

A fund's performance against its stated objective and investment strategy is usually revealing. Mediocre performance while the market is flying can be positive if it illustrates a desired lack of market correlation. Many hedge funds provide a comparison of their performance history versus a benchmark relevant to their particular strategy. This can be extremely helpful. Other funds do not, and many claim that they can't because there is no relevant benchmark.

This can be true, but the absence of performance comparisons will make decisions more difficult. Regardless, performance data always provide worthwhile information. Poor past performance guarantees nothing and may reverse in the future, but I wouldn't chance my money on a terrible firm that claims it can reverse its past mistakes. Solid past performance certainly seems like a more attractive indicator than past failure.

When analyzing past performance trends, analyzing a few key time periods can be revealing. For example, how did a firm do during the 2008 meltdown? How about the 2000–2002 Internet crash? Similarly, what do comparisons with very good years reveal?

Fees can be another issue. Since most offerings available to individuals will be fund of funds, be sure to delve down through the different levels of fees. Returns can't be guaranteed, but fees tend to be much more predictable. Overly high fees that drag down returns always lessen investor returns.

Manager commitment, through investment of personal funds subject to the same conditions as individual investors, can make hedge funds more attractive. Incentives are powerful, and hedge funds generally lack aligned incentives. Although investing alongside the fund manager doesn't guarantee success, the removal or at least a lessening of disincentives likely increases the odds for success.

Allocation to this sector needs to be driven by investors and investment availability. A very solid offering can improve a portfolio design. Even the consideration of a hedge fund, however, requires access to a high-quality offering. When an investment earns a high level of confidence, allocations are likely best kept under 10 percent of a portfolio. Although many endowments exceed this level of allocation, they currently enjoy much greater access to diversified, quality funds than do individuals. They also benefit from far-more-sophisticated assessment tools than do individuals. Keeping absolute return expectations and exposure at reasonable levels is a wise thing to do.

Other Options

Although hedge funds have been the primary investment vehicle associated with absolute return strategies, additional investment strategies are growing in popularity. Investor demand for noncorrelated assets is high. Like hedge funds, these strategies seek to produce equity-like returns with a low correlation to the stock market. The most popular and fastest-growing investment option is managed futures.

Managed Futures

Most investment strategies for investing in managed futures take both long and short positions in futures contracts as well as options on futures contracts in the global equity, commodity, interest rate, and currency markets. For the uninitiated, this can sound complex and intimidating. The investment strategy, however, is surprisingly easy to understand.

The vehicle used by managed futures funds to gain exposure to markets is normally a futures contract. As we covered earlier, a futures contract is simply a contract agreed to today between two parties to buy or sell a specific amount and type of asset at a specified future date at an agreed-upon price. Although a futures contract is a financial instrument commonly employed by corporate America, few individuals have any use for it. Futures contracts provide managed futures funds the widest and most flexible means to gain upside and downside exposure to virtually any tradable asset class across the globe.

Futures contracts are just a tool. Like holding a share of IBM gives any investor exposure to IBM's future, holding a futures contract on Brazilian wheat simply provides the holder exposure to this asset class.

Value is created only through application of value-adding strategies. Most managed futures firms seek to create investor returns through something called "trend following." This strategy is essentially just what it sounds like: Traders attempt to benefit from long-term asset price trends that often occur in various markets across the globe. Strategies seek to take advantage of trends regardless of direction. It doesn't matter whether prices are going up or down. The only requirement is a trend that continues long enough to create benefit from holding or shorting (i.e., benefiting when the price goes down) the underlying asset. The strategy is simple: Ride the trend wherever it's going.

Although this sounds easy, consistent return generation requires considerable skill. Identifying a trend, figuring out how best to take advantage of it, and determining how long to ride one all require sophisticated risk management techniques. Within the industry, this is called "position sizing"; it involves determining how many contracts to trade, when to increase numbers, when to decrease contracts, when to take profits, and so on.

Similar to investors managing an individual portfolio, the managed futures industry relies heavily on diversification across many different asset classes. Futures managers usually maintain concurrent exposure to a wide array of global assets, including energy, agricultural commodities, short-term interest rates, long-term interest rates, stock indexes, and currencies. Futures traders maintain exposure to a wide degree of markets in search of the next trend. In addition, because diverse markets are unlikely to produce the same trends, the fund diversifies its risk.

Even so, investment returns tend to be unpredictable. Some markets and circumstances produce desirable trends that give attractive returns, while other markets simply don't. Moreover, not all strategies use trend-following approaches. Other strategies employ pricing pattern recognition; arbitrage strategies, which attempt to take advantage of mispricings between two related and often correlated securities; option writing, which uses options rather than futures contracts to implement strategies; and fundamental or discretionary pricing strategies, which analyze global supply and demand, macroeconomic indicators, and geopolitical forces to uncover mispricing opportunities. Regardless, all these strategies can produce attractive returns in some markets and dismal results in others.

Performance

Over time, performance of managed futures has been very solid, which has resulted in increased interest in the sector. From 1980 to 2010, managed futures produced an annual return of 14.52 percent as measured by the CASAM CISDM CTA Equal Weighted Index. This was more than double the S&P 500's return over the same time period.[7] As a category, managed futures outperformed all other categories over this time period with the possible exception of private

Figure 11.1   Gains and Losses of Stocks versus Managed Futures During Times of Stress

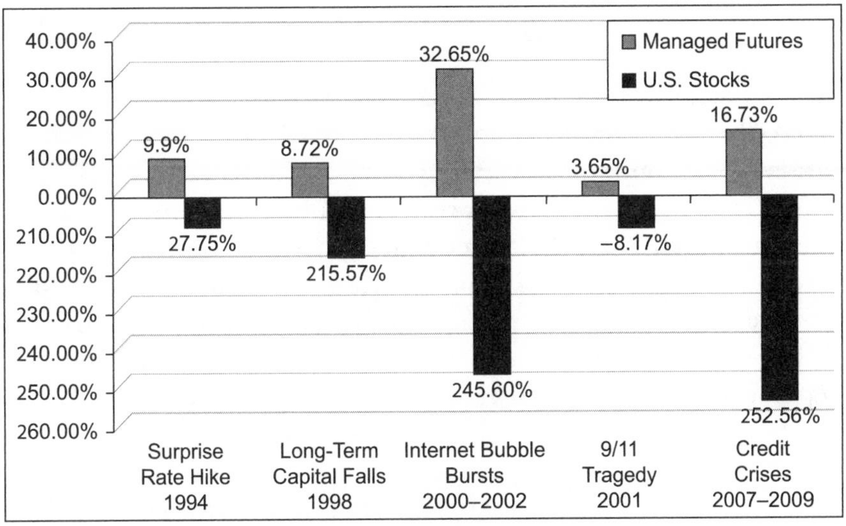

equity. Moreover, these numbers are net of fees and represent performance assessable to individual investors.

The potential benefit of managed futures becomes more apparent given their past returns during periods of large stock market losses (see Figure 11.1). More than any other asset class with the possible exception of gold, managed futures have excelled during various periods of severe market losses.

The good performance of managed futures during bad times for the stock market often arises because of an increase in trends during very volatile periods. When markets decline, volatility is often at its highest. There's an old saying that the only thing that goes up during a down market is correlation. All these trends usually provide great opportunities for managed futures. As a result, it's not surprising that managed futures often excel during down markets. This can make them an excellent addition to a portfolio.

Yet they are far from perfect. At times their lack of correlation is frustrating. During the S&P 500's strong market recovery of

26.5 percent in 2009, managed futures declined 7.89 percent as measured by the Altegris 40 Index. When the market increased nearly 29 percent in 2003, managed futures didn't even earn half the market's return.[8]

Correlation

When the correlation of managed futures with U.S. stocks is analyzed, they really shine. Using the Altegris 40 Index as a representation of the commodities trading advisor performance reveals low to negative correlations with stocks and bonds. From December 1986 to March 2011, the correlation of managed futures with U.S. stocks was negative at 0.12 while correlation with bonds was slightly positive at 0.22.[9] Other time periods and indexes produce somewhat different numbers, but low correlation is quite consistent. The conceptual benefit of this asset class is convincing.

Fees

One note of caution: As with hedge funds, fees charged by managed futures funds can eat into profits. Many managed futures programs structure their fees in a way very similar to hedge funds. Usually, this isn't good for investors. As always, fees need to be assessed with any investment, and managed futures are no exception. Their performance has been strong enough to compensate for the fees in the past, but this may not continue, and fees always act as a drag on performance.

Access

A major difference between this asset class and hedge funds is access. Numerous high-quality managed futures programs have been available to individual investors for decades. Moreover, the playing field is fairly level between institutions and individuals. Institutions definitely have more access, but individuals can invest in some of the best-managed futures programs available. This isn't the case for hedge funds.

When the various characteristics of managed futures are assessed, the overall impact to most portfolios appears to be very positive. In fact, over the past 20 years, most individual investor portfolios would have benefited from holding managed futures, as their strong returns and lack of correlation would have elevated total return and lowered volatility.[10]

Liquidity

Another advantage for most managed futures programs is reasonable liquidity. Although exact liquidity terms vary by fund, most offer some version of short-term access. Optional monthly redemptions are quite common. Higher liquidity can make portfolio planning somewhat more flexible than with other asset classes. Managed futures, however, should definitely be treated as a longer-term investment, like the stock market, largely because of its volatile performance. In fact, a downside to easier access can be a greater propensity by investors to panic when inevitable bad months occur. Hopefully, this isn't a problem for an investor savvy enough to include the asset class.

Allocations

Given the history and diversification benefits of managed futures, it might seem somewhat puzzling that the asset class isn't more widely known and accepted. Managed futures have become a more common part of higher-net-worth portfolios, yet they are mostly lacking in smaller portfolios. Part of this situation results from regulatory limitations. Many managed futures programs are available only to accredited investors, although increasing numbers of programs are available for investors who meet the same requirements as non-traded REITs. Evolution of products within the category will undoubtedly continue, and offerings will certainly change over time.

Volatility can also scare some investors. Managed futures are generally somewhat volatile on a monthly basis. From 1990 to 2010 their annual standard deviation has been 9.45 percent as measured by the Altegris 40 Index versus the S&P 500's 19.3 percent. This would seem to suggest a more stable asset class, but few professionals view managed futures this way. Volatility over shorter time frames can be quite high. Monthly pricing changes over 10 percent are not uncommon.

Furthermore, managed futures' lack of correlation with more traditional asset classes gives the appearance of a more volatile asset. The combination of potential volatility and lack of correlation can make managed futures unnervingly unpredictable. Sometimes they are great; other times, they are awful. Most other asset price changes, even commodities, can be fairly easily understood, at least in retrospect. This simply isn't the case for managed futures. They go up and down for seemingly unknown reasons. The managed futures manager may understand that the Thai Baht currency or molybdenum metal trends drove profits, but investors will rarely know of the trends or a fund's exposure to them.

As a result, the prices of managed futures often appear to vary independently from anything else. When the stock market is down, at least most investors can draw some reasonable conclusion regarding the reasons for the downturn, and they usually have a lot of company. This doesn't hold true for managed futures.

Furthermore, managed futures are not well understood even within the financial services industry. Financial professionals sometimes shy away from the asset category, as futures in general are still considered a more exotic investment type. Although an investment in managed futures is not an investment in futures, the use of futures can create unease.

The lack of wide acceptance and understanding of the category further contributes to its slow adoption in other ways. Earlier, I mentioned E&O insurance carriers' reluctance to provide coverage for hedge funds. Managed futures face a similar problem, although not as severe. E&O carriers worry that the investors will not understand what they are buying and may complain when the investment does what it's expected to do—go up and down independent of nearly anything else. For this reason, E&O carriers may limit the use of managed futures by individual investors. While the limits are generally high enough to allow investors to accomplish their diversification goals, the existence of the limit illustrates the ongoing caution surrounding the asset class.

Moving On

I believe managed futures can be an excellent means to add an absolute return asset to a portfolio. The potential performance and correlation characteristics can provide a very desirable addition to the performance side of the asset mix in a portfolio. In addition, this isn't a new asset class. It's been around for decades and has built a substantial performance history across all kinds of markets.

If the decision to invest in managed futures is made, the next question is: How much to invest? For most investors, an allocation of 10 percent is probably the upper limit. Starting with a lower allocation of 5 percent or less can be a great way for investors who want to gain a bit more experience to build confidence and comfort with the investment. Most managed futures companies seem to agree with this, as they generally recommend allocations around the 5 to 10 percent range. Managed futures are not meant to be the anchor of a portfolio but instead an independent, if unpredictable, portfolio enhancer.

The big question for most investors will be whether to move forward at all. It seems very reasonable to expect nearly any portfolio to benefit from the addition of this asset class. Any investor, however, will have to be convinced of the benefit and maintain a high-enough comfort level to last through volatile periods. Managed futures offer a compelling absolute return solution for those who can get comfortable with the asset class. At the least, they warrant serious consideration for any well-constructed portfolio above a minimal size.

We are just about at the end of the performance side of portfolios. After that, we will address bonds. Before covering bonds, a traditionally important part of portfolios, I'm going to address a few common investments that don't neatly fit into the already identified categories.

12

Miscellaneous Types of Investments

GIVEN THE FINANCIAL WORLD'S COMPLEXITY, SOME INVESTMENTS escape classification, even with the broad categories employed by endowments for performance-oriented assets. Those, again, are domestic equities, developed market equities, emerging market equities, real assets, private equity, and absolute return. Investments that don't fit these categories may still offer attractive combinations of risk-adjusted returns and lower correlation with other investments.

The previous sections covered various types of investments that are worth researching and considering for your portfolio. In contrast, possibilities in this section, such as income investments, debt with equity investments, equipment leasing, and distressed debt, represent opportunities that may or may not be available, depending on numerous factors. Consistently good vehicles may be hard to find, and specific investor circumstances are more likely to impact investment decisions.

Ideally, no more than 10 percent of a portfolio should be filled with any combination of these investments. And individual investments should remain under 5 percent of the portfolio. There can be exceptions to these suggested figures; just be sure to use lots of wisdom. The less standard nature of this class warrants greater caution on the part of the investor.

Since no amount of stretching and torturing a "miscellaneous" category can cover all possibilities, I will stick to a few common investment types. These categories will certainly evolve, so if an investment isn't addressed somewhere in one of these sections, don't exclude it from consideration. Hopefully, the frameworks provided will help you assess the potential value of any additional investment.

Many opportunities will be smaller and involve less money and fewer investors than others. In cases in which the investments are larger, the investment category probably lacks sufficient size or precedence to establish meaningful performance data. Although these investments may be attractive and can be good additions to a portfolio, assessment of performance and risk are likely to be more challenging given the lack of relevant or comparable data. In spite of the less standard nature of the investment concepts in this section, you'll probably find all of them to be familiar since they are generally combinations of investments or opportunities already addressed.

Debt Investments

Excluding the traditional fixed-income market, which will be addressed in the next chapter, numerous debt vehicles provide alternatives to more traditional bonds. Investors are clamoring for more means to earn income, and product sponsors are responding with new opportunities. Multiple products offer investments that vary by interest payments, offering duration, asset backing type, investment structure, and so on. Given the rapid increase in recent demand, new possibilities should continue to multiply.

The unique potential benefits of these investments come with unique risks. The potential negatives are quite obvious. The borrower may stop making payments and may not return all borrowed principal as originally agreed. Even if all funds are eventually received, timing can be delayed or the investment quality can change, raising fears about future payments or return of principal. In addition, reliable and widely applicable data is harder to find in this category, so assessing the attractiveness of an investment can be challenging.

Structure

Debt investments offer investors returns through interest payments rather than capital gains. Investments are often senior to other debt or equity, which provides greater protection for the investment. In exchange, investors usually accept limited ability to participate in the venture's success—just as with a standard bond. The value of seniority—the first claim on all assets—is also highly specific, depending on the kind of investment. Some investments are backed by multiple junior levels of debt as well as by equity. Other investments may offer only collateral, which may or may not provide a strong backing.

Collateralized loans tend to be attractive because investors receive some assurances that the assets can be sold to repay them if the borrower struggles. Real estate is probably the most obvious example of collateral backing a loan. Various other forms of asset-backed financing operate under a similar arrangement. Loans are secured by specific assets, which can be used to pay off investors in turn if the original investment intention goes awry. Good collateral can include almost anything that can hold value outside of the company, including machinery, inventory, property rights, patents, and even cash flows from other assets.

Seniority can also provide security. High levels of subordinated loans or equity can provide a cushion if the borrower runs into problems. Seniority can be particularly valuable if the borrowers have a significant amount of their own net worth and funds subordinate to your money. Borrowers will likely exercise additional caution and diligence to protect their own funds, thereby rewarding you in the process.

Performance

Investors often find debt investments attractive because they usually pay fairly high interest rates commensurate with expected long-term stock returns. Lack of expected correlation with other performance-oriented investments provides another draw. Success is usually easy to determine. If payments are made as promised and principal is returned according to original terms, the investment is likely considered to be a success.

Returns are also higher to compensate for lack of liquidity. These are not tradable, traditional bonds. Holding periods often extend for several years and may possibly last up to a decade. For investors able to accept less liquid assets, the illiquidity premium can provide a higher return for a given level of risk. Of course, if liquidity is needed, this probably isn't an acceptable option. Altogether, the positives can be very compelling.

Deal structure can also be important. Simple covenants can be invaluable. Prevention from future borrowers securing seniority to you as a current lender or another lender gaining access to collateral that backs your loan can be essential. They can make the difference between whether you walk away with all your investment or part empty-handed if a deal goes bad.

Past Problems

An example would be helpful. While it would seem that debt that is fully collateralized should be safe, the category as a whole has seen failures. A particularly notable recent example is Medical Capital, a debt offering backed by accounts receivables from medical doctors, which would seem to be a very safe investment. The investment started out fine in 2003 and paid investors attractive interest yields until the firm ran into problems making payments in 2009. The investment was revealed as a Ponzi scheme when investigators discovered that some funds from new investors were used to pay investors in older funds. Since the firm raised more than $2 billion from 2003 to 2009 through various subsidiaries, the eventual implosion was quite spectacular, causing widespread damage that affected not only unfortunate investors but nearly everyone associated with the offering.

In this case, investors and firms facilitating the investment likely would have been spared much pain if they had required something called a PCAOB (Public Company Accounting Oversight Board) audit to confirm the existence of assets and source of payments. After this and a few other recent failures involving fraud, these audits have become a standard requirement for nearly all investments. Any offering you consider should be audited.

Risks

While return *on* your principal is important, an emphasis on return *of* your principal is particularly helpful in assessing this category. In nearly all cases, investments, even terrible ones, pay investors interest for some time period. You want to make it as likely as possible not only that you will keep receiving interest payments but also that you will get back all your money down the road.

Also, risks will differ wildly by individual deal. If a lender is the only provider of capital, it may be the senior note holder, but it is effectively also the most junior. If borrowers have little of their own capital in the deal, investors could be the only people facing risk of loss. If the venture does very well, the lenders receive their interest payments and original principal while the borrower reaps all the upside from success. Conversely, failure may cost the lenders everything while the borrowers simply walk away.

Contrast this situation to a deal in which the lender backs borrowed funds by equity and ownership capital on a 10 to 1 basis, and the loan is further backed by collateral that can be easily transferred. This type of deal may offer a lower return than the first structure, but the risk to lenders would likely be much lower.

Correlation

Diversification assumptions also need to be realistically assessed. These deals are assumed to have minimal correlations to other types of investments. Often this is true, but not in every case. A more realistic assessment could reveal the likelihood of higher correlation with other investments. For instance, a promissory note collateralized by real estate may face risks similar to the real estate sector. Likewise, a major economic slowdown could adversely impact debt repayment while also leading to a stock market plunge. Exact correlation data won't exist, so common sense should be amply applied.

Industry Scrutiny

One last piece of information can highlight the need for exercising caution. Earlier, I mentioned errors and omissions (E&O) carriers that provide coverage to brokerage firms. As a category, they often treat debt investments differently than other types of investment and may require a more thorough review before providing coverage. Part of their wariness results from a perception that investors are more likely to misunderstand this product than they are many others.

Fortunately, greater scrutiny of these offerings as a result of recent failures seems to have strengthened their overall quality. As a result, errors and omissions carriers' confidence in investment quality has increased, and coverage is expanding. Regardless, different standards by more-experienced risk assessors suggest that any investor should seek extra comfort with this investment before proceeding.

Allocation

As mentioned, any allocation to one specific offering of a debt investment is best kept below 5 percent of a portfolio. In the high-profile examples of fraud and severe investor losses, the most heart-breaking stories are nearly always those telling of investors placing nearly all their net worth into one single investment. That's just not smart no matter how good a possibility looks. There are always so many attractive investment alternatives that no single offering should get the bulk of your total assets.

Debt with Equity

Combined debt *and* equity investments have been around for just about as long as debt *or* equity investments. As soon as someone offered interest for using a resource, someone else figured out a way to get interest and some of the upside.

Over time, offerings have gotten considerably more sophisticated. A few of the more common possibilities are investments that start as debt and can be converted into equity by investors. Another deal structure provides lenders income and also offers warrants or some version of equity that could become worth something if the venture achieves a certain level of success.

These structures are usually created to give borrowers seniority and greater downside protection if the borrower struggles. Simultaneously, they provide a desirable upside possibility if the venture is successful. But this combination doesn't come free. Greater security usually means that investors don't participate fully in a company's upside potential. Also, in exchange for some form of participation in a company's success, interest paid on debt may be lower. These structures are rather traditional and can be found in private or direct deals and also on public secondary markets. Convertible notes represent an entire asset class of bonds.

Notes with equity kickers tend to be more common in the private equity world. Just as with a regular loan, a lender may provide capital secured by specific assets. In addition to interest and a promise of principal repayment, however, the lender receives warrants—the right to buy stock at a specific price in the future directly from the company. This combination of different funding agreements can give investors a less risky means to participate in a private equity offering.

Newer Possibilities

Some investments pool investors' funds to build a portfolio of combined debt and equity holdings in the private equity space. These have become common recently. The goal is to generate returns that exceed expected returns for debt but present lower risk than an all-equity investment. Investors hope to earn profits via receipt of interest payments on loans and then eventually capital gains on equity positions. By pooling investor funds and investing across multiple companies, the investment seeks to limit risk associated with an investment in a single or small number of convertible bonds.

Managers of the invested funds generate returns through lending money and taking equity positions in borrowers. For loans, funds are provided to private companies at rates attractive to both the lender and the borrower. Rates are often 8 to 10 percent above Treasury yield rates. While this sounds high, total costs are often more attractive than other loans for midsize and smaller companies.

The loan terms also provide the lender with an equity stake in the borrower that eventually will be sold back to the borrower or other investors. Usually, investors in this sector have actively sought out firms that are growing and will benefit significantly from an addition of capital. Assuming this arrangement works, the injection of capital helps the borrower grow. Over time, the borrower pays back the loan and enjoys an increase of its equity value. The increased equity value also benefits the investors who frequently sell the shares back to the company.

The structure of the combined debt and equity investment can offer some unique benefits. Multiple investments provide diversification into the area. Total return targets tend to be well above expected stock market returns but lower than most private equity return targets. Because the investment utilizes lending as a key component of the investment structure, significant cash flow is expected. This provides returns throughout the investment's holding period rather than only at the investment's end. Often, about half of the investment's total return comes through income, which can make the vehicle desirable for particular investors.

This investment type can also provide another advantage through its offer of limited liquidity. Under some structures, the loans must be valued daily according to valuations on a liquid market. The ready access to a liquid market as well as other features of the investment can allow investors to redeem their purchase quarterly or even more frequently. The redemptions may have a cost, or investors may receive back less than they invested, but the availability of liquidity for an investment linked to private equity can be attractive. For investors not interested in this feature, a likely loss of some principal during redemption and only sporadic redemption periods still provides a liquidity premium.

Obviously, this investment also poses unique risks. Because smaller private companies are often involved, they usually have more concentrated risks than would a larger entity. As a result, their business conditions may change more quickly, which can cause struggles in repayment of debt or the making of payments. Just as with other private equity firms, their future company valuations are likely to vary more than a larger company's, resulting in less predictable future values for investor equity positions. Yet the structure can offer a very interesting alternative to an investment that is either pure debt or private equity.

Equipment Leasing

Companies often prefer to lease different types of equipment rather than buy them. Leasing can help companies focus more resources on their own business. It does so by shifting capital away from more costly purchases and focusing management time away from equipment maintenance to higher value-adding activities. Additional advantages may also include tax benefits and increased financial engineering capabilities. Assets can be moved off the balance sheet, and superior cash-flow management may be possible. A familiar example of equipment leasing is found in the airline industry, which frequently employs leasing to secure extra capacity when needed, thus avoiding the financial burden of airplane purchases.

Whatever the reason for equipment leasing, this common corporate practice is big business, and investors have multiple different options with which to participate. The concept is straightforward. As with investments previously addressed, most individuals invest by providing a management team funds to purchase equipment that is leased to end users. The lease income is paid to investors, and investor capital is eventually returned when the equipment is sold. It sounds simple.

There is a large potential flaw in this arrangement. Does most equipment appreciate or depreciate? If we consider a car lease, the car's value obviously declines over time and with use. Similarly, aircraft don't become more valuable as they are flown, and most equipment wears out.

There are exceptions. Some equipment actually appreciates over time. Large and complex machinery used to produce microchips can increase in value because of manufacturing and capability advancements added into the machines. Various other types of equipment follow a similar pattern.

Regardless of the type of equipment considered, accurate projections of residual values are extremely important. If management assumes equipment will depreciate 30 percent over time, and if it instead declines by 50 percent, total returns will be reduced. Conversely, residual values that exceed expectations can boost returns. If equipment depreciates, the residual will be less than the original purchase price, which results in investors receiving back less than they invested. If investors know this at the beginning of an investment, why would anyone choose to invest?

In spite of investors receiving back less than what they invested, total returns can be very attractive because higher lease payments during the lease term can compensate investors for receiving only partial principal repayment. When lease payments include a return of principal, they provide income during the investment holding period greater than many other types of investments.

Because the offerings are so diverse, finding meaningful performance information is challenging. In addition, the category has seen its share of unpredictability. Over the past few decades, some periods of poor returns resulted when residuals were realized below expectations. In more than one instance, technological change caused unexpectedly fast equipment obsolescence. The industry has learned from these mistakes, and current offerings are thought to be better designed. But the world will certainly continue to change, providing opportunities and potential pitfalls to any management team. Just as with any other investment, the selection of good managers is very important.

In my experience, this type of investment benefits even more from thorough up-front planning than do most others. The reason is simple. Many, if not most, equipment leasing investments offer higher up-front income in exchange for a probable smaller return of principal. Most people don't like holding a shrinking investment, even if it does provide outsized income.

Moreover, even the best investors and financial professionals can be seduced by ongoing financial statements when they continue to list the value of the investment at the original purchase price. Even if everyone involved consciously remembers that the value is likely to decrease in the future, the day of reckoning can still deliver an unwanted jolt. Adjustments downward can be even more painful if investors don't really understand the dynamics of the investment or if they simply forget. This investment's unique investment structure requires special attention to make it a successful addition to most portfolios, but its unique structure can make it very desirable.

Distressed Debt

Most people are familiar with various types of standard debt offerings made available to investors through different bonds. Generally, investors earn a return by loaning money to corporations at a set rate. The investment will set the terms for return of principal, and the investment return is derived solely from the interest payments on the bond. Although there are deviations from this basic arrangement, most debt offerings follow a similar pattern of interest payments and return of principal according to an original agreement. Companies may borrow from individuals through public bond offerings or directly from institutional lenders in the private market.

Within the debt markets, borrowers often differ from one another in very significant ways. Some borrowers are public companies with very extensive public and audited information readily available. Much greater regulatory requirements for public companies result in much more extensive disclosure than generally exists for private companies. The additional public and audited information required can make analysis of a potential borrower easier.

In contrast, private companies often present different opportunities to lenders able to provide debt according to differing amounts and types of information. There are also many differences across all types of companies, whether private or public, and borrowing terms can vary tremendously.

At the time a firm borrows money from any individual or institution, specific terms are agreed to that are often very dependent on that specific firm's credit worthiness and expected future ability to pay. Regardless of how well future risk is assessed and understood, the future never evolves exactly as expected. If a firm runs into difficulties, it may fail to make payments and repay loans per the original agreement. Even firms that abide by all original terms may experience substantial deterioration of their creditworthiness, which can force a lender to recategorize the value of the ongoing interest payments and loan principal.

If a company stops paying interest, it is said to be in default. It enters a new category of loan called "distressed debt." The category includes loans in default, loans under bankruptcy protection, or loans believed to be heading toward either of these conditions. Bonds and bank debt are the most common type of distressed debt. While there is no exact categorization of distressed debt, generally any fixed-income instrument with a yield to maturity 10 percent greater than the yield on Treasuries is considered to be distressed debt.

For lenders, these loans can present challenges. Valuing and managing problem debt frequently requires very different skills and resources than valuing and managing performing loans. And bad debts adversely affect bank balance sheets. For these and other reasons, distressed debt holders frequently seek to offload these types of riskier loans to companies or individuals that specialize in managing this type of debt.

In a capitalistic society, one firm's challenge is nearly always another's opportunity. Over time, many firms have developed specializations in pricing and managing problem loans. Given the size of the assets involved, high levels of focus in the arena aren't surprising. The ability to effectively consolidate, price, and manage billion-dollar portfolios of distressed debt provides ample opportunity to add value.

The allure of distressed debt investing is very easy to understand. If an investor can buy loans for 50 cents on the dollar and eventually sell or liquidate the portfolio for 80 cents on the dollar while collecting interest payments based on the original loan value, profits can be tremendous. Of course, the risk can be high as well. Some or even all of the loans may be in default, and value can go down rather than up. And even if the value increases, if the costs of selling or realizing the profit are too high, distressed debt investors can still lose money.

As you might expect, this type of investment tends to be most popular during times of economic distress. The recession beginning in 2008 released a wave of distressed debt that will take years to work its way through the financial system. Investors in distressed debt normally attempt to generate current income and perhaps also eventual long-term capital appreciation, if loans increase in value.

The possible combinations of these investments are nearly endless. Some investors and managers will focus on very low debt quality in which loans may be purchased for pennies on the dollar. Other firms may focus on much higher debt quality in which the debt may be discounted only a few percent. Other permutations also include securitized versus nonsecuritized debt, varying levels of seniority, and collateralization.

The structures of these offerings will vary. Some emphasize interest payments with possible capital appreciation, and others focus almost exclusively on generating future capital gains. The possibilities are nearly endless with structures heavily affected by the type of debt available and the particular managers' expertise.

There isn't a one-size-fits-all approach to this opportunity because every combination of crises and managers will create different opportunities. As with other opportunities, managers' expertise and experience are exceedingly important. The opportunities can be tremendous, but that's because there is risk associated with the opportunity. A manager or management team with a successful past track record should be a minimum requirement. Obviously, a compelling story about why the investment will work is a good idea, too.

Other Possibilities

There are many additional categories of miscellaneous investments. And many more will undoubtedly arise as the global economy evolves and matures. Some of the entries mentioned previously could also become standardized enough to enter into more accepted categories or create their own categories. Don't let exact classification drive you into or away from an investment that offers a desirable combination of performance, risk, and diversification.

These areas may present opportunities, but don't try to force them into a portfolio. They are likely to become available through circumstance or a relationship with the right financial professional. They can provide excellent flavoring to many portfolios. Their unique and potentially less familiar nature, however, likely dictates using them to add spice to a portfolio rather than using them as the major ingredient.

13

Fixed Income

Up to this point, all discussions on different investments have focused on performance-oriented investments. An increased emphasis on holding highly diversified performance-oriented assets with low(er) correlation is the fundamental basis of the endowment model. Fixed income, however, still has a place in most endowment models, and many individual investors can find it much more beneficial than do endowments because of its complete liquidity and lower volatility.

What Is Fixed Income?

Before jumping into the category, let's be sure we are using a common definition. I'm using the term *fixed income* to refer to any type of investment that (1) is not equity, (2) requires a borrower to make payments according to a predetermined schedule, and (3) requires an eventual repayment of the borrowed principal. Technically, (2) and (3) can be combined, but that arrangement isn't very common. When looking at this definition, it's easy to understand why the name *fixed income* arose, since the income is set at the outset by the original borrowing terms.

Within the fixed-income category there are numerous subdivisions because many different entities borrow capital using a wide variety of structures. The largest single borrower in the United States is the government in various forms. Beyond federal borrowing, government-sponsored enterprises such as the Federal Home Loan Mortgage Corporation (Freddie Mac) and the Federal National Mortgage Association (Fannie Mae) facilitate home loans through pooling mortgages and selling them in securitized form to investors. Unfortunately, lax origination standards and overzealous lending by these entities was a primary cause of the housing bubble, but that discussion will be left to other books.

Local and city governments borrow money through municipal bonds. Muni bonds, as they are generally called, are unique in that their income is usually exempt from federal taxation and state taxation by the state that issues them.

Corporate bonds issued by companies are the last major category. The term is usually applied to longer-term debt instruments with maturity dates extending out at least a year from the issue date. The term *corporate bonds* tends to be used as a broad description that includes all nongovernment bonds, but it technically refers only to corporate bonds.

Commercial paper is another major category of bonds, referred to as "notes," that has a short duration of 1 to 270 days. It is sold by corporations and large banks to meet their short-term funding and working capital needs. The debt is unsecured and backed only by a firm's promise to repay. Since there is no collateral involved, almost all borrowers have excellent credit ratings. This form of security is normally held in money market accounts and can act as another form of cash holding for large entities.

The size and level of complexity of the fixed-income market can be overwhelming. Books, textbooks, college courses, and entire careers are devoted to small categories within the broad sector. Fortunately for most investors, this category can be vastly simplified, especially if the endowment model is employed, which results in a smaller bond allocation.

Categorization

Bonds can be broadly categorized by risk and maturity date or duration. U.S. government bonds are the safest, at least for now. Investment-grade bonds come next, followed by non-investment-grade bonds. Various ratings agencies determine an entity's ability to repay its debt according to broad categories. The highest rating, AAA, indicates that a borrower has an extremely strong capacity to meet all its financial commitments. The next level down, including AA+, AA, and AA–, rates firms as having a very strong capacity to meet financial commitments. Categorization continues with this same pattern from A+ to BBB to B to C or D, depending on the rating agency. Anything BBB– or above is investment grade, and anything below is high-yield debt, often called "junk bonds."

The U.S. government has been one of 13 countries rated AAA although Standard & Poor's, one of the major ratings agencies, lowered that rating to AA+ in August 2011, citing the country's seeming inability to address its budget deficit and long-term debt. A few companies still carry the AAA rating, and most corporations fall within the investment grade rating.

The categorization of bonds significantly impacts borrowers and lenders. For investors, a higher rating provides greater confidence in the borrower and normally reduces their expected return. Borrowers with higher credit ratings usually have better and cheaper access to capital.

Duration also affects interest rates. Longer-term debt usually pays a higher interest rate because borrowers compensate lenders for the increased uncertainty associated with future interest rates. When short-term rates are higher than longer-term rates, the yield curve is said to be inverted because a chart showing interest rates versus time slopes down as time increases. An inverted yield curve isn't interesting in itself, but it tends to garner a lot of attention since it nearly always indicates a coming recession.

Investment Vehicles

Most bond investors hold a combination of bonds with different risks and maturities either directly or through some form of vehicle that pools investor monies to buy individual bonds. Some investors like the control and exact nature of individual bonds. Investors know the interest rate and exact maturities of their holdings, which provides an excellent ability to create and understand the bond portfolio. For other investors, high investment minimums and greater management requirements make mutual funds a better choice and worth the management fees associated with the vehicle. Recent years have seen a tremendous increase in the availability of bond ETFs offering low fees and excellent diversification.

Whether using individual bonds, mutual funds, or ETFs, investors can build a portfolio with specific risk and duration characteristics. Research indicates that holding as few as 10 bonds of investment-grade corporate securities provides enough diversity to prevent extreme default loss.[1] Mutual funds have been the most popular vehicle traditionally, and many good options provide investors sufficient exposure and diversification with reasonable costs. My preference tends toward ETFs because the fees are lower, diversification is excellent, and the variety of ETF offerings allows investors to build a portfolio that targets particular risk and duration characteristics.

I'm not adamant about a particular fixed-income vehicle. My perspective is fairly easy to understand when bond risk and reward potential is viewed.

A successful commodities strategy versus a flawed approach can mean the difference between negative returns for a decade versus double-digit compounding returns. Different stock, real estate, or private equity strategies can also produce very different results, especially if an investor is prone to panic and mismanagement.

Bonds, by contrast, are generally hard to mess up badly. They don't offer as much performance potential over time as an investment category, and there's less risk involved. Very simply, they offer lower upside and downside potential. Standard investment approaches can't change this basic dynamic.

Admittedly, more sophisticated strategies can easily add a percentage point or two per year, which can add up. And there can be exceptions if more exotic fixed-income approaches are employed. For now, I'm assuming more standard investments are employed, and therefore the differences will be small compared to most other categories.

Performance

Assessing fixed-income performance can be a bit confusing because the term describes such a broad category. Fortunately, there are several standard benchmarks similar to those used for stocks.

The most common bond benchmark is the Barclays Capital U.S. Aggregate Bond Index, formerly known as the Lehman Aggregate Bond Index. When Lehman Brothers collapsed in April 2008, kicking the financial meltdown into high gear, it left a lot of assets available to the survivors. Barclays Capital bought this portion of the defunct firm and now maintains the index. As an aside, many investment professionals struggle to remember to use the new name, and usage of the old one is still common.

The index represents investment-grade bonds traded in the United States, including various government and corporate bonds. Numerous ETFs and index mutual funds track this index and are available to investors.

The index performance serves as the common proxy for the bond market. During the last 30 years, it has done quite well, largely because the conditions have been near perfect for bonds. In the early 1980s, interest rates were at record highs, and by mid-2011 they were at record lows after steadily declining for decades.

It doesn't get much better for bonds. First, rates started out high, which rewarded bondholders with good income. Second, as rates declined, existing bonds with higher rates became more valuable, which increased their price. Bondholders earned positive returns through interest yields and capital gains.

During the 30-year period ending December 2010, the Barclays Capital U.S. Aggregate Bond Index (again, this was the Lehman Aggregate Bond Index for most of this time) returned an amazing average of 8.92 percent per year. In fact, during the depths of the 2008–2009 financial crisis, 25-year bond returns exceeded stock returns. After stocks recovered, this advantage disappeared, but the short-term disparity garnered a lot of attention because that is not supposed to happen.

Bonds also offer various other advantages. Correlations with most performance-based investments are low and sometimes negative, which provide excellent diversification. In addition, bonds enjoy greater stability than common performance categories such as stocks; losses are also less frequent and smaller. Lastly, most bonds are quite liquid, although individual holdings often have a smaller market, which results in greater spreads between buy and sell prices.

Looking forward, bonds face a much more difficult future. While the last 30 years have seen near-perfect conditions, the next 30 years offer much less appealing prospects. By nearly any measure, interest rates are at or near record lows, which provides investors with limited interest returns. As the recent financial crisis recedes, rates are expected to rise. Furthermore, given the vast expansion of the Federal Reserve and injection of money into the money supply, inflation is a growing threat. As rates rise, current bond holdings become less valuable. The combination of low initial interest rates and likely future capital losses means bonds are likely to produce fairly anemic returns for the foreseeable future—the exact opposite result of the last 30 years.

This doesn't mean that bonds are worthless as an investment. Their liquidity and stability combined with some income can still make them a valuable component of portfolios. But performance and income expectations will need to adjust, as future returns will likely differ markedly from those of the past 30 years.

Bonds appear to be used increasingly as a safe haven rather than as a return asset. It's not that bonds produce no return. It's more that the return is not as important as the bond's ability to provide valued safety when other assets are struggling. Bond values reflect this, as increased risk in various markets drives riskier asset values down while government bond values tend to increase as investors flee to safety.

Treasury Inflation-Protected Securities

Treasury inflation-protected securities—or TIPS for short—will likely perform better than others during a rising rate environment. These securities are one of the many bonds issued by the government, but they are unique in that the principal adjusts up or down according to changes to the consumer price index (CPI). The actual bond coupon remains constant. A different amount of interest results when the constant rate is multiplied by the inflation-adjusted principal. The bond promises to shield the bondholder from some of the effects of inflation, although the consumer price index excludes notable contributors to inflation, such as food and energy.

Foreign Bonds

The challenges facing the domestic bond market are leading many investors to seek alternatives elsewhere. Just as foreign equity markets have drawn investor interest, increasingly so have foreign bonds. Similar to equity markets, foreign bonds now represent about 60 percent of global fixed-income investment possibilities. Also, just as with foreign equities, foreign bonds provide several potential advantages.

In past decades, the perceived strength of U.S. debt markets, particularly U.S. government debt, combined with very solid performance, overshadowed foreign debt. That resulted in little interest in this asset class. Now, near-record low domestic interest rates, downgraded U.S. government debt, and the devaluing U.S. dollar combine to make foreign debt much more interesting to alert investors.

Higher interest rates in many countries are likely to provide greater income than available through similarly rated bonds in the United States. In the past, higher foreign rates were often accompanied by significantly lower credit ratings. Now the situation is reversing, and the argument can be made that many foreign countries are managing their debt much better than the United States. Changes are particularly apparent in many emerging markets in which their recent governments' fiscal discipline completely outshines budget management in virtually all developed countries.

Moreover, the long-term devaluation of the U.S. dollar against nearly all currencies should provide fixed income denominated in foreign currencies an additional boost. As with many trends, gains due to exchange rate changes will likely benefit emerging markets most, as their economies are growing the fastest.

Finally, foreign bonds provide some level of diversification within the fixed-income sector and an overall portfolio. Yields and price changes may differ dramatically from U.S. fixed income. As with stocks, foreign bonds react differently to global events and face unique risks in their home market.

As always, performance differences can be good or bad. Like U.S. bonds, foreign bonds are subject to credit risk and interest rate risk. Strong warnings regarding potential political and economic instability have commonly accompanied foreign bonds, especially those in emerging markets. These warnings are likely to still apply but probably need modifications given our nation's recent struggles and the growing emerging market strength.

Foreign fixed-income risks differ today from risks faced decades ago. Political and economic risk remains. However, it's morphed into a different animal. Twenty years ago, foreign bond risk nearly always originated when undisciplined emerging markets finally collapsed after bingeing for too long. Today, this problem appears more prevalent in developed markets.

Moreover, today, when emerging market debt struggles, it's usually the result of investors fleeing to the safety of U.S. government bonds, ironically because of issues such as downgrading U.S. government debt. While investors' reaction in this case seems ridiculous, as the prudent are punished while the profligate are rewarded, the flight to the dollar in times of crisis has been a pattern for many decades that won't change overnight. Even if emerging markets have acted responsibly, in the short term their debt may be punished during times of panic.

This brings up the major potential weakness of foreign fixed income. Most investors hold investment-grade bonds as a safer and more secure asset to balance the risks of other holdings. Unfortunately, during more extreme economic dislocations, seemingly all asset classes lose value other than U.S. government bonds and gold. Often, this includes foreign fixed income, which could lead to losses in value for an asset class held to provide safety. Yet if investors keep their wits about them, pricing usually reverts back to more standard levels quickly, but it may take a few days, weeks, or even months (in extreme cases) for this to occur.

This isn't always true, and less severe economic problems often force foreign fixed income up as expected for a traditionally safer asset class. As global investors become more comfortable with foreign debt, I expect that foreign markets will increasingly follow traditional trading patterns of domestic bonds. While this may benefit portfolios by providing more stability, it may also lessen some of the opportunity within the asset class. On balance, diversifying fixed-income holdings with foreign debt likely provides several benefits.

Investment Vehicle

When venturing into foreign fixed income, most investors benefit from using some type of packaged product rather than building their own foreign fixed-income portfolio with individual bonds. As with individual foreign stocks, accessing individual bond characteristics, including credit quality, is much harder internationally. Again, I like exchange-traded funds, given the breadth and quality of low-cost options. Mutual fund companies, however, offer some solid options, and good managers may be able to find unique opportunities.

Allocation

As with equity allocations, there's no right or wrong answer to allocation percentages with foreign fixed income. If you have decided this category makes sense for you, your desire to increase your expected return and willingness to accept a bit more risk will likely drive your choice of percentages. If your time horizon is greater than six months, I believe adding international fixed income will likely decrease your fixed-income risk, especially if you are not prone to panic during inevitable market dislocations. Given the rapidly changing nature of this asset class, there's not a lot of meaningful data on correlation. Chinese, Brazilian, and Spanish debt all represent very different risks and opportunities than they did a decade ago, and the trends suggested by detailed analyses are likely inaccurate.

Setting upper and lower bounds of your total bond portfolio may be more useful than determining an exact percentage. Since this asset class isn't meant to provide strong performance, going above a 60 or 70 percent foreign bond allocation doesn't make much sense. Doing so potentially removes part of the safety element of fixed income. Similarly, if you are going to add the asset class, having anything less than 20 percent doesn't really accomplish much. While these numbers represent only general starting points, ranges between 20 and 60 percent seem reasonable given the category's purpose in a portfolio. Most investors will probably best be served by ranges around 40 to 50 percent, given the likely performance of the asset class, but levels above that may defeat the purpose of holding bonds.

Structured Products

This category doesn't really fit neatly into any of the endowment model sectors, but its performance and risk characteristics closely resemble fixed income. Most structured products and their close cousins, structured notes or market-linked investments, offer a unique value proposition. The investment can increase in value when a specified asset changes in value, but investors face no, or limited, risk of loss. Obviously, many investors find this very interesting. Who wouldn't?

There's a catch. In exchange for guarantees of principal, gains are limited. Limits may come in the form of caps on gains, fees deducted from gains, reduction of gains by fixed percentages, some other condition, or a combination of any of these.

As an aside, the insurance industry offers a similar product in the form of a fixed index annuity (FIA). FIAs are a narrow subcategory of structured products that increase in value if an index or indexes goes up. The products will usually require much longer holding periods and enjoy some of the tax benefits of annuities.

Most structured products work in the same way, although some designs are much more complex. Using investors' funds, managers buy safe assets such as government bonds and use the interest to purchase options on a higher-risk asset such as a single security, basket of securities, options, index, commodities, fixed income, currencies, or just about anything you can imagine. In some cases, the products are structured so that investors benefit if prices move up or down, or if they stay beneath certain limits. Some designs lock in gains annually, ratcheting up annual values, while others may provide value increases only at final liquidation. Design possibilities are endless.

Regardless, most structures keep the original investment safe through investment in very conservative bonds while the interest secures exposure to the risky asset. If the risky asset price increases, investors win. Declines result in the option expiring worthless, and the only loss is the option premium. The principal guarantee usually exists only if the security is held to maturity, although some products offer early redemption if a fee is paid that may be less than investment returns, which enables a full return of principal.

Performance

The concept of structured products is simple, and the promise of gains without risk sounds great. Yet in reality, the strategy faces challenges as should be obvious from the fact that not everyone puts all their money in this guaranteed investment.

One drawback is liquidity. Some strategies provide no access to capital until maturity while others may provide limited access. Time frames may be as short as a year, or they may approach a decade. Some insurance-based offerings can run over 15 years or more. Yet, as mentioned earlier, liquidity issues can be planned for and effectively addressed.

Limited performance potential is the real drawback to structured products. In exchange for safety, investors lose upside potential. These types of investments seek to perform about the same as the bond market does, although sometimes they are positioned as a performance asset by the financial and insurance industries. Exceptional annual or specific product performance will inevitably arise at times, given the breadth of possible offerings. Aberrations may lend credence to claims of high performance. But any thorough analysis of the broader category quickly reveals these instances to be anomalies.

Today's interest rate and market volatility also make life particularly difficult for structured product managers. Given today's ultralow interest rates, yields on the original bond investment generate very limited funds. Not only must managers secure exposure to risky assets with very limited income, the dividends must also cover running expenses such as salaries, legal, trading, research, custody, and sales. In addition, market volatility has generally increased the cost of purchasing options. These two factors severely limit return possibilities.

This doesn't mean this asset doesn't or can't create value in a portfolio. It's more a question of purpose. Most uses of this product either focus on an ultraconservative investment (since they offer guarantees beyond bonds) or provide a much more conservative means to secure exposure to an asset that might otherwise be avoided.

Performance expectations need to be realistic. This investment can provide unique exposure or a great safety net in a portfolio. But the investment will rarely generate strong returns; it's not designed to. As usual, there's no free lunch.

Correlation

The design of structured products results in some strange correlation numbers. Given a design that locks in exposure on the upside, it would seem that correlation with asset price increases should be nearly perfect. Yet various structures frequently result in no or limited value increases when the linked asset value increases. Perhaps minimal fee hurdles were not overcome or performance caps may have limited gains. As a result, upside correlation is surprisingly weak. More positively, for many designs, downside correlation is pleasantly absent.

In addition, the tremendous diversity of products combined with the category's much shorter history complicates correlation statistics. Because of this, it's very difficult to establish meaningful data on the category's performance relative to other assets. For most product designs, correlation will likely be highest with risk-based assets because their increases drive value increases. This likely decreases the diversification benefit of the product, since most people add this asset class to balance riskier assets. Yet, complete downside protection may compensate for other shortfalls.

High-Yield Debt

This category could arguably have been included in the previous section that addressed more performance-oriented assets. Its highly liquid nature and frequent inclusion in fixed-income portfolios, however, suggests this classification makes more sense.

Decades ago this asset developed only when firms experienced trouble, thereby increasing their risk of default. Reduced credit ratings caused price declines, but the firms continued to pay interest, so the bonds never entered the distressed debt category. Since the bonds paid the same interest rate but their price had declined, the resulting yields were higher versus the current value. The new category was referred to as "high-yield bonds." Over time, high-yield bonds also have come to be called "junk bonds" because their credit quality is lower than investment-grade bonds.

Investment-grade bonds are rated AAA to BBB–. High-yield bonds are rated BB+ or lower. Investment banker Michael Milken recognized that junk bonds were routinely valued at less than their likely value. Essentially, they deserved a lower credit rating than investment-grade bonds, but ratings agencies went too far and reduced credit ratings too much, overestimating the likelihood of potential defaults.

As Milken gained experience in working with junk bonds, a larger market for these speculative-grade bonds emerged. Over time, he and other partners at Drexel Burnham Lambert began helping firms issue bonds that began life as speculative-grade bonds. Other firms followed their lead, and high-yield bonds became a common form of financing higher-risk firms that wanted to complete mergers and acquisitions or leveraged buyouts.

To raise capital, some firms with lower credit ratings and lack of access to traditional investment-grade bonds markets also issued junk bonds rather than investment-grade bonds. Many firms such as MCI, McCaw Cellular, Time-Warner, Mattel, Cablevision, News Corporation, and Barnes & Noble aggressively used high-yield bonds to finance various forms of growth. This method of financing has become so prevalent that high-yield bonds now represent as much as 25 percent of the U.S. corporate bond market with about $1.1 trillion in outstanding value.[2] It's a major asset class.

Performance

High-yield bonds are simply another type of bond that trades on a secondary market. They can be bought and sold very easily and are completely liquid just like investment-grade or government bonds. Yet their differences are very significant. Their performance characteristics tend to correlate much more closely with equity or risk investments, particularly small-cap stocks, than with fixed-income investments.[3]

During the recent financial crisis, the value of government bonds and many corporate bonds increased as investors fled to safety. In contrast, prices of high-yield bonds plummeted as investors panicked over the creditworthiness of riskier bonds. Some high-yield bonds and bond funds experienced much greater losses than did the stock market; then, as the crisis passed, they also saw greater returns.

High-yield bonds also offer a couple of different means to earn returns. Yields are frequently quite high and may approach and even exceed average stock market returns. In addition, the value of the underlying principal fluctuates, which adds to or subtracts from investment returns through changes in the investment value.

As is the case with many assets, understanding performance of this asset class isn't as simple as might be expected. Over the 25-year period from January 1985 through the end of August 2009, comparisons of high-yield bonds with investment-grade bonds reveal some unexpected results. Even though the standard deviations of high-yield bonds were more than double those of investment-grade bonds, at 15.4 percent versus 5.9 percent, respectively, the average returns of both asset classes were very similar with both returning between 8 percent and 9 percent per year.[4] Given the differences in volatility, similar return numbers are a surprise.[5]

If we look further, the anomaly in the performance numbers results from some unexpected behavior within the high-yield sector. Returns have been the exact opposite of expectations for certain subcategories. The higher-quality junk bonds produced higher returns, and lower-quality junk bonds produced lower returns in spite of their higher risk. This isn't supposed to happen over longer time periods. Higher risk should be rewarded; with junk bonds, however, it was punished. Moreover, the lowest-rated bonds produced the worst return.[6] This appears to result from an incredibly high default rate of 52.2 percent on the worst junk bond category, Caa.[7]

Unfortunately, the lack of higher performance across the category of junk bonds poses a challenge. Is the additional risk incurred worth the potential return? For the asset class, the answer would seem to be no, but for select sectors, the answer could be yes. Before you decide what to do with the asset class, let's assess another important characteristic.

Correlation

As mentioned, high-yield bonds correlate more closely to equity markets, particularly small-cap stocks. Estimates of correlation with the S&P 500 are about 0.50 versus a slightly negative correlation for a very large bond fund ETF that mimics the Barclays Capital Aggregate Bond Index.[8] Correlations with the high-yield bonds and the Russell 2000 small-cap stocks are even higher at 0.61 from January 1985 through August 2009.[9]

By contrast, high-yield correlations with Treasury (government) bonds are only 0.18 for the higher-quality Ba bonds, 0.03 for B-rated bonds, and −0.09 for Caa-rated bonds.[10] Anything below 0.20 is generally viewed as being statistically insignificant. So high-yield bonds clearly represent a different asset category than investment-grade bonds.

Ironically, the lack of correlation between investment-grade bonds and high-yield bonds can make the addition of high-yield bonds to a bond portfolio very desirable. This can be especially valid if investors can successfully identify the better risk versus reward subclasses within the high-yield sector.

While the correlations between high-yield stocks and bonds are significant, they still appear to provide some meaningful diversification with values around only 0.5 to 0.6. Another factor, however, becomes important within this asset class. Correlations with equities during periods of high volatility rise considerably.

In 2008, when the U.S. stocks fell off a cliff, high-yield bonds plummeted right along with equities. Correlations with the stock market rose to over 0.90 in late 2008.[11] Unfortunately, during various other periods of economic uncertainty, standard deviations of high-yield bonds also leaped. Nearly all the difference in risk of high-yield bonds versus investment-grade bonds seems to show up during periods of economic and political uncertainty. Obviously, this isn't a desirable outcome, especially if you are holding this asset to provide stability.

One last issue regarding high-yield bonds also deserves attention. Much if not all the return from high-yield bonds is taxed as ordinary income. Many other performance assets derive much or all of their returns through more attractively taxed capital gains. Depending on an investor's tax bracket, tax treatment can significantly lower this investment's allure.

Given all the performance, correlation, and even tax data, high-yield bonds don't seem to stand out as a particularly desirable asset class. Yet inclusion of high-yield bonds in a bond portfolio could make a lot of sense, and high-yield bonds can be utilized very successfully by some investors. The category simply can't be easily eliminated or whimsically included.

Investors and advisor experience can be major factors in determining whether or not to include this asset class. Familiarity by either or both parties with the fixed-income asset class may substantially raise the likelihood of successful inclusion of this asset class. The ability to better target specific high-yield bond exposure and gain access to the better risk and reward assets within the sector could substantially enhance the effectiveness of this asset class within a portfolio.

In addition, the potential of this asset class for generating higher income can make it more attractive for the right portfolio. While the higher income generally comes with higher risk, wise asset selection can help substantially in tipping the risk/reward ratio favorably, and good portfolio design can further help the investor. The simplest and clearest action for most investors is most likely to include it in measured levels, if their advisors are comfortable with the asset class, or to avoid it if not.

Lastly, the complexity of the category suggests that a good manager can add substantial value. In that case, mutual funds can offer the best investment means, especially if investor or advisor expertise in this area isn't high.

Preferred Stocks

Preferred stock is a unique hybrid security that is senior to common stocks and subordinate to all forms of debt, including high-yield debt. Other common names for the category include preferred shares, preference shares, or simply preferreds. Although preferred stocks are technically equities, investors nearly always view and use them as fixed-income substitutes since they pay dividends and share in none of the upside of the company's success as do equities.

Much like bonds, preferred stocks are rated by the major credit rating companies. Their ratings are almost universally lower than similar bonds since preferred dividends lack the same guarantees on interest payments that bonds have, and preferreds are junior to all creditors. Unlike bonds, preferreds may or may not offer a determined expiration date, so investors often lack a promise to receive their full investment back in the future.

Many other more complex characteristics may differentiate one preferred from another, but the meaningful preferred stock features are simple. Preferred stocks don't enjoy as strong a protection as bonds, and they don't share in the upside potential of stocks. The benefit? Since they carry higher risk, preferred stockholders receive higher interest payments on their funds.

Historically, most individual investors have shunned preferreds, as they are somewhat difficult to understand and don't offer a high premium over most fixed-income investments. Very simply, why bother? Yet they have had their fans. Around 2003, I attended a certification program in which a speaker highlighted the benefits of substituting all of a fixed-income portfolio with preferred stocks. And some people with more experience within the sector enjoyed solid success with the category until 2007, as we will see.

Going back a bit further, the preferred stock world shifted dramatically after a regulatory change in the mid-1990s allowed banks to count preferred stock as tier 1 capital, the core measure of a bank's financial strength. Incidentally, this arcane definition became a bit more familiar to many people during the 2008 financial crisis when it routinely hit the front page of many nonfinancial papers. After the change, financial institutions became the dominant issuers of preferred stocks, increasing offerings from just 9 in 1994 to over 500 in 2009.[12] By June 2009, the financial sector represented over 82 percent of the S&P U.S. Preferred Stock Index and 95 percent of new issues of preferred stocks. Given the damage suffered by the financial sector over the recent downturn, investors encountered numerous problems.

Performance

From March 2005 to March 2007, the yield on preferred stocks fluctuated between 5.7 percent and 6.7 percent. This compared favorably to the Moody's AA Corporate Bond Index, which varied between 4.9 percent and 6.0 percent, and the U.S. government 20-year Treasury yield, which varied between 4.2 percent and 5.4 percent. Doing just a bit of math reveals small premiums of only around 0.8 to 1.5 percent per year paid to preferred stockholders in 2006 and 2007.[13] Investors assumed that preferreds were not much riskier than bonds.

The economic expansion from 2003 to 2007 seemed to endorse these assumptions as volatility for the S&P Preferred Stock Index remained reasonable until July 2007. Preferred stock volatility averaged about twice that of Treasury securities and high-grade corporate bonds, and it stayed a bit higher than junk bonds. Given the higher coupon rates of preferreds, the risk/reward trade-off remained reasonable for fans of the sector.

But the economic contraction from 2008 to 2010 dramatically changed this pattern and inflicted significantly more damage to preferreds than to other fixed-income categories. While the volatility of all asset classes increased during the downturn, the volatility of preferred stocks increased far more than that of either high-quality bonds or junk bonds. Investors feared their low seniority and lack of protection. The subordinated status of preferred stock to all bonds gives it risk characteristics similar to common stock in times of financial stress or uncertainty. [14]

Unfortunately for most holders of preferred stock, after August 2007 the S&P U.S. Preferred Stock Index became more correlated with the volatile and declining S&P 500 and S&P Financial Index and less correlated with bond markets. The timing and severity of this change inflicted much pain on investors as common stock volatility of all equities, and particularly financial firms, increased significantly in the summer of 2007. The S&P 500 Financial Sector Index volatility approximately doubled during August 2007 alone.[15] Since financial institutions were the primary issuer of preferreds, performance was terrible. Moreover, this recent pattern suggests a very unattractive ongoing attribute of the category.

Is Preferred Stock Worth It?

Since most bond portfolios are built to shield investors from risk, preferreds don't seem to be an attractive option. They seem to lack the key safety element required of this category. In retrospect, it seems that many preferred stock investors enjoyed a free ride for many years before the jolt of the 2008 financial meltdown.

While some situations may always be exceptions, I recommend that investors avoid this category unless they possess a high level of expertise in the area or work with an advisor who does. Why assume risk commensurate with stocks for returns barely above bonds?

Moreover, preferred stock positions substantially diminish the benefits of holding bonds. This type of investment is probably not worth the trouble.

Bond Portfolio

Let's put this all together. Constructing the bond portion of a portfolio requires several decisions, but none of them is particularly difficult. The choice that carries the biggest portfolio impact will likely be the percentage of the total portfolio allocated to bonds.

In considering the amount to put into bonds, there's no magic number or perfect selection. Traditional, dated assumptions allocate around 50 percent of a portfolio to individuals' retiree portfolios; some endowments, on the other hand, have no bond holdings. For investors adopting any part of the endowment model, the ideal percentage will lie somewhere in between the two just mentioned, with a final percentage likely to approach low double digits or possibly even single digits for some investors. We will cover some example allocations in the next section that pulls everything together.

Next, you will need to determine the types of fixed income to include and what vehicle to use. It's easiest to first decide relative percentages of domestic versus foreign fixed income. Within either category, you will also need to determine if high-yield, preferreds, or structured products will be included.

By category the next key decisions will likely focus on several factors such as credit quality, bond type, and average duration. For the past 30 years, most investors have been fairly well served by nearly any product that delivered performance commensurate with the Barclays U.S. Aggregate Capital Bond Index. This may work well going forward, but more challenging bond markets could present investors with greater challenges. In addition, you will need to choose your investment vehicle from individual bonds, ETFs, mutual funds, or a combination of these.

Because specific interest rate and inflation conditions present different opportunities and challenges in building a portfolio, anything mentioned here will need to be adjusted to existing and expected conditions. Furthermore, there isn't one answer. Various solutions work well.

A solid bond portfolio can be set up with just a few ETFs or mutual funds. I believe that a combination of ETFs provides the best diversification and exposure while still keeping management relatively simple. For domestic bonds, a core ETF following the Barclays U.S. Aggregate Capital Bond Index can act as the foundation of a portfolio. For example, around half of the domestic bond portion of a portfolio might consist of this holding. Various additional holdings can provide exposure to corporate bonds, shorter- or longer-term bonds, inflation indexed bonds, and high-yield bonds.

Next, you will need to develop a foreign bond allocation. While this may seem more challenging given the lack of Barclays U.S. Aggregate Capital Bond Index as a reference, multiple useful broad indexes exist internationally that provide common references and targets for ETFs or mutual funds. Standard & Poor's publishes international corporate bonds indexes, international government bond indexes, and inflation-protected bond indexes. Other firms also provide similar reference points, such as the J.P. Morgan GBI-EMG Core Index, which tracks direct exposure to local currency bonds issued in emerging markets. A combination of a few ETFs or mutual funds in these sectors can provide good exposure and diversification.

If high yield is added to any category, allocations should probably be kept below 25 percent within the respective category. Higher-quality high-yield bonds can help performance and diversification but increase volatility during rough periods. If this is acceptable, they can be a good addition. If not, solid bond portfolios can be built without them. As mentioned, I recommend including preferreds only if you are a devoted fan. The inclusion of structured products likely falls into a different category, as their diversity and purpose varies dramatically by portfolio and investor desires.

Future Purpose

As we have seen, historically bonds have provided income and reasonable performance as well as immediate liquidity and lowered volatility. In spite of the endowments' deemphasis of the category, most of them still maintain some holdings in the area, and most investors will likely want to maintain fixed-income exposure. The primary change for most investors, including endowments, appears to be almost a complete discounting of the asset class's ability to provide returns and a greater emphasis on its value as a safe haven. During brief periods in 2009, 2010, and 2011 we have even seen extremes of this practice as investors have been willing to suffer negative yields in exchange for refuge from risk-based assets.

At this point, I've addressed all the major allocation sections included in the endowment model as well as a brief section on non-conforming investments. All that remains is pulling everything together into a coordinated strategy.

14

Putting It All Together

WE HAVE COVERED A WIDE RANGE OF THE INVESTMENT VEHICLES commonly used by endowments and institutions to achieve their investment aims. Hopefully, you are convinced that there is value in adopting this strategy or at least parts of it. Let's look at some different ways to get started.

A key component of successful application of these various principles can be working with someone who understands them and has experience applying them. If your net worth is well above the accredited investor threshold—remember that means you have at least $1 million of investable assets or suitable income—finding a good financial professional to help you will be easier. But it may still take effort to find the right person. If your net worth is less than $1 million, your options may be more limited, but there are growing numbers of professionals who are developing expertise in this area who can provide excellent information.

Regardless of who may help you or whether you go it alone, the decisions and investments you eventually make will ultimately be yours. Recommendations, information, advice, and counsel can be helpful, but you live with the consequences, not someone else. Your comfort level, confidence, and eventual success according to your definition are the real concern. After all, it's your money!! Always remembering this helps in making good decisions. Never abdicate responsibility for your investments.

In determining how to move forward, I believe applying a basic framework to a few clearly defined goals makes the process easier. An easy place to start can be as simple as determining what you want the money to do for you. While this is such a simple question, developing a constructive answer can be surprisingly challenging. Breaking it down into a few key components can be helpful.

There are countless questions that can be asked about what you want your money to do. Numerous personal factors also enter in: What is your health? Will you retire? What lifestyle do you want in the future? The list can get very long. The following section provides only a cursory overview. Yet the answers can help you get started by categorizing your individual needs along just a few key variables. The following are the primary categories.

Income

The most important issue for many people is determining required income: How much income do you want your portfolio to produce, and when do you need it? This can be an extremely long discussion because so many variables and assumptions must be included. What follows is a basic overview that will suffice for many people, but this is a great topic to take up with a financial professional given the need to adjust to your exact situation.

There can be countless answers regarding original portfolio withdrawal rates, depending on a myriad of factors; a simple number or percentage works well as a starting point. For individuals in retirement, basic percentages are usually easiest to work with. Many studies have been done about withdrawal rates that maximize portfolio income while making it very likely that funds will last through a common retirement. Obviously, these formulas are based on averages, because investors, markets, and portfolios differ. There's no correct answer.

Assuming that retirement begins at age 65 and a lifespan will be an additional 25 years, a 4 percent original withdrawal rate adjusted up annually for inflation has a "very high likelihood" of not running out. Some studies interpret the term "very high likelihood" to mean nearly 100 percent while others are somewhat lower. As these conclusions result from statistical studies of large populations, the exact number isn't as important as the concept.

It's also important to understand what is being stated, as many investors miss the finer points. The *original* withdrawal rate is 4 percent. This withdrawal amount calculated from the original percentage withdrawal is adjusted up for inflation every year. So, if you start taking out $20,000 from a $500,000 portfolio, the next year's withdrawal is not 4 percent of your new portfolio value, it's $20,000 adjusted upward by inflation. Some people get the 4 percent number stuck in their head and continue to multiply 4 percent by their portfolio value to get their acceptable withdrawal rate. While leaving 96 percent of your money in your portfolio every year will ensure that you never run out of money, it's also likely to result in a declining income and an unnecessary lifestyle downgrade.

The 4 percent number also varies, depending on what study is involved. Some put the number at 5 percent, and others go as high as 6 percent. As you increase the withdrawal rate, the likelihood of the portfolio lasting 25 years goes down—it's simple math. One key variable that impacts the assumption is the time period over which the study was done. Linked to this assumption is the overall stock market valuation at the time of retirement, since almost all of these studies assume your sole performance asset is the U.S. stock market. If the stock market is overvalued when you retire, the 4 percent number is assumed to be more applicable. A market priced below historical averages has allowed investors to assume an initial 6 percent withdrawal that lasts throughout retirement with high probability, since greater asset growth provides increased funds throughout retirement.

Most studies show that withdrawal rates below about 2.5 percent adjusted up annually for inflation create a perpetually growing portfolio, which means the portfolio's real value increases after inflation rather than declining. While you may have no desire to do this if you retire early, it provides another frame of reference for consideration.

In your particular case, what percentage should you use? Besides the complexities of your own circumstances your decision can be further complicated by adopting the endowment model. I believe your finances will be stronger if you take that step, but simple formulas and rules of thumb may be less relevant. I've never seen a study try to incorporate the endowment model for individual investors, largely because it's practically impossible to do since many investment options haven't existed for individuals for more than a decade. Given the variety of potential portfolio structures that can be created with the investment possibilities we have covered, a simple formula probably wouldn't be very meaningful anyway.

Fortunately, I believe that adopting the endowment model enables the withdrawal percentage to increase above 4 percent. A higher withdrawal percentage can likely be assumed since there are more performance assets. After all, this is the primary reason endowments employ the model. Still, arriving at an exact number isn't really possible. Only an estimate can be made.

I have a simple suggestion: If you are planning on applying the endowment model to a significant part of your portfolio and the stock market valuations are close to historical averages, with price/earnings ratios below 20, I believe a 5 to 6 percent starting withdrawal rate is reasonable. This is based on a couple of assumptions. Real returns net of inflation in an endowment strategy portfolio should come close to, if not exceed, these numbers. Taxes will decrease the total amount available to the investor, resulting in an actual return that may exceed or trail these percentages, but returns shouldn't fall far enough to jeopardize the portfolio's success. The result should be a portfolio that maintains or only slowly loses its purchasing power over time as withdrawals are increased.

If you are already well into retirement, you can probably adjust the withdrawal percentage upward because your time frame is shorter. (Sorry about that, I'm just talking about the numbers here.) If you haven't retired yet or don't plan to, this discussion just gives you an idea of what assumptions can be helpful for planning.

Obviously, if you withdraw less money, this all becomes easier. Most people actually do. They may not need the income, may want to maintain a higher cushion, or may want to leave a greater inheritance. All these cases, however, are easier if we build a portfolio that meets the most challenging withdrawal requirements.

Aggressiveness

Aggressiveness, or risk aversion, is the next major category. Exactly pinpointing a person's risk profile is surprisingly difficult. It becomes even harder when two very distinct variables are separately identified. The willingness to accept risk and the ability to face the consequences of assuming risk are actually two different issues. Some people are much better at accepting risk than they are at handling the consequences. As you might imagine, this can be a very bad dynamic that causes tremendous stress. Alternatively, some people can handle almost anything but are reluctant to accept risk. They are likely missing great opportunities to better themselves financially.

Often investors start assessing their risk profile by identifying how much loss in percentages they can easily endure combined with their view of time frames. Since the stock market is so familiar to many investors, it can be a great example, although recent years have certainly dampened people's enthusiasm for the category. Does a 10 percent loss cause worry? How about 20 percent? What is the confidence level that the market will eventually recover? Are daily or weekly losses painful, or are they even noticed? If multiple different stocks are owned, do losses in one hurt more than the overall gains in an account? Unfortunately, even the most sophisticated questionnaires struggle to help people get much more advanced in risk assessment than categories beyond aggressive and moderate.

In my experience, I have found it is often easiest to start with a vague assumption about a risk profile and then reassess according to a particular portfolio design. An assumption that an investor wants some growth but doesn't want to be very aggressive seems very ambiguous, but it can provide a reasonable starting point from which to build several sample portfolios. As always, there will be pros and cons to each different portfolio, and the level of comfort with different options can help further identify which levels of risk are most appropriate for an investor. Risk seems to become more meaningful when illustrated through specific portfolio designs.

Liquidity

In a traditional portfolio that consists solely of stocks and bonds, the liquidity factor doesn't exist because everything is liquid. An endowment strategy portfolio that utilizes alternative investments is much more likely to require investment decisions that affect liquidity. As mentioned earlier, few investors need complete portfolio liquidity. Rather, sufficient income and access to emergency funds are paramount.

As with risk, willingness to assume illiquid assets can often be better understood with real examples. Analyzing several different portfolios with differing liquidity characteristics can be very helpful in crystallizing acceptable levels of liquidity.

Start Somewhere

Building portfolios is often best done on an iterative basis. Start with something, and then adjust to make it fit. In the paragraphs that follow, I'm going to build a portfolio assuming few restrictions on either liquidity or aggressiveness. While this may sound very optimistic or unreasonable, I think you may find that the results are surprisingly acceptable and provide a fair amount of flexibility. You may believe that one or more of these investments just don't make sense for you, but if so, they'll probably be marginal components of the portfolio that easily can be eliminated or substituted. If the portfolio doesn't have enough safety or traditional assets, you can just ratchet back the performance assets and add bonds or make other substitutions.

If we assume a fairly traditional endowment portfolio model, it could look something like Table 14.1.

Using the assumptions shown in Table 14.1 for the yields on the different investments, the portfolio produces an expected yield of 3.4 percent. Assuming a 5 percent initial withdrawal rate leaves us short by 1.6 percent. A $1 million portfolio will produce $34,000 in income, leaving the investor $16,000 short in income. The combination of stocks, bonds, and commodities puts 60 percent of the portfolio in assets that can be liquid in a couple of days. Depending on the exact vehicle used for the absolute return portion of the

Table 14.1 Traditional Endowment Portfolio Model

Asset Class	Percentage Allocation	Expected Yield
Domestic stocks	24%	2.5%
Developed market stocks	12%	2.5%
Emerging market stocks	12%	2.5%
Real assets: real estate	14%	6.5%
Real assets: commodities	7%	1.5%
Real assets: oil and gas	6%	10.0%
Private equity: traditional	5%	0.0%
Private equity : debt & equity	5%	7.0%
Absolute return: managed futures	10%	0.0%
Fixed income: domestic investment-grade bonds	2.5%	4.0%
Fixed income: foreign investment-grade bonds	2.5%	6.0%

portfolio, another 10 percent could be immediately liquid, although some investments could take 30 days to access. Depending on what vehicle is used for the private equity debt and equity portion, another 5 or 10 percent could be liquid within a maximum of 90 days, putting the total at 75 or 80 percent.

The income shortfall can be addressed through a sale of various assets just as is normally done with a traditional stock and bond portfolio. In this case, however, we have the choice of domestic stocks, developed market foreign stocks, emerging market stocks, commodities, two distinct classes of bonds, potentially absolute return assets, and two classes of private equity that could be used. None of this even includes the other 20 percent of the portfolio—real estate and oil and gas investments—that will become liquid at some point in the future.

If we assess the likely performance of this portfolio during the 2008–2010 meltdown, the assets that would appreciate in the portfolio just mentioned would be the investment-grade bonds, parts of the commodities holdings, and the managed futures. I'm assuming all the foreign bonds would decline, although this scenario would be very unlikely. In this example, we would have $25,000 of bonds, $100,000 of managed futures, and possibly another $5,000 to $10,000 of commodities available to meet an annual shortfall of $16,000.

We may also want to make more conservative assumptions. The income may not stay the same. Some stocks might cut their dividends during this period, although the vast majority do not. Probably more important, the real estate dividends might change. Some companies would increase their yields during this period, but more would decrease them. The result would be that your income could also decline, although it probably won't change much.

A downturn like that of 2008–2010 provides a clear and very severe test case, as financial markets are terrible and present many unprecedented challenges to portfolios. Assuming you have no other options or flexibility at the time and have to withdraw needed funds throughout the year, you would get through the first year and most of the second using only your domestic bond holdings. Realistically, many if not all the foreign bonds would be available immediately, and they would go up in value, not down over this time period. It's possible that you may have to sell some bonds at a slight loss, but it's much more likely you would see reasonable gains across the bond category. If managed futures are a part of the portfolio, they could also be sold at a gain, as they likely would be the portfolio's best-performing asset.

By the beginning of the third year, stocks would recover some, but they would still be underwater from their highs regardless of whether you look at them at the beginning of the year or halfway through it. This extreme example highlights the reasonable durability of this portfolio, but it also shows potential limitations. The different asset classes provide nearly two years of protected income from domestic bonds and probably more than three years from the total bond portfolio. Managed futures or other hedge funds could address several more years of income, as they likely could be sold at a gain.

To be very conservative, I will assume that only the bonds are available and not managed futures. If you don't need income, are building a portfolio exclusively for growth, or are comfortable with a somewhat more aggressive portfolio design, the previous design may be fine. But if you depend on your income, are a more conservative investor, or simply desire greater flexibility, you may want a higher level of safer assets that could be used to supplement income.

Normally, when I build a portfolio that must produce immediate income, I like to build in at least three years and preferably five years of income coverage from assets with very low risk of loss. In addition, additional flexibility can be added through inclusion of assets that are likely to liquidate over the five-year time horizon. That would provide access to funds that hopefully would have retained or increased their value.

In this case, we could fairly easily adjust the portfolio to give us five years of access to government and investment-grade bonds, thereby adding more protection against a repeat of the world falling apart. Again, in calculating these values, I don't include any precious metals or absolute return assets, which usually increase during times of economic distress. In other words, my assumptions are pretty pessimistic.

Taking a more conservative approach by increasing the bond allocation would reduce our expected returns, but not by much. As a first guess, covering five years of liquidating approximately $15,000 of bonds every year requires about $75,000 in bonds, or 7.5 percent of the portfolio. But, the $50,000 annual withdrawal will likely increase over time to account for inflation, so the withdrawal amount would actually be more. Some of the liquidated bonds would also be providing income. As they are liquidated, the income generated by the portfolio decreases a bit. As a result, the $75,000 allocated to cover five years of income shortfalls will be a bit short, so I'm going to raise it to $80,000. That should get us close.

If we rebalance the portfolio, we might come up with something like what's shown in Table 14.2.

This $1 million portfolio is estimated to produce $35,150 in income, which leaves the investor $14,850 short, or slightly less than the previously assumed $15,000 shortfall. Even if all risk-based assets are excluded as potential sources of funds, this design should cover income needs for about five years from bonds alone. The $80,000 invested in government and investment-grade bonds provides ample access to liquid capital. Realistically, if a major economic disruption causes most commonly held assets such as stocks to struggle for five

Table 14.2 Rebalanced Endowment Portfolio

Asset Class	Percentage Allocation	Yield
Domestic stocks	22%	2.5%
Developed market stocks	12%	2.5%
Emerging market stocks	12%	2.5%
Real assets: real estate	16%	6.5%
Real assets: commodities	5%	1.5%
Real assets: oil and gas	5%	10.0%
Private equity: traditional	5%	0.0%
Private equity: debt & equity	5%	7.0%
Absolute return: managed futures	10%	0.0%
Fixed income: domestic investment-grade bonds	4%	4.0%
Fixed income: foreign investment-grade bonds	4%	6.0%

years, the total portfolio that holds numerous noncorrelated assets would likely enjoy greater return numbers than assumed, and some of the assets probably would increase in value even if stocks didn't. I've assumed everything other than bonds declines over a five-year period, which is highly unlikely and therefore a very conservative assumption. This fairly aggressive portfolio provides many options and significant downside protection during very poor markets while also offering much upside potential during more normal periods. If this portfolio is still too aggressive, it easily can be made more conservative by ratcheting up bond holdings.

Is there anything magical about these numbers? Absolutely not. In fact, you will notice that I'm approximating many asset values and incomes. Building a portfolio that balances and predicts future income and returns down to the penny creates the illusion that projections are known facts rather than estimates. Over time, returns will vary, interest rates will change, and all asset values will fluctuate, which will make every prediction ultimately wrong.

Focus on the Concept

The previous model is a concept that provides a robust design framework rather than a specific and constant answer. You may also look at some of these investments and decide you are not comfortable with real estate, commodities, high-yield bonds, oil and gas, or some other asset category. Or you may want fewer stocks and more alternative assets because you don't like the volatility of the markets and you don't require higher liquidity. You may prefer other investments or opportunities available when you are implementing your portfolio. Any of these changes are fine. Remove what you don't like, and include what works for you as long as you are making reasonable assumptions and modifications.

The concept is the greater point. This portfolio provides significant amounts of diversification across numerous performance assets. These should do well over longer time periods while also providing income and access to safer assets that should be available during inevitable downturns, even those as severe and longlasting as the last collapse. Remember, the economic meltdown and corresponding plunges in many asset values that we have just gone through are the worst since the Great Depression. Yet a well-designed portfolio would have thrived during the preceding decade and weathered this very severe storm.

If we revisit the recent market turmoil, and assume that you had implemented this portfolio before the downturn, some of the portfolio assets such as stocks would have declined in value, but your income would have been fine. Moreover, some of your performance-oriented positions such as the absolute return managed futures and parts of the commodities portfolio could have actually done quite well during 2008. The Barclays Capital U.S. Aggregate Bond Index would have also increased quite a bit while providing income.

Withdrawing income from a portfolio also offers opportunities to actively manage your assets in ways similar to endowments. If your portfolio contained managed futures in 2008, their excellent performance during the year probably would have dictated your taking much or all of your 2009 income from this asset class rather than selling bonds. This not only practices selling high, it also extends the capability of the bond position to satisfy income needs in future years. This is a natural and expected result of good portfolio design. Not everything always works, and history never repeats exactly, but good strategy makes success more likely.

Illiquid assets might have just sat there even though their underlying values might have been changing. Their lack of mark-to-market pricing and associated volatility might have made you feel better even though their asset values might have been adversely affected by the numerous economic challenges.

Going forward, designing a portfolio to handle extreme volatility, inflation, and economic dislocation seems prudent given the increasing pace of change, ongoing international instability, and U.S. government challenges. In addition, increasing lifespans, likely inflation increases, and the decline of the dollar probably necessitate portfolio performance that produces quite good returns over a long time period while satisfying immediate income needs.

With all this said, if you look at this portfolio and decide that you are still not comfortable with all these different assets, some basic steps can still help you make significant portfolio improvements over the designs most investors employ. First, diversify your stocks to include developed and emerging markets. This is likely to increase returns while reducing risk. Second, diversify your fixed-income portfolio for the same reasons. These two actions will help, but you are still at the mercy of fully liquid traditional markets.

Given the likelihood of future inflation, adding real assets would be a great next step. Real estate is quite acceptable to most people and provides an easy place to start. The commodities strategy using equities can be a great addition and is also liquid, but it may make conservative investors uncomfortable. You can keep going through this same process of acceptance or elimination of other investments to build a much more diversified portfolio.

As you consider investments to add, common sense should play a major role. While your comfort level is critical, realistic return expectations should always be considered. Endowments provide a great example of adjustments to portfolios to increase exposure to investments expected to perform better under circumstances associated with current and expected future economic conditions. For example, in 2009 and 2010, most endowments increased their exposure to real assets such as real estate and commodities because they believed prices in those areas were depressed, which presented good opportunities for future returns. These assets should provide excellent inflation hedges, which most experienced investors believe is very important given our government's massive increase in the monetary supply. Over the same 2009–2010 time period, most endowments also increased investments in other nontraditional assets such as private equity and absolute return.

By this point, I hope you are convinced that you can appropriate much of the success the endowments have enjoyed by taking highly feasible and practical steps with your portfolio. I believe you will be well rewarded for making the effort. I hope you will agree that the new challenges and opportunities arising in today's economy offer compelling reasons to move forward. Best of luck!

Endnotes

From the Author

1. Market closing value peak on October 9, 2007, was 1,565.15. Market closing value bottom was on March 9, 2009, at 676.53. Percentage loss of 55.38 percent does not include dividends.

Chapter 1

1. For the sake of simplicity, references to any investor refers only to investors located in the United States. While the principles discussed work very well in any country, specific facts referenced will differ depending on your country of domicile.
2. Standard & Poor's, S&P 500 Equity Indices Fact Sheet, December 31, 2008.
3. Rob Wherry, "Our Mutual Fund Report Card for 2008," January 7, 2009, http://www.smartmoney.com/invest/funds/Mutual-Fund-Report-Card-for-2008/.
4. Tiburon Research, *Key Driving Factors: Defining the Role of Consumer Wealth, the Institutional Markets, and Current Events in the Future of Advice*, March 2010, p. 9, http://www.triburonadvisors.com.
5. On March 6, 2009, the S&P 500 fell to an intraday low of 666.79. *The RIC Report, Investment Strategy*, Bank of America Merrill Lynch, March 11, 2011, p. 1.
6. Standard & Poor's, S&P 500 Equity Indices Fact Sheet, December 31, 2009.
7. Barclays Capital, *2009 Barclays Capital Equity Gilt Study. Also* The Investor, "Historical Returns from Corporate Bonds, "*Monevator.com*, August 26, 2009, http://monevator.com/2009/08/26/historical-returns-corporate-bonds.
8. *Harvard University Financial Report*, Fiscal Year 2009, p. 10, via S&P500/ Citigroup US BIG.

9. *The Yale Endowment,* reports for years 2000 to 2009; *Harvard University Financial Report 2009*, p. 10. Also report from the Stanford Management Company, 2009, p. 2.

10. Peter Mladina and Jeffrey Coyle, "Yale Endowment Returns: Manager Returns or Risk Exposure?," *Journal of Wealth Management*, Summer 2010, p. 47.

11. Mladina and Coyle, "Yale Endowment Returns," p. 48.

Chapter 2

1. MSCI (www.msci.com), www.msci.com/products/indices/country_and _regional/dm/

2. MSCI (www.msci.com), www.msci.com/products/indices/country_and _regional/em/

Chapter 3

1. The Yale Endowment (2010), p. 8.

2. Michael Lewis, *The Blind Side*, New York: W. W. Norton, 2007.

Chapter 4

1. *Harvard University Financial Report, Fiscal Year 2009*, p. 10.

2. http://us.ishares.com/product_info/fund/overview/AGG.htm?qt=AGG& ihpq=true.

3. Ibid.

4. *Yale Campaign Annual Report, 2009–2010*, p. 7.

5. Aaron Pressman, "University Endowments Beat S&P 500 Last Year," Leslie Gevirtz, ed., *Reuters.com*, December 10, 2009, http://www.reuters.com/ article/idUSN1019101520091210.

6. *Harvard University Financial Report, Fiscal Year 2009*, p. 10, via S&P 500/ Citigroup US BIG.

7. Shirley M. Tilghman to members of the Princeton University community updating them on the impact of the economic climate, September 29, 2009, Princeton University, http://www.princeton.edu/main/news/archive/ S25/41/94G77/index.xml?section.

Chapter 5

1. Brad Case, "New REIT ETF: Stocks Correlation Only 74% Now," *Seeking Alpha*, January 12, 2011, http://seekingalpha.com/article/246289-new-reit-etf-stocks-correlation-only-74-now.

2. Bradford Cornell, "Economic Growth and Equity Investing," *Financial Analyst Journal* 66, no. 1: 63.

Chapter 6

1. http://www.managedfutures.com/managed_futures_index.aspx
2. InflationData.com, accessed March 10, 2012, http://inflationdata.com/ Inflation/Inflation_Calculators/Inflation_Rate_Calculator.asp#calcresults.
3. InflationData.com, accessed March 10, 2012, http://inflationdata.com/ Inflation/Inflation_Calculators/Inflation_Rate_Calculator.asp#calcresults.
4. InflationData.com, accessed March 10, 2012, http://inflationdata.com/ inflation/images/charts/Articles/Decade_inflation_chart.htm.
5. David Frum, *How We Got Here: The '70s,* New York: Basic Books, 2000, pp. 292–293.
6. Jeffrey Rogers Hummel, "Death and Taxes, Including Inflation: The Public versus Economists," *Econ Journal Watch* 4, no. 1 (January 2007: 56, http:// econjwatch.org/articles/death-and-taxes-including-inflation-the-public-versus-economists).
7. Lars E. O. Svensson, "Escaping from a Liquidity Trap and Deflation: The Foolproof Way and Others," *Journal of Economic Perspectives* 17, no. 4 (Fall 2003): 145–166, in American Economic Association, accessed March 10, 2012, http://www.aeaweb.org/articles.php?doi=10.1257/089533003772 034934.
8. Robert Huebscher, "New Challenges for the Endowment Model," *Advisor Perspectives*, June 7, 2011, http://www.advisorperspectives.com/ newsletters11/22-viceira3.php.

Chapter 7

1. 2009 Dalbar QAIB Study.
2. David Brooks, *The Social Animal: The Hidden Sources of Love, Character, and Achievement*, New York: Random House, 2011, p. 167.
3. Andrea Frazzini and Owen A. Lamont, "Dumb Money: Mutual Fund Flows and the Cross-Section of Stock Returns," Working Paper 11526, National Bureau of Economic Research, January 2005, p. 2, http://www .nber.org/papers/w11526.pdf.
4. Ibid., p. 15.
5. Ibid., p. 18.
6. Ibid., p. 27.
7. Ibid., pp. 31–32.

8. L. Larry Swedro, "Survivorship Bias," April 13, 2001, originally published in the *Wall Street Journal*, April 4, 1997.

9. Daniel Wildermuth, *How to Keep and Grow Your Retirement Assets: A Guide to Investing During the Next Decade,* 2004, p. 45.

10. "Mutual Funds: A Monthly Review, August 2005," *Wall Street Journal*, September 6, 2005, p. R1.

11. "Investors Have Stars in Their Eyes," *Wall Street Journal*, June 1, 2010, p. C7.

12. A hypothetical $1 invested at the beginning of 1927 through year-end 2010 assuming reinvestment of all dividends and no transaction costs or taxes. This is for illustration purposes only and is not indicative of any investments or investor return. An investment cannot be made directly into these indices. From Fama-French Benchmark portfolios. In this chart, growth stocks are represented by the bottom 30 percent of stocks traded on the New York Stock Exchange (NYSE) ranked by book-to-market ratio, plus stocks traded on the American Stock Exchange (AMEX) and Nasdaq with equal or lower book-to-market ratios. Value stocks are represented by the upper 30 percent of stocks traded on the NYSE ranked by book-to-market ratio, plus stocks traded on the AMEX and Nasdaq with equal or higher book-to-market ratios. The median market capitalization of NYSE stocks is used as the breakpoint in classifying stocks as large or small. Index composition is determined in June and rebalanced annually.

13. Frazzini and Lamont, "Dumb Money," p. 33.

14. Ibid.

15. http://www.forbes.com/2002/04/03/0403dividends_print.html.

16. Wellington Management Solutions, Third Quarter 2011, *Do Dividends Matter?*, p. 1.

17. WebCPA staff, "Investors Feeling Better About Advisors," Accounting Today for the WebCPA, June 30, 2010, http://www.webcpa.com/news/Investors-Feeling-Better-About-Advisors-54788-1.html.

18. RJ & MaKay, "Wealthy Investors Increasingly Use Multiple Advisors," RJandMaKay.com, August 16, 2011, http://www.rjandmakay.com/rj-and-makay/wealthy-investors-increasingly-use-multiple-advisors.html. Also Gary D. Halbert, "Use of Professional Financial Advisors Is Changing What You Can Learn from Wealthy Investors," InvestorsInsight.com, May 16, 2011, http://www.investorsinsight.com/blogs/forecasts_trends/archive/2011/05/17/use-of-professional-financial-advisors-is-changing-what-you-can-learn-from-wealthy-investors.aspx.

Chapter 8

1. *Market Insights: Guide to the Markets, 2Q/2011,* as of March 31, 2011, J.P. Morgan Asset Management, p. 47.
2. Fareed Zakaria, *The Post-American World*, New York: W. W. Norton and Company, 2009, p. 20.
3. International Strategy & Investment, *ISI Portfolio Strategy Report*, June 30, 2010.
4. Zakaria, *The Post-American World*, p. 24.
5. Ibid., p. 26.
6. Maria Laura Lanzeni, *The New World: Emerging Markets After the Crisis,* Deutsche Bank Research, April 2010, p. 8.
7. Ibid., p. 9.
8. Ibid., p. 12.
9. Zakaria, *The Post-American World*, p. 20.
10. *Market Insights: Guide to the Markets, 2Q/2011*, J.P. Morgan Asset Management, p. 47.
11. Zakaria, *The Post-American World*, p. 20.
12. "Percent of World Market Cap by Country," Bespoke Investment Group, June 11, 2008. http://bespokeinvest.typepad.com/bespoke/2008/06/percent-of-world.html.
13. Ibid.
14. Ibid.

Chapter 9

1. The Yale Endowment, 2009, p. 5.
2. The Yale Endowment, 2010, p. 8.
3. Harvard University Financial Report, Fiscal Year 2009, p. 10.
4. The Yale Endowment, 2009, p. 15.
5. "Which Asset Hedges Are the Best Inflation Hedges?," *Seeking Alpha*, May 13, 2009, http://seekingalpha.com/article/137323-which-asset-classes-are-the-best-inflation-hedges.
6. http://www.assetcorrelation.com/
7. Frank Shostak, "Commodity Prices and Inflation: What's the Connection?", Ludwig von Mises Institute, July 1, 2008, http://mises.org/daily/3018. Also David John Marotta, "Hedge Inflation Risk with Hard Assets," Marotta Wealth Management, June 4, 2007, http://www.emarotta.com/hedge-inflation-risk-with-hard-assets.

8. James L. Williams, "Oil Price History and Analysis," WRTG Economics, accessed March 20, 2012, http://www.wtrg.com/prices.htm.
9. "Which Asset Classes Are the Best Inflation Hedges?" *Seeking Alpha*.
10. *Market Insights: Guide to the Markets, 2Q/2011*, as of March 31, 2011, J.P. Morgan Asset Management, p. 47.
11. http://www.ncreif.org/property-index-returns.aspx
12. http://www.reit.com/IndustryData/FNUS-Historical-Data/Monthly-Index-Data.aspx
13. http://www.ncreif.org/property-index-returns.aspx
14. Correspondence, Keith D. Allaire, managing director, Robert A. Stanger & Co., Inc., May 13, 2010.
15. http://www.sec.gov/answers/accred.htm
16. Mark Huamani, "Investing in Commodities: The Search for Diversification," J.P. Morgan, accessed March 20, 2012, http://www.jpmorgan.com/tss/General/Investing_in_Commodities/1159337364479.
17. *Market Insights*, p. 47.
18. *Capital Markets Perspectives as of 3/31/11*, Oppenheimer Funds, p. 60.
19. http://bigcharts.marketwatch.com/historical/default.asp OR http://www.standardandpoors.com/indices/gics/en/us
20. John Jannarone, "The Sum of Oil Fears," *Wall Street Journal*, May 12, 2011, C12.
21. "Key Issues and Mandates: Secure and Reliable Energy Supplies: Exploration and Production of Domestic Oil and Natural Gas," National Energy Technology Laboratory, accessed March 20, 2012, http://www.netl.doe.gov/KeyIssues/secure_energy3a.html.
22. "America Is the Third Largest Producer of Oil in the World . . . and There's Plenty to Go Around!," OilheatAmerica, accessed March 20, 2012, http://www.oilheatamerica.com/index.mv?screen=production.
23. Dick Gibson, "Some Interesting Oil Industry Statistics—Imports/Exports," Gibson Consulting Online, accessed March 20, 2012, http://www.gravmag.com/imports.shtml.
24. Ibid.
25. Christopher Helman, "It's Time for the U.S. to Export Natural Gas," *Forbes*, September 27, 2010, http://blogs.forbes.com/christopherhelman/2010/09/27/its-time-for-the-u-s-to-export-natural-gas/.
26. "Modern and Ancient Spot Gold Prices, "OnlyGold.com, accessed March 20, 2012, http://www.onlygold.com/TutorialPages/prices200yrsfs.htm.

27. "Modern and Ancient Spot Gold Prices, "OnlyGold.com.
28. Ibid.

Chapter 10

1. The Yale Endowment, 2010, p. 33.
2. David F. Swensen, *Pioneering Portfolio Management: An Unconventional Approach to Institutional Investment*, New York: The Free Press, p. 235.
3. *2006 Investment Benchmarks Report: Venture Capital,* New York: Thomson Financial, 2006.
4. The Yale Endowment, 2010, p. 20.
5. September 2009, Harvard Management Company Endowment Report, Message from the CEO, p. 2.
6. 2009 Report from The Stanford Management Company, p. 49.
7. The Private Equity Performance Index is based on the quarterly statistics from Thomson Reuters' Private Equity Performance Database analyzing cash flows and returns over 1941 U.S. venture capital and private equity partnerships with a capitalization of $828 billion. Sources are financial documents and schedules from Limited Partners investors and General Partners. All returns are calculated by Thomson Reuters from the underlying cash flows. Returns are net to investors after management fees and carried interest. Buyout fund sizes are defined as follows: Small: 0–250 $Mil, Medium: 250–500 $Mil, Large: 500–1000 $Mil, Mega: $1 Bil+.
8. Tom Idzorek, *Private Equity and Strategic Asset Allocation,* Ibbotson Associates, October 31, 2007, p. 29.
9. *Market Insights: Guide to the Markets, 2Q/2011,* as of March 31, 2011, J.P. Morgan Asset Management, p. 57.
10. Swensen, *Pioneering Portfolio Management*, pp. 226–227.
11. Ibid., p. 227.
12. The Yale Endowment, 2010, p. P8.

Chapter 11

1. David F. Swensen, *Pioneering Portfolio Management: An Unconventional Approach to Institutional Investment*, p. 112.
2. John Sullivan, "Hedge Fund Assets Return to Pre-Crisis Peak," AdvisorOne, April 18, 2011, http://www.advisorone.com/article/hedge-fund-assets-return-pre-crisis-peak?t=alternative-investments.
3. Burton G. Malkiel and Atanu Saha, "Research Shows That Hedge Funds Produce Poor Returns in Long-Term: Performance Data Subject to

Manipulation," Finfacts.com, last modified December 19, 2007, http://www.finfacts.com/irelandbusinessnews/publish/article_10005605.shtml.

4. Mark J.P. Anson, CAIA Level 1, The Official Reading for the CAIA Level 1 exam, Hoboken, NJ: John Wiley and Sons, Inc., 2009, p. 240.

5. *Market Insights: Guide to the Markets, 2Q/2011*, as of March 31, 2011, J.P. Morgan Asset Management, p. 47.

6. Swensen, *Pioneering Portfolio Management*, p. 192.

7. Ryan Davies, "Managed Futures Consultancy," March 30, 2010, www.alternative-investment.com.

8. http://www.managedfutures.com/managed_futures_index.aspx

9. The correlations are calculated based on the common date range of each pair of indexes being compared with the date ranges of indexes used in this correlation matrix: U.S. stocks: December 1986 to April 2011; managed futures: December 1989 to March 2011; U.S. bonds: December 1975 to April 2011. "CTA Correlations with Stock and Bond Indices," Altegris, accessed March 20, 2012, http://www.managedfutures.com/correlations.aspx.

10. Mark J.P. Anson, CAIA Level 1, The Official Reading for the CAIA Level 1 exam, Hoboken, NJ: John Wiley and Sons, Inc., 2009, p. 386.

Chapter 13

1. Jim Schaberg, *How Many Bonds?*, BondDesk Group, December 7, 2010, p. 1.

2. Frank K. Reilly, David J. Wright, and James A. Gentry, "Historic Changes in the High Yield Bond Market," *Journal of Applied Corporate Finance*, 21, no. 3: 67.

3. Ibid., p. 65.

4. Ibid., p. 69.

5. Ibid., p. 68.

6. Ibid., p. 69.

7. Ibid., p. 69.

8. Michael Johnston, "Junk Bond ETFs: Too Good to Be True?," ETFdb, June 18, 2010, http://etfdb.com/2010/junk-bond-etfs-too-good-to-be-true/

9. Reilly, Wright, and Gentry, "Historic Changes in the High Yield Bond Market," p. 69.

10. Ibid., p. 69.

11. Ibid., p. 70.

12. Guohua Li, Craig McCann, and Edward O'Neal, "The Risks of Preferred Stock Portfolios," Securities Litigation Consulting Group, Inc. Working Paper, 2010, p. 2.
13. Ibid., p. 6.
14. Ibid., pp. 12–13.
15. Ibid., p. 14.

Index

About the Author

DANIEL WILDERMUTH IS THE FOUNDER AND CEO OF THE investment brokerage firm Kalos Capital Inc. and the money management firm Kalos Management Inc., which represent over $1 billion in assets in 12,000-plus accounts across 50 offices managed by a staff of about 250. Kalos Capital provides comprehensive brokerage services including a vast offering of alternative investments, and Kalos Management offers multiple domestic and international equity and fixed-income strategies to financial professionals and individual clients. Mr. Wildermuth serves as Chief Investment Officer for Kalos Management.

His combined firms' average annual revenue growth over the past five years has exceeded 40 percent. Growth drivers include a national reputation and recognized expertise in training financial professionals how to implement the more advanced portfolio strategies covered in *Wise Money.*

He speaks frequently at industry conferences and events and is often quoted as an expert in the fields of alternative investments, the stock market, and the general economy.

Daniel continues to work directly with a small group of investors, and he has been awarded The FIVE STAR: Best in Client Satisfaction Wealth Manager Award every year of its existence.

Daniel and his firm have been profiled on CNBC and the Bravo television networks and, most recently, by *Forbes* magazine for the group's experience in working with advanced portfolio strategies for individual investors.

At his quarterly training programs he enables financial professionals from across the nation to better serve their clients through applying more advanced portfolio and money management solutions.

He serves as advisor for several different industry conferences, helping them to design and produce conferences best suited to financial professionals who are seeking to improve their individual practices.

For approximately two years, Mr. Wildermuth hosted the popular weekly radio show, *Money Talks with Daniel Wildermuth*.

He previously authored *How to Keep and Grow Your Retirement Assets*, which sold approximately 10,000 copies out of his office.

Mr. Wildermuth earned an MBA in Finance from Anderson School at UCLA and an undergraduate degree in engineering from Stanford University. He graduated in the top 2 percent and 15 percent of classes, respectively.

If you are interested in building your own portfolio that follows the strategy outlined in the book, or if you would like to experiment with different portfolio design possibilities, I invite you to use the software we've created that enables easy application of the book's concepts. The software helps you to define estimates for returns and incomes of different investments, and then enables quick creation of a portfolio that provides return and income estimates. You can also define the same inputs for your current portfolio and then compare your current portfolioto a portfolio based on the book's approach.

For more information, go to www.wisemoneybook.com.

**To enjoy a special discount for
readers of *Wise Money*, use the code word Moneybook!
And again, best of luck!**